D1446680

Laurence Sterne Revisited

Twayne's English Authors Series

Herbert Sussman, Editor

Northeastern University

TEAS 532

LAURENCE STERNE
Portrait by Joshua Reynolds, 1760.
Reproduced by permission of the National Portrait Gallery, London.

Laurence Sterne Revisited

Elizabeth Kraft

University of Georgia

Twayne Publishers
An Imprint of Simon & Schuster Macmillan
New York

Prentice Hall International
London • Mexico City • New Delhi • Singapore • Sydney • Toronto

Twayne's English Authors Series No. 532

Twayne Publishers
An Imprint of Simon & Schuster Macmillan
1633 Broadway
New York, NY 10019

Library of Congress Cataloging-in-Publication Data
Kraft, Elizabeth.
    Laurence Sterne revisited / Elizabeth Kraft.
        p.   cm. — (Twayne's English authors series ; TEAS 532)
    Includes bibliographical references and index.
    ISBN 0-8057-7058-5 (cloth)
    1. Sterne, Laurence, 1713–1768—Criticism and interpretation.
    I. Title.   II. Series.
    PR3716.K73   1996
    823'.6—dc20   96-30820
                                                                         CIP

The paper used in this publication meets the minimum requirements of American
National Standard for Information Sciences—Permanence of Paper for Printed Library
Materials, ANSI Z39.48-1984. ⊚ ™

10 9 8 7 6 5 4 3 2 1

Printed in the United States of America.

For Bill

Contents

Publisher's Note

Laurence Sterne Revisited by Elizabeth Kraft draws on new materials made available since the 1965 publication of *Laurence Sterne* by William Bowman Piper. Twayne Publishers is pleased to offer this new critical study.

Preface

Laurence Sterne earned his place in literary history as the author of *Tristram Shandy* and *A Sentimental Journey*. *Tristram Shandy* immediately established Sterne as a literary luminary, a status he maintained until his death. He seems to have enjoyed his fame even though it was attended with the usual by-product—infamy. Before Sterne became an author, he was a minister of the Church of England, and his bawdy, irreverent tales were shocking to some readers of his own day and of later generations as well.

From the Christian perspective, the fundamental ambiguity of human life is the duality of the immortal spirit housed in the very mortal body. It is this ambiguity that Sterne exploits and explores in *Tristram Shandy* and *A Sentimental Journey*. Although Sterne's preoccupation with the sexual body has seemed to some readers and critics incommensurate with his profession as a clergyman, he shares this preoccupation with other clergymen/writers—particularly his favorites, François Rabelais and Jonathan Swift. The body is the locus of longing, desire; it is the means by which we experience and express the erotic love that is one of the chief pleasures of human life. But the body—especially the sexual body—is also the proper subject for laughter, as Rabelais, Swift, and Sterne all understood. In the words of a twentieth-century Anglican moralist, C.S. Lewis, "we must not be totally serious about Venus [that is, about sexual love]. Indeed, we can't be totally serious without doing violence to our humanity."[1] He goes on to explain in terms that Sterne would have understood quite well:

> It is not for nothing that every language and literature in the world is full of jokes about sex. Many of them may be dull or disgusting and nearly all of them are old. But we must insist that they embody an attitude to Venus which in the long run endangers the Christian life far less than a reverential gravity. We must not attempt to find an absolute in the flesh. Banish play and laughter from the bed of love and you may let in a false goddess. (Lewis, 140)

Sterne wrote to encourage play and laughter and joy. He saw the ability to experience pleasure as a gift to be cherished, neither worshiped nor abused. In this sense, his works stand in opposition to what Lewis

calls "doing violence to our humanity," in opposition to what he himself—along with Lewis—calls "gravity."

For over twenty years, Laurence Sterne performed the traditional
duties of an Anglican priest. He delivered sermons that reminded his
parishioners of their duties to each other; he assured them of their wor-
thiness and their accountability to God. It was his job to administer the
rites of the church: baptism, marriage, burial, and communion. It fell
within his purview to take part in the political life of the church, a
dimension of his profession characterized by pettiness, narrow principles, and short views. Of course, like any minister, Sterne spent much of
his time contemplating the eternal: He read scripture each morning and
each evening, and he regularly offered catechism classes for the youth of
his parish. Sterne seems to have fulfilled these professional duties both
reliably and sincerely.

Sterne's life, like most lives, was riddled with difficulty—family quar-
rels, the deaths of children, illness, disappointment, and personal failings—and punctuated with pleasure—recreation, friends, flirtations,
and ultimately, fame. His post–*Tristram Shandy* life took him away from
his village parish, away from his duties as a clergyman, and away from
his family and friends. Yet that book grew out of Sterne's life as a clergyman, his life as a man. This study treats Sterne's masterpieces as the cul-
mination of his life's work, not as a departure from it. For this purpose, I
have devoted two chapters to the early writings of Sterne, his pre–*Tristram Shandy* satires and, most important, his sermons. These chapters
provide an essential context for the following discussions of *Tristram
Shandy* and *A Sentimental Journey.*

I would like to acknowledge those friends and colleagues who have
helped me in completing this book. The editor of this series, Herbert
Sussman, was a joy to work with; his comments were succinct and inci-
sive, and he always had an encouraging word as he read and returned
each chapter. I am especially grateful to Melvyn New who suggested me
to Twayne as a potential writer of this text and then kindly agreed to
read the work I produced in manuscript. I am awed by his generosity,
the thoroughness with which he responded to my argument, and his
knowledge of Sterne and Sterne studies, which, I think, is equaled by no
one in our time. Some of his suggestions I stubbornly resisted; many I
used as the basis to rethink and rewrite parts of my argument. In time, I
will probably regret the stubbornness, but as Sterne himself would put
it, there is no disputing about hobby-horses, and I ride a few of my own
despite the caution of one I am proud to acknowledge as my mentor and

pleased to call my friend. To my husband Bill Free I offer thanks that I well know cannot repay his patience. He encouraged me to do this project when I was approached by the publishers. He never complained about the long hours I spent writing during vacations and on weekends, and he never once even grimaced at my endless requests for just one more reading of just one more revision. He even assisted with the tedious task of proofreading. In appreciation, I dedicate this book to him.

To the University of Georgia's Research Foundation, I owe thanks for a Senior Faculty Research Grant that made it possible for me to devote the summer of 1994 to writing the second chapter. To Hugh Ruppersburg and Douglas Anderson, department head and graduate director of English at the University of Georgia, I am grateful for graduate assistance and for course scheduling that enabled me to complete this project. Patricia Watson Hamilton helped me compile the annotated bibliography, and Eric Rochester assisted at the end with proofreading. I would also like to acknowledge Betsey Weinrich for her unintentional, but important, contribution to this book. To the fifteen hearty members of my Fall 1995 Eighteenth-Century English Novel course who showed up for class the day before Thanksgiving break, I offer my appreciation for their help with this brief preface.

It is with great pleasure that I extend my last thanks. To the students of my Special Topics course in Swift and Sterne (Winter 1995), I acknowledge my most important debt. It is through teaching that we learn what needs to be explained and which explanations actually work. The comments, concerns, and responses of the students of English 489 in a very real sense directed the writing of this book. I hope the members of that class will be pleased with the result.

Athens, Georgia
17 November 1995

Chronology

1713   Laurence Sterne born 24 November in Clonmel, Ireland, first child of army ensign Roger Sterne and wife Agnes.

1723   Enrolled by his father at school in Hipperholme, close to the estate of his paternal uncle, Richard Sterne.

1731   Death of Roger Sterne in Jamaica.

1732   Death of Sterne's uncle, Richard Sterne.

1733   Begins attendance as a sizar at Jesus College, Cambridge, 11 November; sometime during his residence at Cambridge, experiences his first tubercular attack.

1734   Receives vacated Sterne scholarship 30 July.

1735   John Hall registers at Jesus College, Cambridge; beginning of friendship with Sterne.

1737   Receives A.B. degree, is ordained, receives his first clerical appointment as assistant curate of St. Ives.

1738   In February, receives appointment as assistant curate of Catton in Yorkshire; in August becomes vicar of Sutton-on-the-Forest.

1740   Receives Master of Arts degree from Cambridge.

1741   Succeeds to prebendary of Givendale in York Minster; marries Elizabeth Lumley 30 March in the minster; uncle Jaques Sterne starts the *York Gazetteer,* a pro-Walpole newspaper for which Laurence Sterne contributes several essays in controversy with "J.S."

1742   Walpole falls from power; Sterne resigns from the *York Gazetteer,* exchanges his Givendale prebend for that of North Newbald; break with Jaques Sterne occurs due to politics of election; Agnes Sterne begins demanding financial support from her son; Elizabeth Sterne suffers miscarriage.

1743   Poem, "The Unknown World," published in *Gentleman's Magazine.*

1744   Appointed vicar at Stillington in addition to his duties
        at Sutton-on-the-Forest; Agnes Sterne enlists Jaques
        Sterne's aid in pressuring Laurence for money; Lau-
        rence Sterne purchases Tindal Farm at Sutton.

1745   24 July, Charles Edward Stuart and a few Scots soldiers
        and English expatriates land at Eriskay, initiating the
        "Jacobite Rebellion" of '45; 1 October, daughter Lydia
        born to Laurence and Elizabeth Sterne; 2 October
        Lydia buried.

1746   In April the rebel forces are defeated in the notoriously
        bloody battle of Culloden; August–October, treason
        trials conducted in York.

1747   At the church of St. Michael le Belfry, York, preaches
        charity sermon "The case of Elijah and the widow of
        Zarephath, consider'd" in April; the sermon is pub-
        lished in July; 24 October, John Fountayne installed
        Dean of York Minster; Sterne appointed justice of the
        peace; Agnes Sterne, encouraged by Jaques, makes fur-
        ther financial demands of her son and daughter-in-law;
        1 December, Lydia Sterne born.

1748   Matthew Hutton installed as Archbishop of York.

1749   Controversy within York Minster pits Laurence Sterne
        and Dean Fountayne against Jaques Sterne and Arch-
        bishop Hutton; Francis Topham foments the feud.

1750   Controversy continues, this year focused on the issue of
        substitute preaching with Jaques Sterne challenging
        the power of the Dean to appoint substitutes; Hutton
        sides with Jaques Sterne and Topham; Laurence sup-
        ports Fountayne; 29 July, preaches "The abuses of con-
        science" at the annual assizes at York Minster.

1751   Without her son's knowledge, Agnes Sterne jailed for
        debt in January through the influence of Jaques Sterne;
        later in the year Laurence Sterne settles her in York;
        receives commisaryship of Pickering and Pocklington
        over Topham's protests; Elizabeth Sterne's pregnancy
        results in a stillbirth.

1757   John Gilbert becomes Archbishop of York.

1758   Prepares to receive residentiaryship and move his family into the Minster Yard at York; Francis Topham's efforts to procure a preferment for his son are blocked by Dean Fountayne; Topham stirs up controversy; Sterne begins writing *A Political Romance.*

1759   In January, *A Political Romance* appears in print; in February, Fountayne, Topham, and Sterne meet with Archbishop Gilbert and as a result most remaining copies of *A Political Romance* are burned; loses hope of residentiaryship and support of Fountayne; moves family to the Minster Yard in York; writes "Fragment in the Manner of Rabelais"; Agnes Sterne dies 5 May; Jaques Sterne dies 9 June; Elizabeth Sterne suffers mental breakdown; Laurence Sterne begins affair with singer Catherine Fourmantel; late in December the first two volumes of *Tristram Shandy* are printed in York and half the copies are sent to be sold in London.

1760   4 March, arrives in London with Stephen Croft; is lionized as the author of *Tristram Shandy* for the next two months; meets Garrick; has portrait painted by Reynolds; London edition of *Tristram Shandy* with sketch by Hogarth appears on 2 April; receives living of Coxwold; 18 May preaches at the chapel of Serjeants' Inn in London; 22 May, two volumes of *The Sermons of Mr. Yorick* appear in print; late May, returns to York to take up residence in Coxwold at "Shandy Hall."

1761   29 January, volumes 3 and 4 of *Tristram Shandy* published; 3 May, preaches charity sermon in London at the Foundling Hospital, "The parable of the rich man and Lazarus consider'd"; meets Samuel Johnson for the first and only time in November; volumes 5 and 6 of *Tristram Shandy* printed on 22 December.

1762   January, arrives in Paris; in the summer, suffers an attack of pneumonia, followed by a lung hemorrhage; Elizabeth and Lydia arrive in Paris 8 July and the family sets out for Toulouse.

1763   Again ill; Sterne family relocates, after a summer visit to Bagnères, to Montpellier where Sterne makes the acquaintance of Tobias Smollett.

1764   Elizabeth and Lydia move to Montauban; Sterne returns via Paris to England; in Paris, has sentimental love affair and preaches before Lord Hertford, the English ambassador to France, "The case of Hezekiah and the messengers."

1765   23 January, volumes 7 and 8 of *Tristram Shandy* published; in September suffers another hemorrhage; in October sets out for Europe; visits Paris, Lyons, Turin, Milan, Florence, Rome, and Naples; sometime during the journey is reunited briefly with Elizabeth and Lydia.

1766   18 January, *The Sermons of Mr. Yorick* volumes 3 and 4 published; concludes trip to Italy; in August preaches at York Minster, last sermon he would ever preach.

1767   January, volume 9 of *Tristram Shandy* published; falls in love with Eliza Draper; April, Eliza departs to join her husband in India; Sterne writes *Journal to Eliza* and *Sentimental Journey;* undergoes treatment for syphilis; renovates Shandy Hall; October, Elizabeth and Lydia move back to York.

1768   27 February, *A Sentimental Journey* published; Sterne, in London since January to oversee publication, falls ill in early March; 18 March, dies at his lodgings in London.

Chapter One

Laurence Sterne Before *Tristram Shandy:* Personalities and Politics

With the December 1759 publication of volumes 1 and 2 of *Tristram Shandy,* Laurence Sterne became that most modern of entities—a celebrity. By March of 1760, the heretofore obscure clergyman from York was the toast of London. "My Lodgings is every hour full of your great People of the first Rank who strive who shall most honour me—" he wrote to his mistress Catherine Fourmantel, a singer of some renown herself. "[E]ven all the Bishops have sent their Complimt[s] to me . . . ."[1] Young James Boswell, in London for the 1760 social season, commemorated Sterne's popularity in jaunty couplets:

> By fashion's hands completely dress'd,
> He's everywhere a welcome guest.
> He runs about from place to place,
> Now with my Lord, then with his Grace,
> And, mixing with the brilliant throng,
> He straight commences *beau garçon.*
> In Ranelagh's delightful round
> Squire Tristram oft is flaunting found;
> A buzzing whisper flies about,
> Where'er he comes they point him out;
> Each waiter with an eager eye
> Observes him as he passes by:
> 'That there is he—do, Thomas, look!—
> Who's wrote such a damn'd clever book.'[2]

This newfound notoriety delighted Sterne who, as he himself said, "wrote not [to] be *fed,* but to be *famous*" (*Letters,* 90). Sterne adroitly managed his celebrity, playing in public (and in private to some degree) his self-created roles, first of Tristram and later of Parson Yorick. He seems to have grasped almost intuitively the cardinal rules that publicists and other public relations experts have in our day refined into a science: Any publicity is good publicity. Keep your name before the public. Create a public persona and—in public anyway—live it. Sterne's fame, of course, outlasted the eight years, two months, and some odd days that remained of his life in December 1759; through *Tristram Shandy* and *A Sentimental Journey* it continues to endure. But his celebrity was a phenomenon of the 1760s, and while he was alive to exploit the public's interest he created the enigmatic, capricious, whimsical, nervous, feeling, laughing, Shandean personality we think of when we think of Laurence Sterne.

Childhood and Youth

Who was Laurence Sterne before he was the celebrated author of that "damn'd clever book"? This question is more easily asked than answered, for the author left more traces than the man. We do know some facts, however; Sterne left a brief "memoir" of his *"family, and self,"* written, he said, for his daughter Lydia, *"in case hereafter she might have a curiosity, or a kinder motive to know"* the details of her father's life (*Letters,* 5).[3] In this brief account, Sterne got much wrong, particularly with regard to his mother's family, and the very brevity of the memoir— fewer than 2,000 words—suggests that Sterne, like his Parson Yorick, found "telling any one who I am" a "perplexing affair."[4] Certainly, the reader who wants a balanced and documented view of the life of Laurence Sterne must consult the definitive two-volume biography by Arthur H. Cash.[5] Still, Sterne's cryptic account is of interest if only because the few things he does mention tell us something about who he felt the pre-Tristram, pre-Yorick Laurence Sterne to be.

Sterne begins the "Memoirs" as most autobiographers would, with an account of his parentage. Sterne's father, Roger, was an army ensign. His mother, Agnes, was the daughter of a provider of supplies who followed the army from camp to camp and who died while Agnes was still quite young. Her mother soon married a Captain Nuttall who rose to the rank of Major in the British army. Agnes grew up in barracks and encampments, and she seems to have found the life appealing. She first married a Captain Hebert, who left her a young widow, and then she married soldier Roger Sterne. Later on, Agnes would become a nuisance to her son, and Sterne would speak of her with great impatience, even vitriol. But in the "Memoirs," he is restrained, no doubt partly because he wrote them eight years after Agnes's death. Indeed, the picture of Sterne's early life that emerges from the "Memoirs" bespeaks a quite natural bonding between mother and son, even if this bonding occurred in rather strange circumstances. Sterne's earliest memories are closely connected to his mother's travails as an eighteenth-century army wife: the births and the deaths of children, the difficulties of traveling with infants, and disruptions to domestic life caused by military relocations.

Before Sterne was six years old, his family had moved five times. In fact, the day after his birth on November 24, 1713, Roger Sterne's regiment was "broke," that is, disbanded, and Roger was "sent adrift into the wide world with a wife and two children," the infant Laurence and his year-old sister, Mary ("Memoirs," 1). There followed a ten-month sojourn in Elvington near York, on the Sterne family estate. When Roger's regiment was reconstituted, he was sent to Dublin for a month and then ordered to Exeter, to be followed by his wife and children in, as Sterne puts it, "a sad winter" ("Memoirs," 1). After a year, the regiment was sent back to Ireland, and Sterne's mother once more packed up her young family, now including baby Joram, to follow her husband. This journey was as difficult as most eighteenth-century travel. Sterne reports that "[m]y mother, with three of us, . . . took ship at Bristol, for Ireland, and had a narrow escape from being cast away by a leak springing up in the vessel" ("Memoirs," 1–2). The family lived in Dublin for the next year and a half, and they must have lived well, judging from Sterne's comment that his father in this time "spent a great deal of money" ("Memoirs," 2). But in 1719, the regiment was ordered up again, this time to the Isle of Wight, from whence the troops would leave to fight a recently declared war with Spain. At this time, Sterne was nearing the age of six. What he records of this period of his life and onward reflects his own memories and experiences rather than those of his mother. It is no coincidence that the phrase "I remember" appears suddenly.

Yet even these memories are closely bound to the rhythms of his mother's life. Sterne's earliest recollection seems to be of the death from smallpox of his four-year-old brother, Joram. This event was followed by a happier one: "We had poor Joram's loss supplied during our stay in the Isle of Wight, by the birth of a girl, Anne . . ." ("Memoirs," 2). Then came the birth of a brother, Devijeher, in 1720; the death of Anne ("[t]his pretty blossom fell at the age of three years, in the Barracks of Dublin"); the death of Devijeher a year later; the birth of another sister, Susan; and her death, too ("Memoirs," 2). Sterne remembers life in encampments and barracks, a six-month stay in a parsonage with his mother's stepsister, her clergyman husband and their family, difficult journeys by sea and land, and life in an Irish castle owned by a "collateral descendant" of Sterne's paternal great-grandfather ("Memoirs," 3). Yet Sterne also recalls an emerging sense of individuality during this period. He records two early achievements: learning to write at the age of eight while living in barracks in Dublin and experiencing his first taste of fame. This latter event occurred during the spring or summer of 1721, just before the move to Dublin, while Agnes Sterne and her children were enjoying the hospitality of her clergyman brother-in-law. Sterne relates: "It was in this parish, during our stay, that I had that wonderful escape in falling through a mill-race whilst the mill was going, and of being taken up unhurt—the story is incredible, but known for truth in all that part of Ireland—where hundreds of the common people flocked to see me" ("Memoirs," 2).

By the age of ten, Laurence Sterne had experienced all of traditional family life—such as it was—he would experience until his own marriage produced a strikingly different domestic scene. At ten, he was enrolled at school in Hipperholme, near Halifax and also close to the estate of Roger Sterne's elder brother, Richard. Father and son were never to meet again. As if in response to the sense of severance from his immediate family that this enrollment at Hipperholme signified, Sterne becomes at this point in the *Memoir* self-conscious about narrative strategy, for it is here that Sterne's "life" and his "family" diverge onto separate courses. His own young adulthood is dispensed with—momentarily—in the sentence that reports his removal to school, his eventual enrollment at Cambridge: "my father got leave of his colonel to fix me at school— . . . with an able master; with whom I staid [*sic*] some time, 'till by God's care of me my cousin Sterne, of Elvington . . . sent me to the university, &c. &c." ("Memoirs," 3). The dismissive ampersands yield to the "thread of our story," a summary of the salient events of the remaining years—there were eight—in Roger Sterne's life. There was the birth of another child, Catherine, a duel over a goose at the siege of Gilbralter, a fever in Jamaica "which took away his senses first, and made a child of him," and finally his death: "[H]e sat down in an arm chair, and breathed his last" ("Memoirs," 3). Sterne's assessment of Roger Sterne reads like a passage from *Tristram Shandy:*

> My father was a little smart man—active to the last degree, in all exercises—most patient of fatigue and disappointments, of which it pleased God to give him full measure—he was in his temper somewhat rapid,

and hasty—but of a kindly, sweet disposition, void of all design; and so innocent in his own intentions, that he suspected no one; so that you might have cheated him ten times in a day, if nine had not been sufficient for your purpose. ("Memoirs," 3)

Hasty, innocent, sweet, unsuspecting, a soldier, a father, and a little smart man, this Roger Sterne seems a combination of Walter Shandy, Uncle Toby, Parson Yorick, Trim, and Tristram himself. Engenderer of sickly children, his own name (Roger) a slang word for sexual intercourse, his life, by his son's account, a series of disappointments culminating in a ridiculous quarrel and idiocy, the Roger Sterne presented by the "Memoirs" is as wayward and hapless as any of the inhabitants of Shandy Hall. He is a fitting progenitor of the author of *Tristram Shandy,* a prototype, in a sense, of Tristram's inchoate state: the homunculus, the spermatazoic "little man," whose lonely journey, undertaken without the animal spirits dispersed by Mrs. Shandy's "untimely" question, is the beginning of Tristram's own chaotic, meandering existence.

Sterne remembers his life after the age of ten primarily in terms of relationships with more or less satisfactory surrogate fathers: his Hipperholme schoolmaster, Nathan Sharpe; his Uncle Richard; his cousin Sterne of Elvington; and his Uncle Jaques, Roger's younger brother. Schoolmaster Sharpe, Sterne remembers fondly for his response to a bit of schoolboy mischief: Sharpe "had had the cieling [*sic*] of the schoolroom new white-washed—the ladder remained there—I one unlucky day mounted it, and wrote with a brush in large capital *Letters,* LAU. STERNE, for which the usher severely whipped me. My master was very much hurt at this, and said, before me, that never should that name be effaced, for I was a boy of genius, and he was sure I should come to preferment." "[T]his expression," concludes Sterne, "made me forget the stripes I had received" ("Memoirs," 3–4).

In 1731, Sterne's father died, followed in 1732 by his Uncle Richard. These deaths left young Laurence, as he put it later, "without one Shilling in the World" (*Letters,* 34). He appealed to his Uncle Jaques for aid but was refused. Richard Sterne of Elvington, elder son of the deceased Uncle Richard, came to his cousin's rescue. He, says Sterne both in the "Memoirs" and in a 1751 letter to his Uncle Jaques, "became a father to me" ("Memoirs," 3; *Letters,* 34). "[T]o . . . [his] Protection *then,*" Sterne acknowledges, "I chiefly [*sic*] owe What I now am" (*Letters,* 34). Richard made it possible for Sterne to enter Cambridge, where he prepared for a career in the Church of England.

Richard Sterne placed his cousin Laurence at Jesus College, where he himself had studied and where a compelling family tradition encouraged all the Yorkshire Sternes to study. The Sternes' great-grandfather, another Richard Sterne, had been a master at Jesus College in the 1640s and had later become Archbishop of York. This esteemed ancestor had established scholarships at the college for succeeding generations of Sternes. Jesus College, then, was the obvious choice for the impecunious son of Roger Sterne, though he had to work during his first year at Cambridge while awaiting the availability of one of the Sterne scholarships.

As Arthur Cash has pointed out, most of the students at Jesus College, including Sterne, studied for careers in the Church of England. Richard Sterne was an exception, as were other country gentlemen who had no need of a career at all and who usually—as in Richard's case—matriculated without taking a degree. Poor students almost invariably entered the priesthood. In Cash's words, "[p]robably it never crossed anyone's mind that young Laurence Sterne could become anything but a clergyman" (Cash, *EMY,* 44).

Despite his chosen profession, Sterne's Cambridge years were by no means characterized by piety and solemnity. It was at Cambridge, after all, that Sterne formed a friendship—"most lasting on both sides"—with John Hall, later John Hall-Stevenson ("Memoirs," 4). An eccentric, secular, and often blatantly anti-clerical writer of bad verse, Hall was in many ways an unlikely companion for a clergyman, but his friendship would be important to Sterne throughout his life. At Hall's home, Skelton—"Crazy"—Castle, would meet the Demoniacs, a group of men including soldiers, squires, a politician, and Laurence Sterne, who shared a love of sports, eccentricity of character, and a taste for Rabelaisian humor. Periodic visits to the Castle would provide Sterne needed respite from his duties as a clergyman. Although Hall's efforts to ride the coattails of his friend's literary success by publishing offensive verse epistles would prove embarrassing to Sterne, the two remained lifelong friends; indeed, Hall—Eugenius-like—attended Sterne in his final illness.

Sterne's Uncle Jaques exerted the greatest influence on his pre–*Tristram Shandy* life. By the time Laurence Sterne completed his studies at Cambridge, Jaques Sterne had risen through the hierarchy of the Church of England to become the Archdeacon of Cleveland, a fairly powerful position. In fact, as Sterne notes in the "Memoirs," it was to Uncle Jaques that he owed his appointment as vicar of Sutton-on-the-Forest: "I then came to York, and my uncle got me the living of Sutton" ("Memoirs,"

4). In the "Memoirs," Sterne seems to imply that, in our vernacular, he got his first job through his uncle's influence, but in fact, as with most young college graduates, Sterne floundered around a bit before becoming settled. Sterne's period of floundering lasted about six months and consisted of two brief tenures as an assistant curate, first at St. Ives and next at Catton. Some clergymen of the eighteenth-century church spent their entire careers in such lowly offices, but Sterne was lucky. In contrast to his earlier behavior when Laurence had needed him, Jaques Sterne now exerted himself on his nephew's behalf, though probably not out of a sense of family obligation. More likely, during his six months as an assistant curate, Laurence Sterne had begun to strike Jaques as possibly useful to his own career. Perhaps the nephew had been impressive enough in the sermons he preached as an assistant curate for word to have reached his uncle's ears. Or perhaps Laurence Sterne had begun to evidence literary skills that Jaques found promising, a plausible suggestion considering how often the elder Sterne found use for the younger Sterne's pen in the decade to come.[6]

Today, in America especially, we may find it hard to conceive the degree to which church and state were conjoined in eighteenth-century England. Although religious issues may fuel much political debate today—or to put it more accurately, though much political debate is couched in religious terminology today—the fact remains that the institutional structure of our religious life does not and cannot accommodate a true fusion of church and state. Our Constitution denies the possibility by its complete commitment not only to freedom of religion but also to the equality of all religions. In eighteenth-century England one could be Catholic, Quaker, Anabaptist, Presbyterian, or Jewish; and although in general one was not officially persecuted for belonging to any of these groups, there were penalties. Only communicants of the Established Church of England could attend Oxford or Cambridge; only communicants could hold political office. While religious homogeneity did not really exist, the country was organized as though it prevailed: All of England was divided into parishes. The church functioned very much as an arm of the state, inculcating values that were political as much as spiritual (anti-Catholicism, for example). And the state was very much involved in church hierarchy; promotions and preferments were generally bequeathed directly or indirectly for service to the government.

By 1738, Uncle Jaques had earned a reputation as a supporter of the Whig government of Robert Walpole. His position as Archdeacon was one reward for his support, but further glories were possible with further service. No wonder he suddenly looked with favor upon his talented nephew.

Unlike his uncle, Laurence Sterne does not seem to have been keenly interested in politics, though like any young man who has to support himself, he was interested in advancing his own career. After 1741, this interest was even sharper as he had become responsible not only for himself but for a wife as well. In the "Memoirs," Sterne tells his daughter:

> [A]t York I became acquainted with your mother, and courted her for two years—she owned she liked me, but thought herself not rich enough, or me too poor, to be joined together—she went to her sister's in S[taffordshire], and I wrote to her often—I believe then she was partly determined to have me, but would not say so—at her return she fell into a consumption—and one evening that I was sitting by her with an almost broken heart to see her so ill, she said, "my dear Lawrey, I can never be yours, for I verily believe I have not long to live—but I have left you every shilling of my fortune;"—upon that she shewed me her will— this generosity overpowered me.—It pleased God that she recovered, and I married her in the year 1741. ("Memoirs," 4)

Elizabeth Lumley was not wealthy, but she was from a respectable family. Her father had been a clergyman and her cousin was Elizabeth Robinson, better known as Elizabeth Montagu, the famous bluestocking. The Sternes's marriage was marked by periods of sadness caused by the deaths of infants (only one child survived of the three that were born to the Sternes). The marriage also was marred by periods of dissonance caused partly by Mr. Sterne's philandering and partly by Mrs. Sterne's characteristic quick temper. It began auspiciously enough, however, with mutual trust and affection.

The fortune that Elizabeth Lumley had willed to Laurence Sterne was a small one; upon their marriage, she elected to turn the whole of her estate over to her husband's management. By eighteenth-century law, she had a right to a provision in her marriage contract that her fortune would be used for her support and maintenance—as opposed to her husband's needs—and it seems that Sterne offered to, as he puts it, "have her own fortune Settled upon her" (*Letters*, 39). She refused, however, trusting her husband to manage the couple's financial affairs without prejudice to her comfort and security. Uncle Jaques's comment upon hearing of this arrangement was that his nephew should take care to see *"that the Lady should be no Sufferer by such a Mark of her Confidence"* (*Letters*, 39). Sterne took that advice seriously, though his uncle later, in effect, repudiated it.

Laurence Sterne's trustworthiness on the issue was tested early. His mother, who had been living quietly in Ireland with her youngest child, Catherine, was somehow apprised of the news that her son had married "a fortune." She began to write Sterne letters and pay him visits (or send Catherine to pay him visits) demanding money to supplement the £20 annual pension she had received since Roger Sterne's death. Laurence Sterne's adamant refusal to enrich his mother and sister at his wife's expense led to a permanent rift between them. Moreover, it provided the occasion for a serious quarrel with Uncle Jaques, who took Agnes's part in the dispute, though the real cause of the quarrel between uncle and nephew had—as was usual with Jaques—more to do with political than with familial concerns.

Sterne refers elliptically to the quarrel with his uncle in the "Memoirs." After his marriage in 1741, Sterne says, "[m]y uncle and myself were . . . upon very good terms, for he soon got me the Prebendary of York—but he quarrelled with me afterwards, because I would not write paragraphs in the newspapers—though he was a party-man, I was not, and detested such dirty work: thinking it beneath me—from that period, he became my bitterest enemy" ("Memoirs," 4). This statement is quite important, for upon it rests the evidence that Sterne was a writer of sorts before the publication of *Tristram Shandy*. In fact, he wrote a great deal during the twenty or so years between his commencement from Cambridge and his emergence as a celebrated author: sermons, of course; the newspaper "paragraphs" to which he refers; occasional journalistic essays on matters he found of interest or concern; and now and then, a poem.

Three crucial periods of writing deserve remark.[7] In 1741, Sterne experienced for the first time the potency of the pen, but he exerted his power in the service of a cause that was not his own. The Jacobite rebellion of 1745 may have provided another occasion for Sterne to address an audience in print. Finally, the year 1759 saw the production of Sterne's final attempt to influence the course of local events in *A Political Romance* and the transformation of personal experience into a satire that strives for universal appeal in "A Fragment in the Manner of Rabelais," a direct precursor of *Tristram Shandy*.

"Dirty Paragraphs"

It is very difficult and rarely profitable (which probably accounts for the difficulty) to keep political campaigns high-minded. The business of begging for votes is not a pretty one today; it was even less so in eighteenth-century England. There was widespread corruption. Votes were offered in exchange for tangible rewards; powerful squires who virtually controlled the votes of tenants and less powerful freeholders would expect in exchange for delivering a block of votes government preferments—positions, livings—for themselves or members of their families. Ballot boxes were often stuffed with votes from non-residents of the county holding the election; sometimes, in a hotly contested race, the hospitals and insane asylums were emptied as patients were taken to the polling stations and told how to vote. The third plate of Hogarth's *Four Prints of an Election,* "The Polling," shows just such a pathetic scene. Debates during campaigns were almost always in the nature of *ad hominem* attacks, and just as is the case today, the press played a large role.

The 1741 general election was of particular concern to Jaques Sterne because on it rested the fate of Prime Minister Robert Walpole, whose popularity had been slipping in Parliament. The election of 1741 could secure his power if enough Walpole supporters were returned or newly elected to Parliament. The issue was as simple as that. To forward this agenda, Jaques Sterne started a newspaper, *The York Gazetteer,* a pro-Walpole publication, the chief writer for which was his nephew. The opposition *York Courant* represented what was known as the "Country Interest" or the "Country Party" as opposed to the pro-Walpole "Ministerial Party." The election produced a very narrow margin of victory for Walpole; but one of the newly elected officials, Viscount Morpeth, was dying even as he won the seat, a fact widely known throughout Yorkshire and London. So, as early as one month after the May election, before the viscount had expired, the campaigning for the inevitable by-election had begun in earnest. When Morpeth died in August, the Country Interest was ready with their nominee, George Fox, and the Ministerial Party responded by nominating Cholmley Turner. Sterne began to write letters to the *Gazetteer* in support of Turner and Walpole Whiggism in general. Soon he was answered in the *Courant* by someone who signed his letters "J.S. from Leeds," and who wrote in defense of Fox and the Country Interest. A lively paper war had begun.

Sterne's pen proved the stronger. Thanks largely to his energetic responses to J.S., particularly in a pamphlet entitled *Query upon Query* in which Sterne comically dismantled the opposition's criticism of the ministerial candidate, Cholmley Turner won, but not before irreparable damage had been done to the relationship between Jaques and Laurence Sterne. Early on, Jaques had come to the conclusion the J.S. was James

Scott, a clergyman from Leeds, in fact the *only* clergyman from Leeds with the initials J.S. Laurence Sterne, instructed by his uncle, proceeded on the assumption. In *Query upon Query,* Sterne implied that J.S. was a clergyman, and he met all denials with challenges, the most notorious being a letter to the *York Courant* in which "L.S." depicted "J.S." first as a coward who will not own his name and, second, as a "certain nasty Animal in *Egypt*" who, in fleeing strong adversaries, "lets fly backward . . . and thereby covers his Retreat with the Fumes of his own Filth and Excrement" (quoted in *EMY,* 105). Sterne concluded this letter, "As this Creature is naturally very *impotent,* and its chief Safety depends on a plentiful Discharge on such Occasions, the Naturalists affirm, that Self-preservation directs it to a certain Vegitable [*sic*] on the Banks of the River *Nile,* which constantly arms it with a proper Habit of Body against all Emergencies" (*EMY,* 105).

Although this letter might seem harsh to us and, Arthur Cash thinks, rather shocked the editor of the *York Courant* (*EMY,* 105), Sterne seems to have meant it as an almost playful rejoinder to the previous week's attack on him in the *York Courant.* Modifying Alexander Pope's scathing verses on the effeminate Lord Hervey, a correspondent from Leeds (presumably J.S. himself) had addressed the charge that J.S. was a clergyman thus:

> Let L———y Scribble———what? that Thing of Silk,
> L———y that mere white Curd of Ass's Milk?
> Satire or Sense, alas! can L———y feel?
> Who breaks a Butterfly upon a Wheel? (quoted in *EMY,* 104)

Only too glad to couch the political squabble in allusive satire, "Lawry" eagerly matched this Popean display with a Rabelaisian flourish of his own, complete with the scatological imagery so characteristic of *Gargantua and Pantagruel.* He must have been delighted to discover a fellow clergyman with whom to play such literary games.

Unfortunately, to Sterne's chagrin, J.S. was *not* James Scott, but one John Stanhope of Horsforth—not a clergyman but a lawyer. Further, though Cholmley Turner won *his* seat in Parliament in the by-election, Walpole's general support had so weakened that he resigned from office anyway on February 3, 1742. Further still, the following July another elected member of Parliament died, and the Country Interest's old candidate George Fox was elected to fill the vacant seat. He ran unopposed.

Following this election, Sterne, who had resigned from the *Gazetteer* in March following Walpole's fall, sent a letter to the *York Courant:* "Sir," he began, "I find by some late Preferments, that it may not be improper to change Sides; therefore I beg the Favour of you to inform the Publick, that I sincerely beg Pardon for the abusive Gazetteers I wrote during the late contested Election for the County of York, and that I heartily wish Mr. Fox Joy of his Election for the City" (*Letters,* 21). This letter was probably designed as something of a declaration of independence, Sterne's effort to dissociate himself from his uncle's politics. It achieved its end, for it must have irritated and embarrassed Jaques Sterne considerably. "From that period," Sterne says in the "Memoirs," "he [Jaques] became my bitterest enemy" ("Memoirs," 4).

Jaques retaliated in a variety of ways, one of which was to take Agnes Sterne's side in her efforts to wrench a financial settlement from her son. In 1751, Sterne wrote to his uncle, complaining specifically of the support Jaques was giving to Agnes's claims and more generally of "the hardest Measure that ever Man received—continued on Your Side, without any Provocation on Mine—without ever once being told my Fault—or Conscious of ever committing one Which deserved an unkind look from You" (*Letters,* 41). In this letter, Laurence Sterne paints himself as an innocent victim, confused by his uncle's cruelty, himself long-suffering and noble: "notwithstanding . . . the Bitterness of ten Years unwearied Persecution, . . . I retain that Sense of the Service You did me at my first Setting out in the World." He signed himself "Your once much Obliged tho' now, Y^r Much Injured Nephew" (*Letters,* 41). Despite Sterne's pose of ignorance, he clearly is aware of the precise date at which the enmity occurred, both in the letter, written ten years after the events, and again in the "Memoir," written at nearly twenty-five years' remove. He surely remembered the 1741 election as the beginning of a kind of independence for which he paid dearly in terms of his clerical career and for which he reaped enormous benefits as a writer. In refusing to write at the command of his uncle in the sole interest of party politics, Sterne freed himself to find his own subjects, to support his own causes, and to seek his own preferment independent of his uncle's power and position.

Defending the Faith

Aside from letters and the sermons he wrote as a part of his clerical duties, what we know of Sterne's writing between 1741 and 1758 seems to support the notion of Sterne's increasing independence. The truth is, however, that we do not know much. In fact, we can point with unshakable confidence to only one poem published in the *Gentleman's Magazine* in July 1743. The poem is entitled "The Unknown World" and is attributed to the "Rev^d M^r St—n"; and it certainly was not written at the bidding of Archdeacon Jaques Sterne. To speak honestly, it is a poem of little merit or interest other than its authorship. Arthur Cash calls it "the most lugubrious piece" Sterne ever wrote (*EMY,* 152). A sample verse or two will confirm Cash's judgment:

> We talk of heav'n, we talk of hell;
> But what they mean no tongue can tell!
> Heav'n is the realm where angels are,
> And hell the Chaos of despair!
> But what these awful words imply,
> None of us know before we die!
> Whether we will or no, we must
> Take the succeeding world on trust.[8]

Kenneth Monkman attributes Sterne's solemn commonplaces in this poem to the death of a college friend ("Sterne and the '45," 47). Sterne himself says they were occasioned by "hearing a Pass-Bell" tolling the "departure of a soul." Whatever the case, the poem is clear evidence that in 1743, though he had ceased to write "dirty paragraphs," Sterne had not ceased to write.

In fact, the next few years may have provoked a good deal of writing from Sterne. Anyone who had once influenced the outcome of an election by the written word would have been hard pressed to resist having a hand in directing the much more significant events that occurred in 1745. This was the year that Prince Charles Edward Stuart (Bonnie Prince Charlie) arrived in Scotland and proceeded southward with an army for the purpose of reclaiming the throne of England for his father James Francis Edward Stuart. Early rumor reported that the Jacobite forces would travel through York to London; defenders of the crown were on the alert—as were Jacobite sympathizers. Civil war seemed a real possibility.

The roots of this action are traceable to the 1688 Glorious Revolution (so-called because it was accomplished without an actual war), in which the Catholic monarch James II was deposed and replaced by the Protestant King William and Queen Mary. When James left the throne, he had an infant son, also James, whom some in England felt to be the rightful heir to the throne. But others held that the son's right to rule was forfeited when his father was deposed, and he was further excluded by the 1701 Act of Settlement that prohibited any Catholic from sitting on the throne of England. King William was succeeded by Queen Anne in 1702, and after her death in 1714, England turned to Germany and the House of Hanover for her monarch, by-passing once more the now prohibited Stuart line, which had been extended by the birth of Charles in 1720. Sporadically, throughout the eighteenth century, the Jacobites, aided by the French and by Catholic interests in Europe, would assert the Stuart claim to the throne. Roger Sterne had fought against the 1715 uprising; his son would aid the fight against the Jacobites in 1745.

Kenneth Monkman has identified a number of pamphlets, poems, and newspaper paragraphs dating from this period that he feels likely to have been authored by Sterne. We must treat such attributions cautiously, but the material is worth serious consideration. Even if it did not emanate from Sterne's pen, it certainly speaks to ideological and professional truths about the author of *Tristram Shandy*. As an Anglican priest, Sterne was, of course, anti-Jacobite and anti–Roman Catholic; therefore, his emotional commitment to the resistance seems unquestionable. He was also eager at this time for the notice of the new Archbishop, Thomas Herring, who had taken office in 1743. What better way to receive positive attention than by defending the "true faith?" According to Monkman, he did just that.

The six anonymous works identified by Monkman as probably authored by Sterne are all concerned with the dual aim of discrediting the Jacobites and Roman Catholicism in general and of buttressing the loyalist cause. As in most situations of this sort, the greater emphasis fell on the former. In a pamphlet entitled *Seasonable Advice to the Inhabitants of Yorkshire*, the author clearly sets forth the Protestant Englishman's case against Catholicism. In large and bold-faced type the pamphlet enumerates the five occasions in the past when Catholicism threatened the peace and security of England: the reign of Queen Mary (1553–58), the Spanish Armada (1588), the Irish Massacre (1598), the Gunpowder Plot (1605), and the reign of James II (1685–88): "All of you know how he broke through all his Promises; and before the Wax was cold that sealed his Declaration in Council that he would preserve our Constitution, he used his utmost Efforts to break through all the Laws of it."[9] This clearly partisan list is followed by a marginal pointing finger, of the

sort Sterne would employ in *Tristram Shandy,* drawing the reader's attention to the italicized sentence: *"These are all plain and undoubted Matters of
Fact"* (*Seasonable Advice,* 6). *Seasonable Advice* ends with the injunction:

> If You have any Love for Your Religion, if You have enjoyed, and may
> still enjoy the Sweets of Liberty, if You wou'd preserve Your Estates,
> Your Harvest, the Fruits of a Year's Labour, (Just gathered in success-
> fully, and likely to be first ravaged by these hungry and beggarly
> Invaders) from Violence and Outrage: If You love Your Wives and Chil-
> dren, and desire to live with them in Peace and Plenty; Arm, Arm under
> Your Brave Leaders, and stand up to defend King *George* and your Coun-
> try[.] (*Seasonable Advice,* 7–8)

Actually, the "traitors" did not come through York, but this pamphlet, calculated to raise patriotic fervor, was sufficiently inspirational to
sell more than 9,000 copies in two weeks—a phenomenal success. In it,
the author successfully addresses himself to a readership of common
people, in a plain style, without irony and with much emotion. Perhaps,
most especially, a minister would have been accustomed to addressing
such an audience in such a way. As Swift does in the *Drapier's Letters,* the
author of *Seasonable Advice* demonstrates his ability to put rhetoric to
civic as well as spiritual use. It is intriguing to suppose this author is
Laurence Sterne.

The other pamphlets attributed to Sterne by Monkman include two
defenses of the Archbishop's description of the rebels as "Desperadoes"
and "Ruffians," a comment on Louis XV's sanctions against Protestants,
and a dialogue between "A" and "B," who two years after the rebellion
are shocked to hear of toasts raised to "King" James Stuart in the home
of the Lord Mayor of York—an actual occurrence that the pamphlet
humorously debates. Perhaps most poignant, however, is the rather
straightforward reportage of the trials of the Jacobite rebels, which
records the sentencing of seventy rebels to death by hanging ("but not
till you be dead"), disembowelling, decapitation, and quartering
("Sterne and the '45," 101–2). Of those so condemned, twenty-two
were executed and forty-eight were reprieved. Another seventy-eight
were transported. The report, evidence of a stern and brutal system of
justice by our standards, ends with an epitaph and a poem entitled
"Compassion" written according to the reporter by two of the executed
rebels and glossed thus: "every one who peruses these will be affected
with some Degree of the *latter* [compassion], that a Person capable of
writing so well, and of thinking so *justly* on *some Subjects,* should ever

have been engaged in so wicked and unnatural a Rebellion" ("Sterne and the '45," 102).

A Political Romance

If Sterne did write against the Jacobites, he did so for no recognition and without tangible benefit. But Sterne never wrote solely in the service of personal ambition. Certainly he would not have objected to, indeed he quite hoped for, success in his career, movement up the hierarchical ladder within the church, the accumulation of titles, livings, supplemental incomes, and influence; and his failure to advance would continue to rankle for some time. The fact is, however, that Laurence Sterne did not desire this success above all things. Specific occasions, such as the election of 1741 or the rebellion of 1745, might stimulate Sterne to exercise his talents, but when his efforts failed to bring personal reward, he did not redouble them. Instead he turned to books, hunting, gardening, music, painting, friends, and most of all perhaps, women. Sterne lacked the singleness of purpose to prosper greatly in the highly competitive domain of the eighteenth-century church.

Not that he was doing badly. In 1743, he had added to his duties at Sutton-in-the-Forest those of Stillington. For twenty years, as he tells Lydia in the "Memoirs," he did "duty at both places" ("Memoirs," 4). In 1747, Sterne's prospects were further improved by the appointment of John Fountayne, whom Sterne had known at Cambridge, to the deanship of York Minster. Benefits were not immediately forthcoming, however; though Fountayne and Sterne were on very good terms, Uncle Jaques, enemy to both, was still exerting a powerful influence over the affairs of the Minster. By 1758, however, Jaques Sterne was ill and, for the most part, retired (he would die in 1759), and his nephew had renewed expectations of promotion within the church. More specifically, he had his eye on the canon residentiaryship his uncle's death would vacate. This post required that the holder live within the Minster Yard, so in late 1758 the Sternes prepared to move to York.

The close of 1758, then, found Laurence Sterne on the brink of success. The residentiaryship would bring not only more income but a great deal more power, and though his candidacy would have met some opposition, Sterne would almost surely have been voted to the post by the other residentiaries, including the Dean of York Minster, his friend Fountayne. But it was not to be. The success Sterne envisioned for himself and the success he achieved turned out to be vastly different things.

What changed the course of Sterne's life, and the course of literary history, was a squabble at the center of which was a grasping manipulator by the name of Francis Topham. Topham was a lawyer, a commissary (that is, a judge) of the spiritual court, and the father, in 1757, of a seven-year-old boy whose future he wished to ensure. He came up with a scheme for doing so: to have his commissaryship entailed on his son, so that at Topham's death, his child would simply succeed to his position without having to earn that preferment or another for himself. The plan was opposed by Dean Fountayne and denied by the Archbishop, for good reason. As must be apparent by now, the exercise of power in the church was dependent on the ability to confer favors and rewards. If posts were settled for generations to come, what patronage could archbishops, deans, residentiaries, and so on offer?

Topham, illogically angered by the refusal, began to remember other occasions when he had been "wronged" by the church establishment. True, he held a commissaryship, but he had been passed over for two such positions before he secured the one he held. Those positions had been conferred by Dean Fountayne and the other residentiaries on William Stables and on Laurence Sterne. A pamphlet warfare broke out, with accusations leveled by Topham and his champions and a defense mounted by Fountayne and his supporters, one of whom was, of course, Sterne himself.

A Political Romance brought to a stop the pamphlet bickering. Topham, Fountayne, and Sterne were called to London for a conference with the archbishop, who was wintering there. When they returned, copies of the *Romance* were burned, and Sterne did not receive his residentiaryship after all. Composed in Fountayne's service, *A Political Romance* was apparently written without his approval. The nature and tone of the satire must have revealed to him that the unpredictable and reckless side of his friend Laurence Sterne, which he probably enjoyed privately, could be publicly embarrassing or worse. Sterne felt betrayed and vowed to write no more for "an ungrateful person." In fact, he wrote to a "Mrs. F." in November of 1759: "I am tired of employing my brains for other people's advantage" (*Letters,* 84). By then he was well into the work that would secure his own fame, and in a few months' time, there would be no question of his ever using his talents in someone else's service again.

A Political Romance is interesting for the role it played in Laurence Sterne's "turning author," as he put it, but it is also a skillful satire that reveals Sterne's powers as a writer at full maturity (*Letters,* 84). It lacks broad appeal only because it is so tied to the politics and personalities of

York Minster that we have difficulty understanding some of the subtleties of the attack. Still, the broad outlines of the satire are clear and
the strategies by which Sterne sought to expose Topham's follies are a
foretaste of things to come in *Tristram Shandy* and *A Sentimental Journey*.
The satire is divided into four parts: a letter containing the romance
itself to which is appended a postscript, a key to the satire, a dedication
in which Sterne owns authorship, and a rather straightforward letter
addressed to Topham. The romance rehearses the "Fending and Proving
we have had of late, in this little Village of ours" by assigning allegorical
equivalents to the major players and issues involved in the brouhaha.[10]
Topham becomes Trim, "our Sexton and Dog-Whipper"; Fountayne is
"*John,* our Parish-Clerk"; the commissaryships that Topham had not
received are represented by a pulpit cloth, a cushion, and "an *old-cast-
Pair-of-black-Plush-Breeches*"; the commissaryship that Topham wished to
have settled on his son is "an old *Watch-Coat,* which had many Years
hung up in the Church, which *Trim* had set his Heart upon"; and the
archbishop is the "Parson of the Parish" (*PR,* 197–98).

The story begins when Trim asks the parson for the watch-coat from
which he wishes to have made a petticoat for his wife and a jerkin for
himself. The parson is inclined to give it to him—"for no sooner did the
distinct   Words—*Petticoat*——*poor   Wife*——*warm*——*Winter*   strike
upon his Ear,——but his Heart warmed"; yet he does not know if, as he
says, "'tis mine to bestow upon you or not" (*PR,* 198). The parson
assures Trim the coat is his as soon as inquiries determine "if any one had
a *Claim* to it;—or whether . . . the taking it down might not raise a
Clamour in the Parish" (*PR,* 199). Trim, it turns out, knows he has no
right to the coat and begins to pressure the parson into making a quick
decision before he too can discover the truth about the matter. But the
parson delays, having become suspicious that Trim's impatience could
mean "that all was not right at the Bottom" (*PR,* 199).

The truth is revealed to the parson by an unexpected hint. One of his
parishioners, a laborer "past his fifty-second Year," in order to avoid
being retained on the "Militia-List" (drafted, that is), comes to the vic-
arage "with a Groat in his Hand, to search the Parish Register for his
Age" (*PR,* 199). The parson, who has been ruminating on the problem
of the watch-coat, wonders suddenly if the Parish Register might offer
some insight into the matter: "He had scarce unclasped the Book . . .
when he popp'd upon the very Thing he wanted" (*PR,* 199). A black
letter memorandum follows, in which we (and the parson) learn that the
watch-coat was quite old—over two hundred years—and had been

given to the parish for the use of the "Sextons . . . and their Successors, for ever" to wear on cold winter nights when they were required to go outside to ring the bells (*PR,* 200). Just as the parson is congratulating himself for refusing to act precipitately on the matter, Trim appears with the watch-coat in two pieces, one cut in the shape of a petticoat and the other of a jerkin. The parson, full of "Astonishment and honest Indignation" (*PR,* 200) calls a hearing at which Trim defends himself by saying " 'That the Parson had absolutely promised to befriend him and his Wife in the Affair, to the utmost of his Power' " (*PR,* 201–2). The parson replies:

> "That nothing was in his *Power* to do, but what he could do *honestly:*— That in giving the Coat to him and his Wife, he should do a manifest Wrong to the *next* Sexton; the great Watch-Coat being the most comfortable Part of the Place:—That he should, moreover, injure the Right of his own Successor, who would be just so much a worse Patron, as the Worth of the Coat amounted to." (*PR,* 202)

Here we have the crux of the matter—of the watch-coat and of the commissaryship.

But, for Trim as for Topham, the issue is not resolved. Afraid to antagonize the parson any further, Trim begins to complain of John, the parish-clerk who, ten years ago, had promised him, Trim says, first a pulpit-cloth and cushion and then a pair of breeches that instead went to William Doe (William Staples) and Lorry Slim (Laurence Sterne), respectively. The breeches are not worth much, being "very thin by this Time," but Lorry who "has a light Heart" values them because they provoke Trim's envy (*PR,* 207).

This matter erupts into a public quarrel between John and Trim, and finally Trim is taken roundly to task by his neighbors for making such a fuss when he was already so well provided for: "Is there a cast-Coat, or a Place in the whole Town, that will bring you in a Shilling, but what you have snapp'd up, like a greedy Hound as you are?" (*PR,* 208) After all, Trim is sexton, dog-whipper, clock-winder, impounder of stray beasts (pinder), and coney-catcher, for which, the mob says, he has no license. Trim, piqued at the accusation, retorts, "I will catch Conies every Hour of the Night," an assertion overheard by "a toothless old Woman, who was just passing by" and who exclaims "*You catch Conies!*" (*PR,* 208). *Conies* is a synonym for *rabbits* and, in Sterne's day, a slang term for *young girls.* The old crone's remark sets the whole town laughing—"except *Trim,* who waddled very slowly off with that Kind of inflexible Gravity

only to be equalled by one Animal in the whole Creation,—and sur-
passed by none" (*PR,* 208–9).

The postscript goes on in much the same vein, with more claims and
charges by Trim, more denials and countercharges by the parish-clerk's
defenders, including "the Wight in the Plush Breeches." By the end of
the postscript, "*Trim* has been so *trimm'd,* as never disastrous Hero was
trimm'd before him" (*PR,* 212–13).

In addition to the name "Trim," which will appear in *Tristram Shandy,*
reassigned to a much more attractive character, there are indications in
this brief topical satire of Sterne's imminent preoccupations. The bawdiness of the concluding joke is but the most significant of the double
entendres in *A Political Romance.* Another of a sexual nature occurs in the
beginning when the letter writer informs his correspondent that the
"Uproar amongst us . . . does not take its Rise . . . from the Affair of the
Breeches;—but, on the contrary, the whole Affair of the *Breeches* has taken
its Rise from it" (*PR,* 197). Scatological jokes are scattered about as well.
The postscript, for example, speculates that Trim will next lay claim to a
close-stool (a chamberpot) "and defend himself behind it to the very last
Drop" (*PR,* 211). The Rabelaisian, Swiftian humor so evident in *Tristram
Shandy* is clearly a guiding force in *A Political Romance* as well.

A Political Romance also makes use of typography in the self-referen-
tial manner so central to *Tristram Shandy.* The language of deeds appears
in official black letter, and the dashes and italics throughout call further
attention to the technology of print. Letters, postscripts, such state-
ments as "I have broke open my Letter" and "When I finished the above
Account," and a dedication that follows rather than precedes the main
body of the work—all these devices bespeak a self-consciousness about
the artificiality of publication and of writing itself, an awareness, again,
that will be at the center of Sterne's masterpieces (*PR,* 210).

Finally, the romance provides evidence of Sterne's interest in thought
processes, association of ideas, and what he later comes to term *hobby-
horses.* The parson's decision to consult the parish register is presented as
an anatomy of ratiocination. The key to the romance develops the
theme further. The romance, according to the key, was discovered in the
York Minster-Yard and brought to a "Political Club in that City" where
it was read aloud and variously interpreted by the members. One fellow
explains it as an allegory of current European affairs; another maintains
that the references are to King William's war earlier in the century; and
yet another suggests that the tripartite structure of the tale signifies
church, rather than state, affairs. Others in the group construe parts of

the satire as insults to themselves or their professions. "Thus," we are told "every Man turn'd the Story to what was swimming uppermost in his own Brain" (*PR,* 221). Or, as Sterne would later express such devotion to a single idea, each rode his hobby-horse in pursuit of the allegory.

"A Fragment in the Manner of Rabelais"

A Political Romance suggests, in the words of Alexander Pope, that "mighty contests rise from trivial things."[11] But, while the dean and archbishop might agree that Topham's behavior was petty and childish, they were not prepared to admit, as the *Romance* insisted, that the whole business of power, politics, and perquisites was trivial. They would have preferred, no doubt, a satire that pursued the theme "trivial contests rise from mighty things," but that is not how Laurence Sterne saw it. He took Christianity quite seriously, but Sterne found some churchmen, including himself at times, to be fit subjects for ridicule. And he would continue to subject them to laughter, sometimes gentle, sometimes harsh, throughout his career as an author.

In fact, it was a satire on sermon-writing, not *Tristram Shandy,* to which Sterne set his hand immediately following his decision to "turn author." We have only a fragment of this work, because that is all Sterne produced, soon redirecting his efforts to Tristram's life and opinions.[12] "The Fragment in the Manner of Rabelais" is in a sense a false start, but it is a telling one as it reveals his continued preoccupation with Jonathan Swift and François Rabelais. Both of these writers were churchmen— Swift, Dean of St. Patrick's; Rabelais, a monk. And both were satirists. In them, Sterne identified the tradition in which he wished to participate—satire that celebrates the fullness of life even as it exposes the limitations, the hypocrisies, and the pettiness of human existence.

The fragment consists of two chapters. In the first, Longinus Rabelaicus asks a gathering of wits, "Would it not be a glorious Thing, If any Man of Genius and Capacity amongst us for such a Work, was fully bent within Himself to sit down immediately and compose a . . . KERUKOPÆDIA," that is, (though he himself does not say so) a manual on sermon-writing ("Fragment," 1088). The proposal sparks a lively discussion between Longinus Rabelaicus and his colleagues, Panurge, Epistemon, Gymnast, and Triboulet—a crowd with Rabelaisian nomenclature if ever there was one. Longinus Rabelaicus is pompous, hyper-intellectual, and pedantic. He is brought down to earth by the plain-spoken Epistemon who points out that "SERMONS . . . [is] but a Word of low

Degree, for a Book of high Rhetoric" and the dim-witted Panurge who thinks the discussion is about sausages ("Fragment," 1088). Gymnast and Triboulet offer refinements on the scheme. When told the Kerukopædia is "nothing but the Art of making" sermons, Gymnast replies, "And, why not, . . . of preaching 'em, when We've done?" ("Fragment," 1088) "This is Half in Half," he is told, that is, one and the same thing ("Fragment," 1088). Longinus Rabelaicus pursues his scheme a bit further. He begins, "[I]f some Skillful Body would but put us in a Way to do this to some *Tune*" by which he means by some code. Triboulet laughs: "Thou wouldst not have 'em *chanted* surely[?]" And Gymnast cries: "No, nor *canted* neither" ("Fragment," 1088). Longinus Rabelaicus envisions a mechanistic aid to sermon writing, a comprehensive manual "put into the Hands of every Licenced Preacher in great Britain & Ireland just before He began to compose" ("Fragment," 1088–89). But before he can elaborate on the advantages of the scheme, Panurge cuts him off: "I deny it flatly." "What? answer'd *Longinus Rabelaicus,* with all the Temper in the World" ("Fragment," 1089). And thus ends chapter 1 of "A Fragment in the Manner of Rabelais"—a ludicrous discussion at comical cross-purposes, the like of which we will see again in *Tristram Shandy* and *A Sentimental Journey.*

Chapter 2 features another character, Homenas, who is in the next room in the throes of sermon-writing himself, for he "had to preach next Sunday (before God knows whom)" ("Fragment," 1089). Unfortunately, he is "quite stuck fast," unable to write, so he "call[s] in for Help" ("Fragment," 1089). Pulling down a volume of the sermons of Samuel Clarke, he copies away happily until he pauses to think what will happen to him if the plagiarism is detected. He imagines the scene graphically as "*a fall from the Pulpit two Stories high.*" The result: "*Homenas* will never preach more while Breath's in his Body!" ("Fragment," 1089). The group in the next room, Longinus Rabelaicus and company, listen to Homenas's sad soliloquy, Panurge with his mouth wide open until Gymnast gives him a "good squashing Chuck under his double Chin" ("Fragment," 1091). And, we are told, "They plainly and distinctly heard every Syllable of what you will find recorded in the very next chapter" ("Fragment," 1091). But, of course, we do not, for here the fragment ends.

This second chapter finds Sterne experimenting with the Swiftian strategy of explaining the emotional parodically, in purely physical and scientific terms. When Homenas's soliloquy is interrupted by his tears, the relief his outburst brings is presented thus:

a Flood of Tears which falling down helter skelter, ding dong, without
any kind of Intermission for Six Minutes and almost twenty five seconds,
had a marvellous Effect upon his Discourse; for, the aforesaid Tears . . .
did so temper the Wind that was rising upon the aforesaid Discourse, . . .
But moreover, the said Tears, by their nitrous Quality did so refrigerate,
precipitate, & hurry down to the Bottom of his Soul, all the unsavory
Particles which lay fermenting . . . in the middle of his Conception, That
He went on in the coolest & chastest Stile (for a Soliloquy, I think) that
ever mortal Man utter'd. ("Fragment," 1090)

Along with the bawdiness and the attack on systematizing that the
Fragment shares with Sterne's later works, Sterne also employs in this
brief satire the temporal suspension for which *Tristram Shandy* would be
noted. For example, fully two paragraphs are devoted to the opening
and shutting of Panurge's mouth.

Laurence Sterne concludes his "Memoirs" with four sentences that
report the writing of *Tristram Shandy,* his appointment to the curacy of
Coxwold ["a sweet retirement in comparison of Sutton" ("Memoirs," 5)]
and his journey to France and Italy ["for the recovery of my health"
("Memoirs," 5)]. In these sentences, Sterne summarizes the events of his
life that justify our interest in him today. But the "Memoir" reminds us
that there was a Laurence Sterne before *Tristram Shandy.* All of his experiences, literary and otherwise, are reflected, however obliquely, in his
masterpieces, *Tristram Shandy* and *A Sentimental Journey.* I have barely
mentioned, however, Sterne's most significant pre–*Tristram Shandy*
activity. Like Homenas (indeed, perhaps too much like Homenas!), Laurence Sterne was a writer of sermons, and it is this aspect of his pre-
Shandy life that the next chapter examines.

Chapter Two

A Theologic Flap Upon the Heart:
The Sermons of Mr. Yorick

Sterne's decision to include the full text of his sermon "On the abuses of conscience" in volume 2 of *Tristram Shandy* struck one reviewer as "masterly," an "expedient" by which "it will probably be read by many who would peruse a sermon in no other form."[1] This approbation was echoed by Horace Walpole, who called the sermon the "best thing" in the book. Walpole, though, was an early anti-Shandean: He complained that *Tristram Shandy* was, in general, "a very insipid and tedious performance"; and he had qualms too about the part he praised. The sermon was, he pointed out, "oddly coupled with a good deal of bawdy, and," he added with implied umbrage, "both the composition of a clergyman."[2]

This note would sound again in the chorus that greeted Sterne's publication of volumes 1 and 2 of the *Sermons of Mr. Yorick* on 22 May 1760. These volumes represent the fruit of Sterne's clerical profession; they contain sermons he had delivered from Yorkshire pulpits over a twenty-year career as an Anglican priest. Yet Sterne clearly was aware that the public's interest in the sermons would be the result of its interest in *Tristram Shandy;* and for that reason, we assume, he published the volumes with two title pages. The first of these sheets attributed the work to Parson Yorick, the second acknowledged the authorship of "Laurence Sterne, A.M. Prebendary of York, and Vicar of Sutton-on-the-Forest, and Stillington near York," a ruse that prompted Owen Ruffhead of the *Monthly Review* to complain of "the greatest outrage against Sense and Decency, that has been offered since the first establishment of Christianity."[3] The invocation of a character from Sterne's "obscene Romance" offended Ruffhead, it seems, even more than the sermons pleased him. But please him, they did, and many others as well. Boswell tells the story thus:

> Next from the press there issues forth
> A sage divine fresh from the north;
> On Sterne's discourses we grew mad—

> Sermons! where are they to be had?
> Then with the fashionable Guards
> The Psalms supply the place of cards.
> A strange enthusiastic rage
> For sacred text now seiz'd the age,
> Around St. James's ev'ry table
> Was partly gay and partly sable.
> The manners by old Noll defended
> Were with our modern chit-chat blended:
> 'Give me some macaroni, pray.'
> 'Be wise while it is call'd today.'
> 'Heav'ns! How Mingotti sung last Monday!'
> 'Alas! how we profane the Sunday!'
> 'My Lady Betty! Hob or nob?'
> 'Great was the patience of old Job,'
> Sir Smart breaks out, and one and all
> Adore St. Peter and St. Paul.[4]

By July, a second edition was called for, and by 1769 eleven editions had been printed. Further, in 1766, a year after the publication of volumes 7 and 8 of *Tristram Shandy,* Sterne would publish two additional volumes of "Yorick's" sermons (*TLY,* 44).

Yorick's sermons discomfited readers like Walpole and Ruffhead by, in a sense, invoking the paradox that Boswell gleefully celebrates: the coexistence of spiritual and temporal (we would say secular) concerns. Though clearly a paradox some eighteenth-century Christians would prefer not to see manifested in their clergymen, it is, after all, a paradox at the heart of Anglican theology, as the ninth of the Thirty-Nine Articles indicates. This article speaks to the belief in original sin, or "birth-sin" as it is also called, and the doctrine is explained as follows:

> Original Sin . . . is the fault and corruption of the Nature of every Man, that naturally is ingendered of the Off-spring of *Adam,* whereby Man is very far gone from Original Righteousness, and is of his own Nature inclined to evil, so that the Flesh lusteth always contrary to the Spirit. . . . And this Infection of Nature doth remain; yea, in them that are regenerated. . . .[5]

The sign of such regeneration is baptism, which confers upon the Christian "the Promises of the Forgiveness of Sin" (article 27) but not the deliverance from sinfulness itself. "[I]f we say we have no Sin, we deceive our selves, and the truth is not in us" (article 15), for though baptized, "we may depart from Grace given, and fall into Sin" (article 16). Yet there is repentance and forgiveness by which we may "arise again, and amend our Lives" (article 16). The church's mission, of course, was to remind its members of their sinfulness, of Christ's sacrifice by which was purchased of God their forgiveness, and of their duty to strive for the amendment of their lives in accord with God's law and Christ's example. Whatever our own beliefs, it is important to understand that Laurence Sterne's entire adult life was intimately bound to the doctrine of the Anglican church. Not only did he, as a priest, administer the sacraments and preach the sermons that celebrated and sustained the doctrine, but he also believed it.

Typically, we encounter Sterne's sermons after we have read *Tristram Shandy;* that was true of many eighteenth-century readers as well. Yet, unlike many of us, the eighteenth-century reader would have had a fairly extensive acquaintance, fostered week by week in his parish church, with homilies, scripture, and the language of Christian worship. Sterne's sermons would have been, more than likely, an "easy read" for the eighteenth-century reader, for whom the discourse was utterly familiar. In fact, the reader may have quite literally read it all before as Sterne's sermons are largely secondhand stuff. That is, they are pastiches of other sermons by other (largely unacknowledged) divines, neither original compositions in the strictest sense of the term nor scholarly theological arguments. As Sterne put it, they are "Sermons . . . hot from the heart"—that is, from his heart and from the hearts of Bishop Hall, John Tillotson, Joseph Butler, and so on (*Letters, 298*).

This borrowing (which we would call plagiarism) was less disturbing to the eighteenth century than it is to us. As Melvyn New points out in the introduction to the University of Florida Press edition of Sterne's sermons, pulpit oratory was expected first and foremost to reflect the doctrine of the Anglican church; originality in content was not even acceptable, let alone desirable.[6] Sterne, like most preachers, relied on commentaries and other sermons for the matter of his own weekly performances. New also explains, however, that the standard for printed sermons was quite different from the conventions of the pulpit. Printed sermons were generally careful to acknowledge borrowings; they were prepared for publication in the sense that still prevails—with full documentation and cited references—and the writer's ideas and expressions were assumed to be his own unless otherwise indicated. Sterne glances at this obligation in his preface to the sermons with, as it were, a negative acknowledgement:

> . . . the reader, upon old and beaten subjects, must not look for many new thoughts—'tis well if he has new language; in three or four passages, where he has neither the one nor the other, I have quoted the author I made free with.—There are some other passages, where I suspect I may have taken the same liberty,—but 'tis only suspicion, for I do not remember it is so, otherwise I should have restored them to their proper owners. . . .[7]

To refresh his memory would have taken too long. Eager to ride the crest of *Tristram Shandy*'s popularity, Sterne rushed the first two volumes of his sermons into print. Volumes 3 and 4 received more of his attention with regard to rewriting or editing the twelve sermons contained therein, but in the later volumes as in the earlier, Sterne left much work for scholars who would strive, generations later, to sort out his various gleanings, debts, and pilferings.[8]

The vexed issue of plagiarism aside, however, Sterne's sermons are of interest to us for the light they shed on the assumptions and beliefs that form the underpinning of *Tristram Shandy* and *A Sentimental Journey.* Moreover, they point us to motifs and images that reappear (often distorted) in Sterne's major works. The sermons are clearly written, logically argued, and yet often quite emotional declamations. Written to be read aloud, to be performed, they are relatively simple—though not simplistic—messages, designed to convey to the hearer the need to look beyond worldly concerns, encouragement to see and correct personal shortcomings and assurance of divine love. If in reading the wildly ironic *Tristram Shandy* and *Sentimental Journey,* we often find ourselves asking "what can he mean?" the sermons offer a reassuring clarity, at least as far as their own meaning is concerned, and perhaps some useful clues for the other works as well.

Because *Tristram Shandy* and *A Sentimental Journey* seem so "modern" to us, so chaotic, so aware of individual alienation, angst, and fragmentation, we are often apt to regard their author as modern in ways that he could not have been. Indeed, he was not even modern in ways he could have been. He was not a deist for whom the power of reason promised glorious achievements for mankind (as was Denis Diderot, for example); he was not impressed to the point of atheism with man's growing ability to explain the world (as was David Hume, for example); he was clearly not a believer in embracing systems of utopian reform, the kind that would flourish and then flounder in the wake of the French Revolution, the kind that would result in America's own (so far) successful experiment in democracy. For, though the principle of liberty on which America is founded was dear to Sterne, he most surely would have objected to the severing of church and state. In his mind, the only assurance that such liberty would be preserved was a state religion that inculcated the virtues of moderation, duty, acquiescence to one's condition in life, and self-restraint, a state religion, in other words, like the Church of England.

In general, Sterne's religious belief as expressed in the sermons can be described as "Latitudinarian." The eighteenth-century Anglican church saw itself as occupying a middle position between two extremes: Roman Catholicism on the one hand and "enthusiasm" on the other. In the Church of England's formulation, Roman Catholicism was characterized by the tyranny of a venal, absolute authority vested in the Church, its officials, and its ceremonies, and by the unthinking, superstitious obeisance and spiritual bondage of the churchgoer, "a pecuniary system, well contrived to operate upon men's passions and weakness, whilst their pockets are o'picking" ("Felix's behavior before Paul," 1:314–15). "Enthusiasm" was a general term for any sectarian effort—often from within the Church of England itself—to attribute spiritual authority to the individual Christian. In Sterne's idiom, "enthusiasm" signified primarily the Methodist movement with its emphasis on the individual's sense of a personal relationship with God marked by a conversion experience such as John Wesley described. For Sterne and other Anglican priests, the pinpointing of "the day of the month, and the hour of the night, when the Spirit came in upon them, and took possession of their hearts" ("Humility," 2.73), or as Wesley put it, when they "felt [their] heart[s] strangely warmed," was an absurd instance of spiritual pride. The Church of England saw itself as balancing the authority of doctrine with the liberty of individual conscience. It was a self-styled *via media*— a middle way—between authoritarianism and anarchy, both spiritual and political in function and intent.

"Latitudinarianism" refers to the position staked out by certain Anglican divines, John Tillotson and Samuel Clarke among others, in which the role of reason in Christianity was emphasized. Latitudinarianism did not signify, however, the transformation of Christianity into a merely rational moral system, as some would have it, for despite their emphasis on reason, Latitudinarians maintained as well the importance of the supra-rational—revelation, grace, and faith.[9] By Sterne's time, the teachings of the divines, controversial in their own day, had become mainstream Anglicanism. They, in essence, contributed to the church's mediation between authority and individual will by an insistence on both the power of reason and its limitations. This insistence is everywhere in Sterne and forms the foundation of all his other expressions of belief.

At this point, it would be useful to list the "articles" of what we might call Sterne's credo as we can extract them from the sermons. These beliefs were in no way unique to Sterne; they were shared by many, if not most, eighteenth-century Christians. For a literal listing of the beliefs of Sterne and his contemporaries we need but look to the Thirty-Nine Articles or even the Ten Commandments, supplemented by the New Testament teachings of Christ. But the sermons contain several fundamental ideas that appear regularly to guide the churchgoers in their daily lives, several notions that Sterne as preacher inculcated into the consciences of his parishioners, those that stayed awake and paid attention, anyway. They could be described as the foundation of a system of practical religion, thoughts to return to periodically in the living of life. This credo is not startling, nor original, nor eccentric. But for many of us, Christian or not, some of the notions seem strange, or if not strange, at least not so central to our spiritual lives as they were to the spiritual lives of Sterne and most of his contemporaries.

The sermons reveal seven fundamental beliefs:

1. Human reason is limited, as are all other human attributes, by man's inherited fallibility: We are capable of doing what is right, but more often than not we prefer what is wrong.
2. True morality is impossible without religion, and religion is based not on reason but on revelation.
3. Our duty to one another requires us to emulate the charity and kindness of Christ.
4. The Christian ideal is humility and meekness; therefore, pride is a particularly offensive sin.
5. God is intimately involved in the lives of men and women and the nations in which they live; in fact, the world is governed by his Providence.
6. Human happiness in this world is incomplete and fundamentally unsatisfying, but Christianity makes available to the individual Christian true happiness after death.
7. Death is certain, as is God's judgment after death.

Of course, each of these homely points masks a complex theological history: One could invoke voluminous discussions of the doctrine of human
depravity, a doctrine that underwrites the sentiment expressed in the
notion that reason is limited (belief 1); whether man was to be justified
by his works or by his faith is the complicated issue behind the injunction to charity (belief 3), an issue that generated much debate among
theologians, philosophers, and even novelists during the eighteenth century. Our concern, however, is not theology per se but theology as the
source of Sterne's "system of values," values that lie behind the erratic
narratives for which he is famous, values that receive positive expression
in the forty-five sermons of Mr. Yorick. The following discussion examines each of the seven premises by looking closely at the sermons themselves.

What Sterne Believed

1. Reason.   In the eighteenth century people generally believed that,
with regard to "our reason and understanding," we were formed by God
"after his own most perfect image" ("Worship," 2:339). But, as Sterne
charges in "Abuses of conscience," instead of using this reason to access
the truth, the knowledge of self, and the knowledge of God for which it
was given us, since the Fall in the Garden of Eden, we have turned reason into rationalization; we have employed our highest faculty to justify
our lowest impulses. If reason were truly the operative principle in the
individual's self-judgment, "the guilt or innocence of every man's life
could be known, in general, by no better measure, than the degrees of
his own approbation or censure" ("Abuses of conscience," 2:102).
Although, according to Sterne's sermons, self-examination should lead
us to true knowledge—awareness of our motives, our limitations, our
desperate need for God—reason is often so clouded by other concerns
that, unassisted, it is of little use. Sterne explains, "We are deceived in
judging of ourselves, just as we are in judging of other things, when our
passions and inclinations are called in as counsellors, and we suffer ourselves to see and reason just so far and no farther than they give us
leave" ("Self-knowledge," 1:55).[10]
    To say to men and women, then, "know thyself," or "be reasonable" is
rather pointless. The "direct road" to such ends is "guarded on all sides
by self-love, and consequently very difficult to open access." "A different
and more artful course" is necessary to get beyond self-love "for a few

moments, till a just judgment [can] be procured" (1:57–58). So Sterne says in praise of "parables, fables, and such sort of indirect applications" (1:57–58) by which the individual is revealed to himself. In "Self-knowledge," Sterne illustrates the way indirection can overcome the force of self-delusion. In this particular sermon, the self-deluder in question is David; the parable-maker is the prophet Nathan, whom God has commissioned to bring to David a sense of his own sinfulness. David's sins were adultery—his love affair with Bathsheba—and what was in essence murder, for David had sent Bathsheba's husband, Uriah, to "the forefront of the hottest battle . . . that he [might] be smitten, and die" (2 Samuel 11:15). He was so smitten, and he did so die. Nathan's job, then, is to make David regard these heinous deeds as sins, for it turns out that a year has gone by without David experiencing the least remorse for his actions.

Nathan's strategy is to tell a story of a rich man with many flocks who is approached by a hungry traveler. Instead of killing and dressing one of his own lambs for the traveler, the rich man takes a lamb from a poor man, the only lamb this poor man had, a lamb, moreover, that this poor man regarded "as a daughter" ("Self-knowledge," 1:59). This lamb was killed for the wayfarer's meal, Nathan tells David. And David's reaction is swift: The rich man shall die for this offense, "because he had no pity" (1:60). It is then that Nathan tells David the parabolic truth: " 'Thou art the man' " (1:62), upon which revelation David "see[s] the necessity . . . of imploring God to cleanse him from his secret faults" (1:68).

Indirection is but one means to self-knowledge; suffering, Sterne says elsewhere, is another. What happens to David through Nathan's agency happens to the prodigal son through the forces of deprivation. Disobedient, headstrong, sensual, and self-centered, the prodigal son does not face his own sinfulness until he finds himself penniless, hungry, and alone. He then returns to his father, aware of his father's wisdom and kindness, brought to such an awareness not by a prophecy but by his own reason deprived of the self-deluding comforts of power and plenty. Such is often the case, according to Sterne's sermon:

> Nothing so powerfully calls home the mind as distress: the tense fibre then relaxes,——the soul retires to itself,——sits pensive and susceptible of right impressions: if we have a friend, 'tis then we think of him; if a benefactor, at that moment all his kindnesses press upon our mind.—— Gracious and bountiful GOD! Is it not for this that they who in their prosperity forget thee, do yet remember and return to thee in the hour of their sorrow? ("Prodigal son," 1:322)

What we should know, we refuse to know unless brought to knowledge through some sort of revelation.

It might strike one as strange (I admit it did me) that Sterne's sermon on the prodigal son should end with a warning to parents that sending a son on foreign travels will quite likely be his ruin instead of his improvement. Yet as the argument advances, we can see that Sterne is simply recasting the lesson of Nathan's prophecy and the prodigal son's suffering: The limitations of human reason make it an unreliable guide. A young man just out of school is too inexperienced, too prone to be distracted by new sights and new acquaintances to serve as his own guide through lands and societies unknown to him. Available tutors are usually too bookish or too rakish to do the youth any good. Wise men in the foreign country itself will not be interested in conversing with a callow youth who does not speak their language. In short, the Grand Tour of Europe, which had been styled for decades as the finishing of a gentleman's education, is described in this sermon as the setting of prodigality and ruin. Without counsel, the guidance of his own clear reason or the disinterested reason of others, it is the young man's inevitable fate to "[return] the same object of pity, with the prodigal in the Gospel" ("Prodigal son," 1:333). And although the prodigal son is made wiser by his suffering, just as David is by Nathan's revelation, parents might be expected to feel that wisdom too dearly bought. Of course, there is a third kind of revelation that makes such purchase unnecessary—the revelation of Christ in which prophecy, suffering, and knowledge are fused.

2. Morality.   Christianity was to Sterne and others of his time a reasonable religion: "[C]ould we," says Sterne in "Temporal advantages of religion," "suppose ourselves to be in a capacity of expostulating with God, concerning the terms upon which we would submit to his government——and to choose the laws ourselves which we would be bound to observe, it would be impossible for the wit of man to frame any other proposals, which upon all accounts would be more advantageous to our own interests than those very conditions to which we are obliged by the rules of religion and virtue" (2:126). Yet reason, without the aid of revelation, is incapable of sustaining for long the insights it can grasp. In "Advantages of Christianity to the world," Sterne points out that while the ancients were able to "discover" the fact that there was "one supreme Being," they were powerless to sustain this reasonable insight, "against the prejudices of wrong heads, and the propensity of weak ones" (2:84–85). They lacked "something to have gone hand in hand with reason, and fixed the persuasion for ever upon their minds" (2:85). That "something" is revelation. Through Christ the world came to learn of the certainty of a future life (2:132), and it is this knowledge that, according to Sterne, binds together religion and morality, enabling us to sustain a system of virtue that reason alone would find difficult to justify.

Sterne explains the impossibility of morality without religion as follows: "the most exalted motive which can only be depended upon for the uniform practice of virtue,——must come down from *above,*—— from the love and imitation of the goodness of that Being in whose sight we wish to render ourselves acceptable." He continues, "this will operate at all times and all places,—— in the darkest closet as much as on the greatest and most public theatres of the world" ("Advantages of Christianity to the world," 2:89–90). This desire to please God is tied to belief in a future life where we will be held accountable for our actions and our thoughts. God must of necessity know these words and deeds, for he must judge us in the end. The inescapable knowledge of God, his awareness of our most secret thoughts and deeds is a vastly more secure basis on which to build morality than mere reason could ever be. As Sterne explains in "Abuses of conscience," reason alone will serve moral ends only as long as it is in one's interest to do so. But if a banker, for example, "without stain to his reputation, could secrete my fortune, and leave me naked in the world," if a doctor, without dishonor "could send me out of [the world], and enjoy an estate by my death," what argument would reason offer to do otherwise? None, Sterne concludes; "we can have no dependence upon morality without religion" (2:112–13).

Nowhere in Sterne's sermons is our moral unreliability more poignantly illustrated than in his discussion of the character of St. Peter. Peter is characterized by his sincerity, his honesty, and his emulation of the Christly virtue of humility. It is indeed this character trait with which Sterne begins his sermon as he describes Peter's refusal to take personal credit for the healing of a lame man. The apostle denies that he himself made the man walk; God's power alone could accomplish that. This humility, this self-effacing abjection, is indeed Christlike, Sterne says, but to describe Peter's character as such seems to ignore the most famous incident of that disciple's life: his denial of Christ.

Sterne explains the seeming contradiction as an example of the limitations of human resolve. To Jesus's warning that his disciples would be in danger of lapsing once he himself was no longer with them, Peter asserted that though he should die for it he would never deny Jesus.

Jesus's answer is the well-known retort, "the cock shall not crow this day, before that thou shalt thrice deny that thou knowest me" (Luke 22:34). And, of course, Peter did just that. Peter thought "his will was in his power, whether God's grace assisted him or not" ("St. Peter's character," 2:173). Jesus, "to rebuke and punish him for it, did no other than leave it to his own strength to perform it;—which, in effect, was almost the same as leaving him to the necessity of not performing it" (2:173). For, "without me," as Jesus had told him before, "ye can do nothing" (2:174).

Peter's general character "was that of the most engaging meekness,—distrustful of himself and his abilities to the last degree[,] . . . a man of great love to his master,—and of no less zeal for his religion" (2:176). That he could fall prey to the temptation to trust himself is, it seems, an indication of how powerful such impulses are, how difficult it is to sustain a truly moral life even with the benefit of the most direct revelation of all, the living presence of Christ.

3. Charity.   Yet Sterne is rarely pessimistic about the human condition. For, like reason, morality is implanted in human nature: As "GOD made man in his own image[,] . . . [the] resemblance he bore was undoubtedly in . . . moral rectitude, and the kind and benevolent affections of his nature" ("Vindication of human nature," 1:113). This attribute, like reason, was "sullied" by the Fall, but it does remain a defining human characteristic, experienced most actively in the living of Jesus's injunction *"whatsoever ye would that men should do to you, do ye also unto them"* (quoted in "The parable of the rich man and Lazarus considered," 2:37). To be touched by the sorrow or pain of another is to recognize our common human condition, for "[t]hat which has happened to one,——may happen to every man" (2:37). And to minister to the unfortunate is to experience "moral delight"; even the wicked do so, though less perfectly than the good whose "disposition and temper" compound the pleasure (2:35).[11]

Sterne's charity sermons, that is, the sermons that clearly were preached to dispose the congregation toward each other in general and toward the poor, the sick, or the orphaned in particular, include "Philanthropy recommended," "The case of Elijah and the widow of Zarephath considered," "Vindication of human nature," "The parable of the rich man and Lazarus considered," and "Follow peace." These sermons not only assert the "link of dependence" that joins man to man, they also often provide imaginative demonstration of the satisfaction attendant

on feeling for others ("Follow peace," 2:321). There are quite a few passages of highly charged emotion in such sermons, passages that no
doubt reduced some of the original congregation to tears. "The rich man
and Lazarus," for example, concludes on such a note of pathos:

> Hast thou ever been wounded . . . by the loss of a most obliging
> friend,—or been torn away from the embraces of a dear and promising child
> by the stroke of death?——bitter remembrance! nature droops at it—but
> nature is the same in all conditions and lots of life.——A child thrust forth
> in an evil hour, without food, without raiment, bereft of instruction, and the
> means of its salvation, is the subject of more tender heart-aches, and will
> awaken every power of nature:——as we have felt for ourselves,—let us
> feel for CHRIST'S sake—let us feel for theirs. . . . (2:38–39)

Given the high rate of infant and child mortality in the eighteenth century, one can imagine the effect of this oration. Given Sterne's own
childhood sorrows and the infants he and Elizabeth buried, one wonders
if he himself remained dry-eyed as he spoke the words from the pulpit.

In other sermons, not specifically addressed to the need for alms-giv-
ing, Sterne paints similar scenes. "The house of feasting and the house of
mourning described," for example, includes—again at the end of the
sermon—a particularly emotional scene. It is the scene of a funeral. We
are asked to "Behold a dead man ready to be carried out, the only son of
his mother and she a widow" (1:31). This image, however, is discarded
for one of yet greater intensity: "a kind and indulgent father of a numerous family, lies breathless——snatched away in the strength of his age"
(1:31–32). But the preacher's interest is not so much in the dead man as
in the mourners, whom he depicts "going heavily along to the house of
mourning, to perform that last melancholy office, which, when the debt
of nature is paid, we are called upon to pay to each other" (1:32). These
mourners, gay and unthinking at other times and on other occasions,
find themselves now "pensive," "susceptible," "full of religious impressions," "smitten with sense and with a love of virtue" (1:32). This attitude is not the "studied solemnity" of "gravity," but the quiet recognition of common sorrow and suffering (1:33). The seriousness of the
mourners is "religious" insofar as it turns their thoughts from this life to
eternal life. Thus, in a sense, fellow-feeling operates much like revelation
in that through pity for and identification with another we are brought
to an awareness of God.

Yet it would be more accurate to say that charity and compassion are
the fruits of revelation rather than sources of supra-rational knowledge

themselves, for ideally duty to others is the result of a principled adherence to divine law, not the impulse of the moment. In two sermons, "Elijah and the widow of Zarephath" and "Philanthropy recommended," we find not only how central compassion is to the religious life, but also how "reasonable" such a principle is. In "Elijah and the widow of Zarephath," we are instructed to consider the death of Christ as the ultimate act of compassion. Jesus "was willing to undergo all kinds of affliction, to sacrifice himself, to forget his dearest interests, and even lay down his life for the good of mankind" (1:87). The inference we make from this example of self-sacrifice is, Sterne says, "unavoidable": "by reflecting upon . . . the instance of CHRIST'S death, we may consider what an immense debt we owe to each other; and by calling to mind the amiable pattern of his life, in doing good, we might learn in what manner we may best discharge it" (1:88–89). In "Philanthropy recommended," we are told that "a charitable and benevolent disposition" is the source of most other human virtues. A compassionate man will be loyal; he will not kill, steal, lie, or commit adultery because "such trespasses, are so tenderly felt by a compassionate man, that it is not in his power or his nature to commit them" (1:51). The compassionate individual, this sermon asserts, follows the law of charity, one of the "great commandments": "Thou shalt love thy neighbour as thyself" (Matthew 22:39). And thus he or she serves "[t]he great end and design of our holy religion, . . . [to reconcile] us to GOD [and] to reconcile us to each other" ("Follow peace," 2:313).

4. Pride.   The beliefs that we have discussed so far have to do with the individual in relation to himself, to God, and to society, and all of these relationships, we have seen, depend upon the mediation of Christ. It is important that we understand before going any further that the whole system of beliefs espoused by Sterne and his fellow Anglicans is Christ-centered. Without Christ's crucifixion there is no redemption from sin, no morality, no reconciliation of self with self, with God, or with others. It is crucial also to note that, important as he is, Jesus has virtues that are about as far from the worldly sense of what it means to be important as one can get.

Many in Jesus's own time failed to recognize his significance, according to Sterne. Expecting a Messiah of worldly power and political significance, they failed to recognize this base-born, homely, poor man as their long-awaited savior ("Sanctity of the apostles," 2:22). But, Sterne asserts elsewhere, "as pride was the passion through which sin and misery entered into the world . . . therefore the Son of GOD . . . began at the very point where he knew we had failed" ("Humility," 2:66–67). That is, he began by exhorting us to be what he himself was: humble, meek, and mild. Jesus appeared "rather as a servant than a master"; he came to minister to, not to be waited upon; he voluntarily assumed a lowliness of birth and a life among the poor; he had "no form, or comeliness, nor any beauty that they should desire him"; he died the ignoble "death of a slave, a malefactor——dragged to *Calvary,* without opposition—— insulted without complaint" (2:67–68). The "only public instance of honour which he suffered to be given him in his entrance into Jerusalem . . . was accepted with . . . humility"; Jesus greeted the homage of the multitudes "in . . . meekness, . . . lowly and sitting upon an ass" ("St. Peter's character," 2:165).

That such is the nature of Christ to be emulated by the Christian makes the sin of spiritual pride particularly objectionable. The epitome of such pride is found in the parable of the "Pharisee and the publican." The Pharisee's worship is all outward show. He prays, fasts, and gives thanks to God that he is not sinful like the adulterers, the unjust, and the publicans, that is the tax collectors, of the world, while the reviled tax collector himself stands aside with a humble heart full of a "sense of his own unworthiness," begging God for mercy ("Pharisee and publican in the temple," 1:97–98). The publican, Jesus tells his disciples, "went down to his house justified rather than the other" (1:98).

When the subject of spiritual pride arises in Sterne's sermons, the Roman Catholics and the Methodists are bound to come in for their share of the abuse. For both, in the Anglican view, are guilty of an unfounded sense of spiritual superiority. The Methodists feel such because they place a high premium on extraordinary personal revela-tions. For the "Christian of a cool head and sound judgment," the involvement of God in human affairs is accepted; the "influence and assistance" of his spirit is also assumed to be the proper object of prayer ("Humility," 2:71, 70). But the notion that we can distinguish God's influence "from the efforts and determinations of our own reason" is, Sterne says, the product of a disordered fancy (2:70–71). In other words, the Methodist who asserts a special relationship with God resulting from a personal, very specific revelation is setting himself up as superior to those who must rely on the general revelation provided by the life and teaching of Christ.

In contrast, the Roman Catholic church's reliance on "ostentatious ceremonies and gestures" offers another avenue to spiritual pride, for "it

is much easier to put in pretensions to holiness upon such a mechanical
system . . ., than where the character is only to be got and maintained
by a painful conflict and perpetual war against the passions" ("Pharisee
and publican," 1:106–7). Sterne elaborates, " 'Tis easier, for instance, for
a zealous papist to cross himself and tell his beads, than for an humble
protestant to subdue the lusts of anger, intemperance, cruelty and
revenge, to appear before his Maker with that preparation of mind
which becomes him" (1:107). Both the Methodists and the Roman
Catholics, according to Sterne, encourage spiritual pride, a particularly
offensive vice considering not only the example of Christ, which enjoins
us to forego it, but also the very nature of man, which does not in any
way justify it:

> Survey yourselves, my dear Christians, a few moments in this light—
> behold a disobedient, ungrateful, intractable, and disorderly set of crea-
> tures, going wrong seven times in a day,——acting sometimes every
> hour of it against your own convictions—your own interests, and the
> intentions of your GOD, who wills and proposes nothing but your happi-
> ness and prosperity——what reason does this view furnish you for Pride?
> ("Pride," 2:54)

5. Providence.   For late twentieth-century readers who are accustomed to various slogans celebrating the "pride" of one personal identity
or another, readers who are encouraged by their society to cultivate a
sense of personal pride as one of the highest of virtues, it admittedly
requires a stretch of the imagination to hear the word as Sterne meant it.
For Reverend Sterne, pride was a temptation to be fought, not a strength
to be acquired. Humility was a virtue difficult but desirable to achieve,
not a sign of weakness but of victory over self. Of course, in Sterne's time,
as in ours, the humble were no doubt denigrated, abused, and exploited
by the arrogant and by those who judged solely by outward demeanor.
The treatment of *Tristram Shandy*'s Parson Yorick by his mean-spirited
parishioners is a handy example suggesting that human nature has not
changed so drastically in the 240 years that separate us from Sterne. But
the sermons do provide a vocabulary and an ideology, if you will, for challenging the bullies of the world. After all, the sermons argue, though
human beings may think they are shaping events, they are really inhabit-
ing a world of "riddles and mysteries," solvable only by God.

Sterne's sermons evince a belief in providence, that is, the participation of God in human affairs. All of life's blessings are the direct result of

God's providence ("Vindication of human nature," 1:123). The same is true of life's pains, as Job's query to his wife suggests: "Shall we receive good at the hands of GOD, and shall we not receive evil also? Are not both alike the dispensation of an all-wise and good Being, who knows and determines what *is best?*" ("Job's expostulation with his wife," 1:243). God's providence overrules the "policies and designs" of men; the swift lose the race, the weak win the battle ("Time and chance," 1:131). These paradoxes prove the intervention of providence, Sterne asserts: "[I]t necessarily follows . . . that there is some other cause which mingles itself in human affairs, and turns them as it pleases; which cause can be no other than . . . the secret and overruling providence of . . . Almighty GOD" (1:131–32). What seems to us to be the result of caprice and chance is in fact the working of God's will: "what his infinite wisdom sees necessary to be brought about for the government and preservation of the world, over which Providence perpetually presides" (1:133).

Such is the case for individuals; such is also the case for nations whose rise and fall according to God's imminent will is traceable throughout the course of history. And, of course, from time to time God singles out a nation or a people to specially favor in accord with his aim of governing and preserving the world, that is, his aim of preserving knowledge of himself and his law by which the world is to be governed. The Israelites were one such chosen people; the English are another.

The argument that the English are the object of God's special providence surfaces in several of Sterne's sermons, including one entitled "National mercies considered," a sermon preached, according to Sterne's note "on the Inauguration of his present Majesty" (1:335). Sterne begins this sermon with a discussion of Moses's injunction to the Israelites that they should keep alive the sense of God's special providence by telling their sons and their sons' sons how "the Lord brought us out of Egypt with a mighty hand" (Deuteronomy 6:21, text of "National mercies considered," 1:335). The rehearsal of God's special favors would guard the Israelites against the cynicism and worldliness bound to occur as time passes from generation to generation. Otherwise, "a long and undisturbed possession of their liberties," the sermon speculates, "might blunt the sense of these providences of GOD" (1:336).

From the Israelites's case, Sterne turns to an examination of God's special favors toward England. The first mark of such providence was, he says, England's deliverance from darkness and idolatry by the Romans, who brought Christianity to the country. Other parts of the world were equal benefactors of the Roman Empire, of course, but the fact that England is geographically so remote from the cradle of Christianity and yet received the teachings of the religion quite close to the time of the apostles' deaths indicates a special providence other nations did not enjoy. Furthermore, the argument continues, Christianity endured in England despite the coming of barbarian tribes; it survived and purged itself of the mistaken notions of Roman Catholicism; even temporary setbacks such as the reign of Bloody Mary did not deal Christianity a death blow. With the long reign of Elizabeth, Protestantism became securely entrenched in England; it would endure the troubled or troubling reigns of several Stuart kings and would reach its apotheosis in the Glorious Revolution, which would deliver England forever from the snare of "Jesuitry" and tyranny.

The sermon ends with a reaffirmation of the importance of religion to national life and an assertion that an awareness of God's direct participation in the affairs of man is essential to both moral and political well-being:

> a sinful people can never be grateful to GOD,——nor can they, properly speaking, be loyal to their prince;—they cannot be grateful to the one, because they live not under a sense of his mercies,——nor can they be loyal to the other, because they disengage the Providence of GOD from taking his part,——and then giving a heart to his adversaries to be intractable. (1:348–49)

Sterne does admit that, for reasons unknown, righteousness may not "profit a nation of men" (1:349). God's providence works itself out over sometimes vast periods of time; several lifetimes may not reveal his full intent. Still, each righteous individual is assured of his own reward,—the ultimate end of all providential design—the salvation of his soul.

6. Happiness.   It is a mark of faith in Christ's revelation to accept the misfortune as well as the good of life as somehow part of the divine will. Such belief, in the end, assures our eternal happiness, and it is no small part of our satisfaction in this life. For such faith is itself a great solace, as the psalmist David observes, "in the course of a life full of afflictions" ("Trust in God," 2:215). Sterne explains, "he declares that he should verily have fainted under the sense and apprehension of [these afflictions], but that he believed to see the goodness of the Lord in the land of the living" (2:216).

Every life is a mixture of good and bad, happiness and unhappiness, pleasure and pain. How these elements balance out for each individual is largely a matter of temperament, a person's "particular turn and cast of mind." Sterne explains, "[y]ou will see one man undergo, with scarce the expense of a sigh,—what another, in the bitterness of his soul, would go mourning for all his life long" ("Providence justified," 2:362). Both Sterne and his contemporary Samuel Johnson would write of the incompleteness of earthly pleasure, but their very different temperaments color their observations as well as, one would suppose, their experiences. Though he had his share of pleasure, Johnson's characteristic view was that "[h]uman life is every where a state in which much is to be endured, and little to be enjoyed."[12] Sterne, though he suffered his share of sadness, was not so gloomy. While it may be *better* to go to the house of mourning than the house of feasting, the house of feasting could be a lot of fun: "Imagine . . . such a house of feasting, where, either by consent or invitation, a number of each sex is drawn together, for no other purpose but the enjoyment and mutual entertainment of each other, which we will suppose shall arise from no other pleasures but what custom authorises, and religion does not absolutely forbid" ("The house of feasting," 1:24). Although Sterne goes on in this particular sermon to recommend the "house of mourning" to turn our thoughts to the next world, one cannot help but feel that as a human being rather than as a preacher he did prefer—like all of humankind—the house of feasting: "Are the sad accidents of life, and the uncheery hours which perpetually overtake us, are they not enough, but we must sally forth in quest of them[?]" (1:19)

Of course they are enough. What is good for us in moderation may poison us in the extreme. Except insofar as it encourages virtue, "sorrow . . . has no use but to shorten a man's days" (1:33), says Sterne in "The house of feasting and the house of mourning described"; and in "Penances," he echoes the view: "a man might, with as much reason, muffle up himself against sunshine and fair weather,—and at other times expose himself naked to the inclemencies of cold and rain, as debar himself of the innocent delights of his nature, for affected reserve and melancholy" (2:258–59).

Nevertheless, Sterne would agree with Johnson's general argument in *Rasselas* that earthly pleasures, the apparent happinesses offered by life, fall short of truly satisfying us. His sermon "Inquiry after happiness" is, in fact, a *Rasselas*-like survey of the possible sources of human pleasure that inevitably fail to live up to our expectations. The pursuits of fashion, money, beauty, business, titles, great works, collecting, all end in disappointment if not ruin: "our pleasures and enjoyments slip from under us in every stage of our life" (1:15–16). In fact, Sterne continues, though we do experience many pleasures in life, they do not bring us lasting happiness, for "[w]e are so made, that from the common gratifications of our appetites, and the impressions of a thousand objects, we snatch [pleasure], like a transient gleam, without being suffered to taste [happiness], and enjoy the perpetual sunshine and fair weather which constantly attend it" (1:16). True happiness is found only in religion, the "consciousness of virtue[,] and the sure and certain hopes of a better life" (1:16).

In fact, in "Our conversation in heaven," we discover that true happiness is experienced only in this "better life" and only by those who have in their earthly existences cultivated virtue to such an extent that they find goodness itself a pleasure. One who is tied to the pleasures of lust, appetite, drink, slander, and so on, is not only "unworthy of so pure a presence as the spirit of GOD, but even incapable of enjoying it, could [he] be admitted [to heaven]" (2:140). The "impure soul," driven "to the last hour" by his "appetites and desires," can never "take pleasure in GOD" (2:141–42). It is only by cultivating a taste for virtue that we can hope to attain true happiness, the "company of heaven," the eternal presence of God (2:146).

7. Death and Judgment.   Sermons are by nature "otherworldly." They exist to remind the Christian of his duty and his ultimate accountability. For the driving moral force behind the enterprise of sermon-making is the coming judgment of God. Given the power to choose between good and evil, the Christian must answer for the choice he has made ("Providence justified," 2:357).

The individual's reason—the proper use of it, that is—is an aid to him in determining the path of virtue. And Sterne assures his congregation that with reflection they will have no trouble balancing their duty to God with the legitimate enjoyment of this life's pleasures. In fact, he insists, innocent pleasures are necessary for the discharging of that duty: "one principal reason, why GOD may be supposed to allow pleasure in this world, seems to be for the refreshment and recruit of our souls and bodies, which, like clocks, must be wound up at certain intervals, . . . [as] such relaxations . . . are necessary to regain . . . natural vigour and cheerfulness, without which it is impossible [we] should either be in a disposition or capacity to discharge [the] several duties of . . . life" ("Penances," 2:264–65). But the overindulgence in such pleasures, the wasting of time in diversions, the "parcelling out every hour of the day for one idleness or another" is not the proper use of the short life allotted us by God (2:266). And we will be called to account for such waste, as St. Peter says, when Christ comes to judge the world.

This day *"will come as a thief in the night,"* that is, it will take each of us by surprise, as death itself often does ("Description of the world," 2:147). The certainty of both death and judgment, Sterne argues, ought to inform all of our behavior, but, he says in "Description of the world," looking around one could never guess one lived in a country that subscribed to such a belief. The higher ranks of society take pride in their irreligion making a jest of morality, refuting the Bible (which they have not, by the way, bothered to read), objecting to revelation, and eschewing public worship. The lower ranks are better, though with their propensity for aping the manners of the "higher ranks" they too will likely soon embrace the scoffing attitude of the aristocracy. When they do, Sterne says ominously, "those who have done the mischief will find the necessity at last of turning religious in their own defence" (2:152). We talk of virtue, he continues, and countenance vice, especially the vices of the wealthy or the powerful; we spend our time in gaming, distractions, a constant round of pleasure. Even the old, who should know better and serve as a model to the heedless youth of the land, participate in the general frivolity. In England, Sterne says, "there is as little influence from this principle which the apostle lays stress on, and as little sense of religion,—as small a share of virtue (at least as little of the appearance of it) as can be supposed to exist at all in a country where it is countenanced by the state" (2:149).

Yet the judgment day will come and each of us, whether rich or poor in this life, must answer for the lives we led. God's constant observance of us and his awareness of our innermost thoughts should combine with the certainty of eternal life to make us better Christians. After all, we do not know when the day will be that all humankind is called to judgment. And, furthermore, we do not know the length of our own days, when the minute will come that puts repentance and reformation forever out of our power:

> [W]e are standing upon the edge of a precipice, with nothing but the single thread of human life to hold us up;—and . . . if we fall unprepared in this thoughtless state, we are lost, and must perish for evermore. (2:159)

Watch and pray, the sermon exhorts, "that ye may be accounted worthy to escape all these things that shall come to pass, and to stand before the Son of man" (2:160).

Preacher/Man

"[P]reaching," Sterne wrote to George Whatley, "is a theologic flap upon the heart, as the dunning for a promise is a political flap upon the memory:—both the one and the other is useless where men have *wit enough* to be honest" (*Letters,* 134). Sermons remind us, Sterne implies, of what we already know, or should know—of the limits of our knowledge, our duty to one another, the inevitability of death. Sterne's sermons make available to us the beliefs to which most of Sterne's contemporaries subscribed. It was his job to remind his congregation of these truths each Sunday, and as he did so, he recalled them for himself as well.

But Sterne was no saint, and certainly he did not live his life in perpetual prayer and holy meditation. He was a human being who found much pleasure in human life, and not all of the pleasure he took was the innocent delight he recommended from the pulpit. Sterne's own particular weakness was lust. His marriage was, apparently, unfulfilling, and through the course of it he quite often gave in to the impulse to find satisfaction with other women. Early on, according to Cash, there were episodes with prostitutes and servants (*EMY,* 135–36). Later, there were a series of more lasting involvements, emotional attachments to young women such as the singer Catherine Fourmantel and his most famous amour, Eliza Draper. Some of these relationships were consummated; others remained sentimental affairs of rhetoric and emotion. Catherine Fourmantel belonged almost certainly to the first category; Eliza Draper to the latter.[13]

In the age of television evangelists, some of whom have been publicly excoriated for their sexual indiscretions, it probably needs to be said that while Sterne was aware such behavior was wrong in the Christian sense, he would not have felt that his failure to conquer lust in and of itself disqualified him from serving his chosen profession faithfully and well. All that was required of him was what was required of any man or woman: that he *strive* to subdue his passions, that he never give up the struggle to emulate Christ, though he could never be completely successful. This paradox is central to Christianity: The individual Christian is required to try to achieve something that he or she knows in advance is not achievable. He or she must meet failure after failure with renewed effort, never accepting defeat, yet never experiencing true victory on this side of the grave.

Did Sterne struggle? Although, of course, we cannot know for sure, I believe that, in a particularly human sense, he did. He treated his weakness as most of us do: When he found it impossible to face it down, he tried to rehabilitate it, to turn his weakness into a virtue. One of his sermons, "The Levite and his concubine" deals specifically with the issue of love outside of wedlock. In this sermon, Sterne rehearses the number of Old Testament patriarchs who had more than one wife or who took concubines. These patriarchs included Abraham, Jacob, David, and Rehoboam. Sterne makes it clear that their concubines were not prostitutes, but rather women who "differ'd little from the wife, except in some outward ceremonies and stipulations," rather like mistresses, we might infer (1:289). Furthermore, the children of such unions were often blessed and favored by God. In the Old Testament, Sterne says, it was not the fact of having a concubine that was wrong, but the abuse of one's ability to do so. He points to Solomon's seven hundred wives and three hundred concubines as excessive.

The story of the Levite and his concubine (Judges 19:1–3), however, is not offered in support of extramarital affairs. It is a story of love and forgiveness. The concubine has been unfaithful to the Levite and has fled to her father's home. The Levite pursues her and "*speak{s} friendly to her, and . . . bring{s} her back again*" (1:286). He loves her in spite of her offense; he forgives her and brings her home. Yet, as Sterne reflects on the Levite and the concubine, we do seem to hear the yearnings of Tristram Shandy and Parson Yorick, yearnings that speak not only of a man's capacity for compassion but of his need for sexual passion as well:

> Let the torpid monk seek heaven comfortless and alone.——GOD speed him! For my own part, I fear I should never so find the way: let me be wise and religious——but let me be MAN: wherever thy Providence places me, or whatever be the road I take to get to thee——give me some companion in my journey, be it only to remark to, How our shadows lengthen as the sun goes down;—to whom I may say, How fresh is the face of nature! How sweet the flowers of the field! How delicious are these fruits! ("Levite and his concubine," 1:290)

In a letter Sterne wrote to his friend John Hall-Stevenson, we hear the same urgency, less delicately phrased. The letter, written as Sterne was on his way to London in December 1760, was originally penned in Latin. It reads, in part: "I do not know what is the matter with me, but I am sick and tired of my wife more than ever—and I am possessed by a Devil who drives me to town. . . . I am unbearably horny—and I am done to death by desire."[14] In this letter, he cautions Hall-Stevenson, who was prey to similar temptations and desires, that "this is not the way to salvation in this world or the next." The statement is somewhat ambiguous (though Hall-Stevenson no doubt understood his friend), for a subsequent thought suggests that it is the resisting of temptation that runs counter to salvation. Solomon, Sterne says, points the true way: "nothing is better in this life than that a man live merrily, and eat and drink and enjoy good things, because this is his portion and dowery [*sic*] in this world" (*TLY*, 106). He with a thousand women at his disposal might well say so!

Was lust the work of the devil to Sterne or the road to salvation? Is desire a sign of our fallen nature? Or does sexual longing spring from compassion, the root of all morality? Was such a theory self-delusion and rationalization or the insight of true reason? These questions are, I think, at the heart of Sterne's struggle with his own weakness and at the heart of his narrative masterpieces. And, for all of his various ponderings on the matter, to Laurence Sterne's everlasting credit, they are questions he never presumed to resolve.

Chapter Three
Tristram Shandy Revisited

The first chapter of *Tristram Shandy* begins with the words "I wish" and ends with the word "nothing," and in a sense the entire narrative is thus encapsulated, for desire and nothingness are the two poles between which *Tristram Shandy* casts itself.[1] Sex and death are the main preoccupations of the narrator as they are, Sterne would assert, of most of humankind. Part of the purpose of *Tristram Shandy* seems to be to celebrate these preoccupations and to revel in the exigencies of life even in the face of death.

Although beginning at the beginning, at the moment of Tristram's conception or as Tristram himself, quoting Horace, puts it, *"ab Ovo,"* *Tristram Shandy* does not proceed chronologically (*TS,* 1.5/1.4). It is possible, however, to devise a sequential time line of the events in *Tristram Shandy,* an exercise completed some sixty years ago by Theodore Baird.[2] Baird's purpose in offering a chronology of *Tristram Shandy* was to show that Sterne was meticulously careful about the sequence of events in the Shandys' lives, that behind the seemingly chaotic presentation of the narrative lay a precisely ordered series of events. Sterne was so "in command" of the lives he invented for his characters, so aware of the way these lives played themselves out against and within the patterns of history, that, as Baird points out, he was only occasionally tripped up by inconsistencies in the narrative.[3] The following is, in abbreviated form, Baird's chronology of *Tristram Shandy.* While reducing the narrative to such a pedantic tool as a chronology is in one sense a hideous violation of the text, in another it offers a sure means of access to *Tristram Shandy*'s artistry. Furthermore, it provides a handy means of orientation for the first-time reader of *Tristram Shandy,* "the great humour of which," in Horace Walpole's words, "consists in the whole narration always going backwards."[4]

A chronology
1689   James Butler (Corporal Trim) joins the army.
1690   Siege of Limerick, August 17–30. After siege, heavy rains for 25 days; Toby Shandy and Trim have fever, September.

1692   Battle of Steenkirk, July 24.
1693   Battle of Landen, July 29. Trim receives wound in knee, falls
        in love with the fair Beguine, and becomes Toby's servant.
1694   Mr. Wadman dies around this time. Young Le Fever born
        this year or the next.
1695   Siege of Namur. Toby receives wound in groin, July 27.
1697[5] Toby retires with Trim to England (London). Walter sets up
        as Turkey merchant. Toby becomes engrossed in sieges.
1698   Toby buys books of fortification. Yorick and wife establish
        midwife in her post.
1699   Toby studies projectiles, leaves off in huff, and begins to
        pursue fortifications only. Dinah married and got with child
        by coachman. Widow Wadman pursues bedroom practices.
1701   Toby to country with Trim to set up residence. Stays over
        with Widow Wadman, who falls in love (Toby doesn't
        return passion until 1713).
1702   Siege of Ruremond, October 7. Siege of Liege, October 14.
        Toby and Trim build drawbridges, gates, and a sentry box.
1703   Sieges of Amberg, Bonn, Rhinberg, Huy, Limbourg. Trim
        builds model town.
1704   Marlborough marches into Germany. Lawsuit over ox-
        moor. Toby adds church.
1705   Toby adds field-pieces.
1706   Dendermond taken by the allies (summer). Lt. Le Fever
        dies. Young Le Fever sent to school by Toby.
1708   Sieges of Lisle, Ghent, Bruges. Trim builds cannon.
1712   Walter writes *Life of Socrates*.
1713   Walter moves to country. Treaty of Utrecht. Demolition of
        Dunkirk (September–November). Toby falls in love with
        the Widow Wadman.
1716   Walter writing dissertation on "Tristram."
1717   Le Fever joins army just before the defeat of the Turks,
        August 5. Walter to London with Elizabeth Shandy, Sep-
        tember.
1718   Tristram Shandy begot, the night between the first Sunday
        and the first Monday in March. Trim and Bridget break the
        drawbridge. Tristram Shandy born, November 5; chris-
        tened. Visitation dinner during which a hot chestnut falls
        into Phutatorius's flap.
1719   Legacy from Aunt Dinah. Bobby dies. Walter begins *Tris-
        trapœdia*.
1721   Le Fever ill. Toby proposes Le Fever as Tristram's tutor.
1723   Window sash episode. Tristram put in breeches.

1728   Toby and fly.
1741   Tristram accompanies Mr. Noddy's son to Europe.
1748   Yorick dies.
1750   Sermon on conscience preached at York by a certain prebendary.
1759–66 Tristram writes.

Tristram Shandy, of course, is as much about the telling of a story as it is about a story told, and to summarize *Tristram Shandy* is to recount narrative strategy as well as narrative. False starts; digressions; interruptions; sermons; legal documents; fables; addresses to the reader(s); lists; blank, black, and marbled pages; diagrams; and riddles—all these and more interfere with our perceiving *Tristram Shandy* as the sequence of events outlined above. Our experience of sequence in this work is analogous to our experience of sequence in a conversation with someone we know rather well. There are digressions, questions, wandering thoughts —interruptions of all kinds in a conversation between intimate acquaintances, yet stories get told and opinions proffered. *Tristram Shandy* is a conversation; Tristram does most of the talking, to be sure, but we readers are the listeners and our part in the conversation is far from negligible.

The following discussion of *Tristram Shandy* will review the narrative in sequence as it was published—two volumes at a time, with the ninth and final volume standing alone. My intent is to provide the reader a full sense of what goes on in each volume, but I will necessarily be offering my own interpretation as I do so. In particular, I will draw on the Sterne I have constructed in the previous two chapters to describe a narrative written by an eighteenth-century clergyman. For, although the twentieth century has tended to view *Tristram Shandy* as the most modern, indeed the most postmodern of texts, it is a text written within the conceptual framework outlined in the previous chapter—the framework of Anglican orthodoxy. Bawdy, iconoclastic, and irreverent though it certainly is, *Tristram Shandy* is nonetheless a book imbued with its author's beliefs and experiences.

Volumes 1 and 2: Then and Now

An aura of nostalgia pervades the first two volumes of *Tristram Shandy*— an aura that makes the work feel perennially contemporary. For who, in imagining his or her prenatal family, does not experience an odd sense of loss, a paradoxical loss of something never possessed? Thinking back to a time prior to our own existence has the same effect as thinking forward to a time just after our death when we are no longer physically among those we have loved in life, yet our presence is felt, invoked by memory or memorial. When we think in such a way, time is a continuum that we join at a certain point and leave at a certain point, and we tend to regret both what we missed and what we will miss by not joining sooner or leaving later. Such imaginative forays tend to overemphasize the simplicity of both past and future, but the past especially, being "fixed" and finished, tends to seem simpler and slower, as though our own individual existences have somehow complicated things and speeded them up as well. In the first two volumes of *Tristram Shandy*, there is a distinct sense of contrast between then and now.

The act of narration occupies the present. Tristram writing, of course, is the primary activity of "now," but our reading occupies that realm also, and Tristram is ever aware of that fact. Tristram's aim in writing, as he states in chapter 6 of volume 1, is "friendship" with the reader. But it is a peculiar kind of friendship, a friendship possible only in the world of print and a friendship that stands in contrast to the relationships of the past as they are configured by Tristram. Tristram addresses us as we read, asking us to "imagine" this and "picture" that. He invites us to pause, reread, answer questions, guess, fill in blanks, and even, late in the book, draw. He constantly calls our attention to the fact that we are readers reading and that he is a writer writing.

One of the first things we notice about *Tristram Shandy*, writer, is his learning. He admits that he is "not a wise man" (*TS*, 1.13/1.8), but he seems to want to strike us as a learned man, conversant with both ancient and modern writers in every field imaginable, including natural science, obstetrics, literary criticism, law, theology, psychology, astronomy, and rhetoric. "You see as plain as can be," he tells us in volume 2, "that I write as a man of erudition;– – – that even my similes, my allusions, my illustrations, my metaphors, are erudite" (*TS*, 1.98/2.2). Among other ostentatious displays of learning in volume 1, Tristram invokes Locke's association of ideas to help us understand why his mother interrupted his father's love-making to ask if he remembered to wind the clock (Walter always did both on the first Sunday night of the month); he mentions "Tully and Puffendorff" in support of his opinion that the homunculus has all the rights of a living person; he includes a document in French relating a ruling by the doctors of the Sorbonne as to whether or not a child can be baptized in the womb (the answer is, according to the Roman Catholic deliberations, yes), and he compares his father's belief that names set one's destiny to Copernicus's explanation of the solar system. These wide and varied references may seem designed to intimidate the reader, especially in light of chapter 20 of volume 1, in which Tristram chastises "madam" for inattention and instructs her to reread chapter 19 to discover where he reveals *"That my mother was not a papist"* (TS, 1.64/1.20). We find on returning to (or reading on in) chapter 20, that the secret was revealed in the statement: " 'It was *necessary* I should be born before I was christen'd,' " for "[h]ad my mother, Madam, been a Papist, that consequence did not follow" (TS, 1.65/1.20), but unless we knew the ruling of the Sorbonne's doctors we could never have inferred the conclusion the narrator insists that we draw. And we may be expected to wonder how many additional insights we are missing, how many other inferences we are failing to draw because our own knowledge is not quite so broad or so arcane as Tristram's seems to be.

Still, Tristram does not intimidate us, and the reason he does not is that he has such a hard time writing his story that we cannot help but find him a bit of a clown. He even encourages that perception by telling us that he will stop occasionally to put on a cap and bells and dance about. And he does so in numerous digressions that are as engaging as the story he proposes to tell.

Further, he attributes to the reader an adversarial role; Sir and Madam often challenge his competence and his opinions, and although he always has the last recorded word, we can be expected to continue to harbor the doubts and reservations of our surrogates. Finally, if we are familiar with Sterne's eighteenth-century predecessors, Jonathan Swift and Alexander Pope, we might recognize in Tristram a "modern" who desires above all things to seem deeply learned though he is shallow read.[6] We might suspect that Tristram is in that sense an object of satire, not a reliable narrator.

Even so, we cannot fully reject Tristram. Although his learning is a bit esoteric, he is usually right about what he says. He is honest, as well, about his limitations. For example, though he invokes Horace in support of his decision to begin the story of his life at the very beginning, he admits too that Horace does not really recommend doing so. Further, Tristram's impatience protects him from too much pedantry. "Pray what was that man's name," he asks in chapter 21 of volume 1, "for I write in such a hurry, I have no time to recollect or look for it,——who first made the observation, 'That there was great inconstancy in our air and climate?' Whoever he was, 'twas a just and good observation in him" (*TS*, 1.71/1.21).

Tristram is much more anxious to add to the aggregate of knowledge than to report servilely what others have discovered or thought. Thus, in the particular instance mentioned above, for example, he adds a corollary to the unknown authority's observation: "this strange irregularity in our climate, producing so strange an irregularity in our characters,——doth thereby, in some sort, make us amends, by giving us somewhat to make us merry with when the weather will not suffer us to go out of doors" (*TS*, 1.71/1.21). He proudly announces, "that observation is my own," and he records for posterity—for future pedants—the precise date "March 26, 1759," and time "betwixt the hours of nine and ten in the morning" that he made the remark (*TS*, 1.71/1.21). Tristram also invents names for rhetorical strategies not covered by ancient and modern learning on the subject of elocution. Uncle Toby's tendency to greet what he considers absurdity by whistling Lillabulero, for example, is labeled by Tristram the *Argumentum Fistulatorium* (the argument of a whistler), which takes its place alongside other of Tristram's inventions, like the *Argumentum Tripodium* (the argument of the third leg) and the *Argumentum ad Rem* (the argument to the thing), made use of only in arguments between men and women (*TS*, 1.79/1.21). This last example of Tristram's contributions to the fund of human wisdom suggests yet another reason that we tend not to find him intimidating. He is bawdy, constantly distracted by the sensual, and he assumes we are the same. To revise my earlier assertion slightly, to read *Tristram Shandy* is to have a conversation peppered with the titters, giggles, blushes, leers, rib-pokings, winks, and smirks that typically greet double entendre and suggestive jokes.

Tristram exists in the present tense, and thus it is very difficult for him to harness time. He rushes, he tells us, "making all the speed" he possibly can, and still he is behind: "I declare I have been at it these six weeks, . . . —and am not yet born" (*TS*, 1.42/1.14). It is just not as simple a thing to write the story of his life as he thought it would be upon first setting out, for distractions and obligations abound: "there are archives at every stage to be look'd into, and rolls, records, documents, and endless genealogies" (*TS*, 1.41/1.14). Tristram's writing—like our reading—is in a constant state of interruption, though, as he explains it, the interruptions serve to forward his purpose as much as they distract from it. He describes his work as a machine that runs by two contrary motions, "thought to be at variance with each other" but in fact reconciled by what he represents as the skill of the narrator: "[M]y work is digressive, and it is progressive too," Tristram brags, "and at the same time" (*TS,* 1.81/1.22).

Indeed, what he says is true enough, at least in volumes 1 and 2, in which the digressions, with two notable exceptions that will be discussed below, are related to the Shandy family and serve to forward our understanding of the characters and circumstances of Walter, Toby, and Elizabeth Shandy. But it is also true, as Tristram goes on to observe, that the managing of a narrative can be distressing to an author: "For, if he begins a digression,———from that moment, I observe, his whole work stands stock-still;—and if he goes on with his main work,————then there is an end of his digression" (*TS,* 1.81/1.22). And while he does not approve of the taste, Tristram is aware from the outset that many of his readers would prefer to read straightforward; for all that he believes that the digressions are "the soul of reading" (*TS,* 1.81/1.22), he knows his readers want "fresh adventures" (*TS,* 1.66/1.20). His narrative, later on, becomes more and more subject to lengthy interruptions, some of which have the most tenuous relationship to the Shandy family, yet which displace their story for page after page (Slawkenbergius's tale in volume 4 is a handy example). And we are to see these interruptions, I believe, as characteristic of the present moment that Tristram the writer inhabits. The present is, like Tristram himself, contingent, spontaneous and impulsive, predictable only in its unpredictability. The past is fixed and quite predictable only because it is the realm of memory, not the realm of existence.

The elder Shandys inhabit Tristram's past; none of them is alive in Tristram's "now," and as a result, they exhibit a steadiness of character that Tristram lacks. Tristram emphasizes this reliability by the manner in which he chooses to describe them, particularly his father and his uncle, whose characters he draws by describing their "hobby-horses."

A hobby-horse, as Tristram defines it, is something more than a hobby but less than an obsession. Tristram explains that a "man and his HOBBY-HORSE . . . act and re-act exactly after the same manner in which the soul and body do upon each other . . . so that if you are able to give but a clear description of the nature of the one, you may form a pretty exact notion of the genius and character of the other" (*TS,* 1.86/1.24). Walter is in a sense the sum of his theories and Toby of his fortifications.

Walter's character and his theories dominate volume 1. He feels that an individual's nature and physical fortune are determined at the moment of conception and that Mrs. Shandy's ill-timed question lay the "foundation . . . for a thousand weaknesses both of body and mind" in her unborn child (*TS*, 1.3/1.2). Walter also believes that names are another determinant of personal fortune—Tristram being the worst of all possible names in that regard. And he believes that national political power should not be concentrated in London and that domestic authority should accrue to the husband and father of the family—both of which notions support him in his insistence that Tristram be born at Shandy Hall. Walter is a great systematizer, but he does not oversimplify the human condition. Indeed, one might say he does just the opposite. His theories act on and react to one another in a constant series of negotiations and modifications. Although he believes that a baby's fate is determined at the moment of conception, he tries to counteract Tristram's bad luck there first with a particularly lucky name—Tristmegistus—and, when that fails, with a complete encyclopedia of education—the *Tristrapædia*. Walter's war on the dominance of London is aided by his wife's compliance with the marriage settlement's stricture that having taken her husband to London on a false alarm she must "lie-in" in the country the next time she gives birth; but his insistence on his own authority yields to his wife's desire to be assisted in the birth by a midwife rather than the doctor-practitioner Walter would have preferred. In the end, they compromise: "my mother was to have the old woman,—and the operator was to have licence to drink a bottle of wine with my father and my uncle *Toby Shandy* in the back parlour" (*TS*, 1.55–56/1.18). Walter is enamored with theoretical thought, but when forced up against practicality, he resigns his theories or develops new ones. The theory itself is much more important to him than the practical application, anyway.

In this respect, he differs from his brother Toby, for whom theory must be enacted to be compelling at all. Thus, Toby's hobby-horse is, first, a series of maps, books, and instruments, and then an actual model of a military fortification built on the bowling green at Toby's country house near Shandy Hall, a project that had a rather long gestation period. During the four years that Toby recuperated from the wound in his groin received at the Siege of Namur, he gradually immersed himself in the study of military science. He was led to do so first by the confusion that ensued each time he tried to describe his wounding at Namur to the guests Walter sent to his room. To sort out the scarps from the counterscarps, the half-moons from the "ravelins," he pasted "a large map of the fortifications of the town and citadel of *Namur*" upon a board and began to study not only this map, but maps of other fortified towns, books on military architecture, and even, for a little while, books on projectiles as well (*TS,* 1.96/2.1). He also began to accumulate compasses and other instruments that aided his study until one night his equipment fell off of the small table on which it customarily lodged. This frustrating event prompted Toby's servant James Butler (called Trim) to suggest the bowling-green scheme. Toby, after four years' convalescence, suddenly decided he was well enough to leave London for the country, and he and Trim embarked to enjoy Toby's newly acquired hobby-horse in the retirement of the country. The description of Toby's hobby-horse accounts for almost all of his character, according to Tristram, except for the stroke of placidity (so unusual in a soldier) commonly expressed in the saying "he wouldn't hurt a fly." Indeed Toby would not hurt a fly, as Tristram vividly remembers:

> Go,–––says [uncle Toby], one day at dinner, to an over-grown [fly] which had buzz'd about his nose, and tormented him cruelly all dinnertime,—and which, after infinite attempts, he had caught at last, as it flew by him;–––I'll not hurt thee, says my uncle *Toby,* rising from his chair, and going a-cross the room, with the fly in his hand,–––I'll not hurt a hair of thy head:—Go, says he, lifting up the sash, and opening his hand as he spoke, to let it escape;—go poor Devil, get thee gone, why should I hurt thee?––––This world surely is wide enough to hold both thee and me. (*TS,* 1.130–31/2.12)

Because of the hobby-horse to which Toby refers everything from the sudden appearance of Dr. Slop to the rapid increase of obstetric knowledge, he, like Walter, seems fixed and finished, especially next to Tristram's own life of exigency and contingency. But scenes like the one between Toby and the fly or Toby's wounding at Namur remind us that the past was once the present—momentary, capricious, and spontaneous. Tristram's memory alone has fixed the incidents and awarded them significance, as it is natural for the mind of a human being to do. Thus, his memory gives him a sense of stability in the chaos of the present.

With Toby's hobby-horse established, Tristram is ready to pursue the thread of his narrative, picking up in chapter 6 of volume 2 where he left off ten chapters before with Walter and Toby in the parlor awaiting the birth of Tristram. The brothers, informed that Mrs. Shandy is in labor, send Obadiah for the man-midwife, Dr. Slop, whom the servant meets by surprise, causing the doctor to fall off his horse. This "squat, uncourtly," muddy papist of a doctor joins the Shandy brothers at the fireside as Mr. and Mrs. Shandy had agreed he would do (*TS*, 1.121/2.9). Obadiah is again sent away—this time for the doctor's surgical instruments, while the three men talk, distracted first by Toby's comparison of Dr. Slop's arrival to Stevinus's "celebrated sailing chariot" (*TS*, 1.135/2.14) and second by a sermon that falls out of the copy of Stevinus that Toby has Trim fetch for the doctor's elucidation. Trim's reading of the sermon occupies most of the rest of the volume.

The sermon is attributed to Parson Yorick and is meant to remind us of the parson whose story we read in an extended digression in volume 1. Yorick's story and his sermon are related thematically in that both are about interpretation and misunderstanding. Parson Yorick is Sterne's self-portrait, an idealized and allegorized version of the way he felt he had been mistreated and misunderstood with regard to the politics of York Minster, at the hands of his Uncle Jaques in particular and perhaps in the Topham-Fountayne quarrel as well. Yorick is much as Sterne seems to have been, given to wit and satire, basically good-hearted but careless about the way others perceive him. Consequently, Yorick is "misread" by his parishioners, who place the worst possible interpretation on his actions. His charity is invariably decried as selfishness; his lightheartedness, as malice; his honesty, as pride. He has one friend, Eugenius, who warns him that the opinion of the world can indeed damage one. Revenge, cruelty, malice, and cowardice could combine against him:

> the best of us, my dear lad, lye open there,––– and trust me, ––––trust me, *Yorick, When to gratify a private appetite, it is once resolved upon, that an innocent and an helpless creature shall be sacrificed, 'tis an easy matter to pick up sticks enew from any thicket where it has strayed, to make a fire to offer it up with.* (*TS*, 1.32/1.12)

Easy, because we all, like Yorick, have shortcomings; we have all done and said things that can be exploited by those who wish to harm us or discredit us. And so it happens to Yorick. He is attacked by his enemies until he finally dies, brokenhearted. In the black page that commemorates his death, we see our own fate.

The "Abuses of conscience" sermon makes a corollary point. If others are apt to interpret our characters and actions ungenerously, we are likely to treat ourselves with too much leniency. We know the motives of our misbehavior all too well; the impulse that can override our sense of propriety or morality can also assuage the sting of conscience. Conscience must be buttressed, not by interpretation, but by religion, by the spirit of Christianity. We might be tempted to point out to Yorick that Christianity has been subject to various interpretations itself and, of course, he acknowledges that much wrong has been done in the name of religion. Yet he also asserts that the "spirit of Christianity" is a clear and immutable law that conscience, directed by belief, not self-interest, can readily determine (*TS,* 1.163/2.17). The interpretation of self and others is finally less important than the judgment of God, just as, Yorick would say, the past and the present are both less significant than forever.

Volumes 3 and 4: Curses

The first two volumes of *Tristram Shandy* teach us much about reading between the lines. We learn that gaps, pauses, and silences are at times as meaningful as the words of a text. In the space between the beginning of a sentence and the end, between the end of one chapter and the beginning of the next, between the comment of one character and the answer of another, much can occur. Tristram's narrative does not hurtle headlong from cause to effect so much as it reels, stumbles, and jumps from pause to pause to pause. As we have noted, Tristram's narrative style depends on the technique of stopping the forward movement of the narrative in order to "fill in the gaps" in our knowledge of character or past event, as when Tristram interrupts his uncle's "I think" with a ten-chapter review of Toby's hobby-horse. Other pauses are not properly Tristram's, but our own, though they are manipulated by Tristram as he forces us, for example, to stop to contemplate the black page or to reread a chapter. Still other pauses belong to his characters. For instance, Walter's sudden awareness of his wife's fear puts an end to his enthusiastic description of Cesarean birth. Pauses create the space for contemplation, elaboration, and mutual understanding; they also make room for mischief to operate and mayhem to flourish.

In the gap between the publication of volumes 1 and 2 and that of volumes 3 and 4, much had occurred. Sterne had been lionized and lambasted; he had become, in the space of a year, both famous and infamous. *Tristram Shandy* was well received, but the parson who wrote it was reviled in some quarters, particularly when he printed his sermons under the name of the Cervantick Parson Yorick. Such a lighthearted gesture seemed designed, to some, to trivialize religion itself. Sterne, of course, had no such intention, but like Yorick, he "would never . . . take pains to set a story right with the world, however in his power" (*TS*, 1.385/4.27). Instead, he became even more outrageous. The gaps in the text become, in volumes 3 and 4, increasingly difficult to fill with contemplation and understanding as we are left to elaborate salacious hints that, whatever Tristram says in his mock-innocence about noses being noses and nothing more, will not sustain pristine interpretation. Madam's "Fy Mr Shandy!"—her tendency to fill in any blank space with the "dirty" option of the various possibilities on offer—becomes in volumes 3 and 4 the only option available. All pretense of decorum and modesty is exposed for just that—pretense. Toby's modesty is sincere—whether as the result of a wound or his nature—but there are few Toby Shandys in the world. Most of us are by nature less modest than Toby, our thoughts never far from the preoccupation of sex. Admit it and damn the consequences, these volumes seem to say. Or deny it and be damned yourself!

A curse is the opposite of a blessing and, as such, it can refer either to the invocation of evil (as in the curse I have written above) or to the condition of misfortune itself. Volumes 3 and 4 of *Tristram Shandy* are almost exclusively concerned with imprecations and blights. The cursing begins with Dr. Slop. Mrs. Shandy's delivery being imminent, the doctor is driven by impatience and frustration to curse Obadiah for rendering his forceps, squirt, *tire-tête,* and so on difficult to retrieve by tying knots in the surgical bag: "Pox take the fellow! I shall never get the knots untied as long as I live" (*TS*, 1.198–99/3.10). This malediction directed toward Obadiah is followed by a cursed event: In trying to cut through the knots with a penknife, Dr. Slop slashes his thumb. The injury provokes more excoriation: "I wish the scoundrel hang'd——I wish he was shot——I wish all the devils in hell had him for a blockhead" (*TS*, 1.199/3.10).

Walter's passion for systems, it turns out, leads him to pursue various rather unexpected lines of inquiry. He happens to have, among his collection of books, an anathema—a comprehensive system of cursing, as it were—authored by one Ernulphus, a Roman Catholic bishop. Walter, who is in truth offended by Slop's damning of Obadiah, insists that the papist doctor read aloud from Ernulphus. "Small curses," he tells Dr. Slop, "are but so much waste of our strength and soul's health to no manner of purpose" (*TS*, 1.199/3.10). Ernulphus will teach him to swear in a fashion commensurate with the provocation. Of course, Walter (and Sterne) is ridiculing the Roman Catholic practice of excommunication as well as the general human tendency to blame anyone other than ourselves for our misfortunes. And the image of the squat, muddy Dr. Slop uttering the stentorian phrases of eternal damnation is truly a ludicrous one:

> May he be cursed inwardly and outwardly.—May he be cursed in the hair of his head.— May he be cursed in his brains, and in his vertex, . . . in his temples, in his forehead, in his ears, in his eyebrows, in his cheeks, in his jaw-bones, in his nostrils, in his foreteeth and grinders, in his lips, in his throat, in his shoulders, in his wrists, in his arms, in his hands, in his fingers. (*TS*, 1.209/3.11)

Such a curse, offered in this context, is as pointless as it is extreme. It is a curiosity to Walter, a relic of the past devoid of any real conviction. For no one—not the Shandys, not Slop, not the reader, not the hapless servant himself—believes Obadiah eternally damned as the result of Ernulphus's formula. But the "gusto," the exaggerated, meticulously thorough, ice-cold ire of the passage is a perfect introduction to the first day of Tristram's life, which is to be full of bad luck, frustration, and misery—at least from Walter's point of view. And it is a perfect ironic response on Sterne's part to the "monthly Reviewers" who had been "cut[ting] and slash[ing] . . . [his] jerkin" for "these last nine months together" in mean-spirited reviews of *The Sermons of Mr. Yorick* (*TS*, 1.190–91/3.4).

Knotted bag and cut thumb notwithstanding, Dr. Slop manages to retrieve his forceps, armed with which he goes upstairs to assist the midwife. Meanwhile Walter and Toby fall asleep. "Peace be with them both," the narrator says (*TS*, 1.226/3.20), taking the occasion of this brief narrative pause to include "The Author's Preface." In this digression Tristram/Sterne follows up on his earlier reference to the critics' damnation of his work. Then Tristram had answered a curse with a blessing and promised to continue to do so: "God bless you;—only next month, if any one of you should gnash his teeth, and storm and rage at me, as some of you did last MAY . . . —don't be exasperated, if I pass it by again with good temper" (*TS*, 1.191/3.4). Tristram promises to demonstrate the forbearance of his uncle Toby and say to his critics—"get thee gone,———why should I hurt thee? This world is surely wide enough to hold both thee and me" (*TS*, 1.191/3.4).

But in the Author's Preface, he defends himself, and he does so in terms that enlighten our understanding of the curses that befall Walter and Tristram on the day of Tristram's birth. Life is a mixture of laughter and sorrow, of pleasure and pain, of blessings and curses. *Tristram Shandy* reminds us of that truism at every turn. But as universally accepted as the maxim is, Sterne implies, we do not sufficiently recognize the need for a comparably mixed response to the exigencies of life. We emphasize judgment, like Locke, seeing wit as an unimportant—even a distracting, slightly annoying—human propensity. In *The Essay Concerning Human Understanding,* Locke defines wit as "the assemblage of *Ideas,* and putting those together with quickness and variety, wherein can be found any resemblance or congruity." Judgment, on the other hand, consists of "separating carefully, one from another, *Ideas,* wherein can be found the least difference, thereby to avoid being misled by Similitude, and by affinity to take one thing for another."[7] Wit appeals through metaphors and allusions to the fancy, according to Locke, while judgment through reason arrives at truth.

As Sterne complains in the preface, for Locke, wit and judgment are obviously distinct operations of the mind and, as obviously, Locke prefers judgment over wit. For Locke, similitude—metaphors and allusions—is nothing more than pleasant, gay, and distracting: "it is a kind of affront to go about to examine it, by the severe Rules of Truth and good Reason" for "it consists in something, that is not perfectly conformable to them" (Locke, 157). But Sterne's skepticism about the sufficiency of rational thought (which receives its clearest articulation in the "Abuses of conscience" sermon) leads him to a different conclusion. For him, true reason must be a combination of wit and judgment; it is not the province of judgment alone.

The preface ends with the author's illustration of the "affair of wit and judgment" by the analogy of a cane chair (*TS,* 1.235/3.20). The chair has "two knobs on the top of the back of it, . . . the highest and most ornamental parts of its *frame,*——as wit and judgment are of *ours,*——and like them too, indubitably both made and fitted to go together, in order . . . *to answer one another*" (*TS,* 1.235–36/3.20). To remove one knob is to render the chair ridiculous; to be worth anything at all, the chair must have two knobs. One is worse than none would be. And, Sterne argues, so it is with wit and judgment.

The vile rumor that wit and judgment cannot coexist, Sterne further argues, was invented and is perpetuated by the "grave" to the disadvantage of wit simply because they are unable to achieve wit themselves. With a "deep and solemn" cry, they denigrated the *"poor wits"* in "one of the many and vile impositions which gravity and grave folks have to answer for hereafter" (*TS,* 1.237–38/3.20). Sterne, having been accused

by the critics of sacrificing all claim to moral seriousness by his use of
Yorick's name on the title page of his sermons is here fighting back. The
conceit—the wit—in no way compromises the theological validity of
the sermons themselves. And *Tristram Shandy*'s point is the same—
laughter and morality not only can coexist, they must do so or morality
becomes gravity, that is, spiritual pride. It is worth pointing out here too
that Sterne probably had in mind Pope's argument for the compatibility
of wit and judgment: "For *Wit* and *Judgment* often are at strife, / Tho'
meant each other's Aid, like *Man* and *Wife*."[8] Sterne's examination of
morality and wit is decidedly focused on concupiscence.

The curses that rain down on Walter Shandy on his son's birth day
are reminders of human frailty and fallibility. From the squeaky door
hinge to Tristram's squashed nose to the mis-christening of the child,
disappointment abounds. And all is the result of human limitations—
Walter's neglect in oiling the door, Slop's mishandling of the forceps,
Susannah's "leaky" memory, and so on. The natural course of life brings
much misery, but our imaginations compound the difficulties almost
past bearing: "Inconsistent soul that man is!—languishing under
wounds, which he has the power to heal!—. . . his reason, that precious
gift of God to him—. . . serving but to sharpen his sensibilities,——to
multiply his pains and render him more melancholy and uneasy under
them" (*TS,* 1.239/3.21). Certainly, without his theory of noses and
names, Walter would have suffered much less trauma during Tristram's
early hours. Indeed, we might say, with the single exception of Bobby's
death, all of the hardship Walter endures in volumes 3 and 4, he brings
on himself.

Lest we be too critical of Walter Shandy's inability to govern his
imagination, however, Sterne provides ample evidence that he is not
alone in this weakness. On the pretext of introducing a document val-
ued by Walter for its contribution to the doctrine of noses, Sterne begins
volume 4 with "Slawkenbergius's Tale," the story of a man with a big
nose who travels from "Strasburg" to "Frankfort" and back, his large
proboscis provoking comment and obsession wherever he goes. That
one can tell the size of a man's penis by the size of his nose is lore more
ancient than *Tristram Shandy,* and Sterne has already invoked the association in volume 3 as Slop, Toby, and Walter worry over the potential
mutilation of baby Shandy's anatomy should the hip present itself or
should the baby arrive head first (*TS,* 1.221/3.17). As it turns out, in
Walter's mind, it is all one, for he reacts to the injury to Tristram's nose
as though the child's future potency has been compromised. The acci-

dental maiming of a symbol is to Walter's mind the same as the destruction of the thing itself. Similarly, in "Slawkenbergius's Tale," the symbolic completely dislodges the actual.

"Slawkenbergius's Tale" provides an example of the absolute triumph of wit over judgment. Imaginations inflamed by the stranger's large nose, the "Strasburgers" "could not follow their business." They left their homes and their work and "men, women, and children, all marched out to follow the stranger's nose" (TS, 1.324/4. "Slawkenbergius's Tale"). While they were so preoccupied, they were literally occupied: The French "marched in" and conquered the town. Slawkenbergius's gloss on the event invokes a bawdy pun: "it is not the first—and I fear will not be the last fortress that has been either won——or lost by NOSES" (TS, 1.324/4. "Slawkenbergius's Tale"). We snicker at the sexual innuendo, following our own noses, as it were. For while we take "the dirty road" that Sterne has mapped out for us, we forget that a nose is, as Tristram has warned us, "a Nose, and nothing more, or less" (TS, 1.258/3.31). Ingenuity, "art or wile" might "put . . . other ideas" in our minds, but judgment should step in at some point to correct our fancy (TS, 1.258/3.31). It is true that in the sex act women are penetrated by men, and so, metaphorically, one must admit that a fortress may be won (from the man's point of view) or lost (from the woman's) by a nose. But if such metaphors are really meaningful, they are, Sterne suggests, more than simply witty. They are a proper subject for serious reflection—for the operation of judgment—as well.

In volume 2, Toby, unable to tell the right end of a woman from the wrong end, fixes his eye on a crevice in the chimney-piece. In volume 3, Eugenius points out to Tristram that the passage has a double meaning. Tristram responds by defining a nose, and we focus our attention on noses for the rest of the volume and through "Slawkenbergius's Tale" in volume 4, taking, of course, the "dirty road" as we do so. But just as dirt in a sense improves Dr. Slop, that is, it corrects his (to Sterne) superstitious, papist practice of crossing himself, dirt gives us our "comeuppance" as well. Like Walter we spend much time on our high horses (or hobby-horses) concocting theories, systems, plans, and counterplans when, because of our natural human limitations, most are destined to fail, to fall. That we cannot keep our minds clean should correct any tendency we have to pride ourselves on any account, to place any hope in our own ability. After all, the various afflictions that plague us in life are, in the orthodox view that Sterne held, but the result of the first curse of all, God's curse of mankind in Eden.

Walter's efforts to ameliorate his own and his son's suffering are doomed. Walter will not, like Toby, rely on "the grace and the assistance of the best of Beings" to help him through his troubles (*TS*, 1.332/4.7). Instead, he counts on his own ingenuity, "that great and elastic power within . . . of counterbalancing evil" (*TS*, 1.334/4.8). To so counterbalance Tristram's injured nose, Walter chooses a lucky name—Tristmegistus—but Susannah's poor memory renders his scheme worse than pointless. Because she can remember only the "tris" and because the curate himself happens to be named Tristram, Walter's child ends up with not just the wrong name, but the name Walter holds to be the unluckiest name in the world. "Tristram" derives from "triste," or sorrow, which is perhaps the reason that Walter so abhors the name. Whatever the case, it is certain that the news of Tristram's christening is occasion for Walter to mourn: "child of wrath! child of decrepitude! interruption! mistake! and discontent!" (*TS*, 1.354/4.19)—carried by a mother anxious about the midwife, brought into the world head first with 470 pounds of pressure on his small brain, wounded on the nose, and then christened with the wrong—and the worst possible—name. "O *Tristram! Tristram! Tristram!*" Walter moans (*TS*, 1.356/4.19).

Volume 4 draws to a close with a description of a "great dinner" attended by Yorick, Walter, and Toby for the purpose of consulting powerful church officials about the possibility of changing a child's name once he is christened. The dinner provides Sterne another opportunity to satirize "learned" speculative discourse: The scholars reach the height of absurdity when they pronounce "[t]*hat the mother is not of kin to her child*" (*TS*, 1.390/4.29). This ridiculous edict piques Walter's curiosity, and Toby's *Lillabulero,* but in the end Tristram is still Tristram. The dinner is also notable for a hot chestnut that falls into Phutatorius's lap, through the aperture in his breeches, which Tristram refuses to name but which the editors of the Florida edition of *Tristram Shandy* identify for us as a fall or a flap.[9] The terms resonate interestingly. Phutatorius's curse "ZOUNDS!" interrupts Yorick's comments on sermon writing. The passage is worth looking at in some detail as it draws together the notions of birth, the right and wrong ends of thing, and Yorick's sermons—the theologic flap upon the heart that Sterne had published to much criticism the year before. Yorick says to Didius:

> I have undergone such unspeakable torments, in bringing forth this sermon . . . upon this occasion,—that I declare, *Didius,* I would suffer martyrdom—and if it was possible my horse with me, a thousand times over,

before I would sit down and make such another: I was delivered of it at
the wrong end of me—it came from my head instead of my heart—and
it is for the pain it gave me, both in the writing and preaching of it, that
I revenge myself of it, in this manner.—To preach, to shew the extent of
our reading, or the subtleties of our wit—to parade it in the eyes of the
vulgar with the beggarly accounts of a little learning, tinseled over with a
few words which glitter, but convey little light and less warmth—is a
dishonest use of the poor single half hour in a week which is put into our
hands—'Tis not preaching the gospel—but ourselves—For my own
part, . . . I had rather direct five words point blank to the heart. (TS,
1.376–77/4.26)

Yorick delivers his sermon in as much travail as Mrs. Shandy in child-
birth; but unlike Mrs. Shandy, he would have had an easier time, had he
delivered it from the right end, from the heart rather than from the
head. Mrs. Shandy has no such option, as the original Edenic curse
makes clear: "in sorrow thou shalt bring forth children."[10] In sorrow and
for sorrow, so she does. Yet Yorick's difficulty and the curse of womankind have one thing in common: They both result from misdirected
desire, in Eve's case, the desire for knowledge of good and evil; in
Yorick's, the desire to seem learned and witty.

Interrupted by Phutatorius's curse, Yorick stops speaking. Phutatorius's imagination transforms the heat of the chestnut into the sting of a
reptile—an interesting reminder of the fall of mankind—and he flings
the chestnut from him, only for Yorick to pick it up. Phutatorius, whose
name incidentally (but not coincidentally) means "copulator," hence
blames Yorick for the chestnut's falling in his lap in the first place, and
others at the visitation dinner concur. Knowing that Yorick had long
disliked Phutatorius's treatise on the keeping of concubines, some
insisted "that his chucking the chestnut hot into Phutatorius's ***—
*****, was a sarcastical fling at his book—the doctrines of which, they
said, had inflamed many an honest man in the same place" (TS,
1.384/4.27)

Sterne believed, as we have seen, that because of original sin and the
curse it provoked, the inclination of our nature is toward lust, sensuality,
desire.[11] That this inclination is sinful does not stop sex from being fun
or funny, but it is an indication of our fallen state. Yet, as such, it is natural to us and, as the ninth article of religion goes on to point out
"although there is no Condemnation for them that believe and are baptized, yet the Apostle doth confess, that Concupiscence and Lust hath of
it self the Nature of Sin." We are sinful and in need of forgiveness. Ser-

mons exist to point that out, and if publishing sermons under the name of Parson Yorick entices some to read who otherwise would not do so, all the better. If the name "Yorick" associated as it is with jesting and mortality offends the grave and spiritually proud, all the better too. There is nothing in Yorick's sermons or in *Tristram Shandy* itself that is threatening to morality or religion, Sterne seems to be asserting in volumes 3 and 4, unless the threats themselves are brought to the books. The moral of the marbled page, different in every edition, is that interpretation is various, ever-changing, and ultimately unreliable in contrast to the clear and permanent truth of the black page, which commemorates the certainty of mortality.

Volume 4 ends with a blessing *and* a curse. Walter, after all of the suffering associated with his infant son, suddenly receives a piece of unexpected good news. Aunt Dinah has left him a legacy of a thousand pounds. He is thrown immediately into a quandary as to how to spend it: draining the ox-moor or completing his elder son Bobby's education. Troubled almost beyond endurance by the arguments on both sides, Walter is ultimately relieved "by a fresh evil"—Bobby's death. Truly, as Tristram says "[w]hat is the life of man! Is it not to shift from side to side?—from sorrow to sorrow?" (*TS,* 1.399/4.31). Certainly, curses abound, but the volume ends with a blessing large enough to counterbalance the vexation and trouble of life:

> Was I left like *Sancho Pança,* to chuse my kingdom . . . —. . . it should be a kingdom of hearty laughing subjects: And as the bilious and more saturnine passions, by creating disorders in the blood and humours, have as bad an influence, I see, upon the body politick as body natural—and as nothing but a habit of virtue can fully govern those passions, and subject them to reason—I should add to my prayer —that God would give my subjects grace to be as WISE as they were MERRY; and then should I be the happiest monarch, and they the happiest people under heaven— (*TS,* 1.402/4.32)

For "virtue and laughter," we can read "judgment and wit," and thus we find as much philosophy in this "roasted horse" of a tale as Phutatorius should find in the chestnut that falls into his flap.

Volumes 5 and 6: Lines, Ligaments and Threads

"Are we for ever to be twisting, and untwisting the same rope? for ever in the same track—for ever at the same pace?" Tristram asks in chapter

1 of volume 5 (*TS*, 1.408/5.1). Complaining about plagiarisms and imitations of his work, Tristram quotes Burton's *Anatomy of Melancholy* without acknowledgment, setting a plagiary against a plagiary, or as he says later, "*a thief to catch a thief*" (*TS*, 2.514/6.11). The answer he would seem to be looking for is "no!" Why not strike out in new directions? But the answer he gets is "yes." To some extent we will always twist and untwist the same rope. Look at Toby; look at Walter; look at Tristram himself who proceeds to tell us a story about whiskers that merely reiterates the point of "Slawkenbergius's Tale": "the word ['whiskers'] was ruined" through "accessory ideas" (*TS*, 1.414/5.1). Habits of mind and hobby-horses guarantee a certain amount of redundancy, and moreover, life's great variety is punctuated often by regularity. As for Walter Shandy, the first Sunday of the month brings concupiscence and clock-winding, so for the rest of us daily life has a predictable pattern as well.

As if to further underscore this point, volume 5 brings us face to face with mortality again. The black page commemorating Yorick's death becomes Trim's hat falling in illustration of Bobby's sudden demise: "Are we not here now, . . . — . . . and are we not . . . —. . . gone! in a moment?" Trim says as he drops his hat, and Tristram enjoins us in terms every bit as elegiac as "Alas, Poor Yorick!" to "meditate . . . upon *Trim's* hat" (*TS*, 1.432–33/5.7). We revisit too in Trim's "harangue" the message of "The abuses of conscience," Trim's earlier moment of moving eloquence—we human beings are of mixed nature, divine and corrupt:

> Are we not, continued *Trim,* looking still at *Susannah*—are we not like a flower of the field—. . . is not all flesh grass?—'Tis clay,—'tis dirt . . .
> —What is the finest face that ever man looked at!—I could hear *Trim* talk so for ever, cried *Susannah,*—what is it! (*Susannah* laid her hand upon *Trim's* shoulder)—but corruption?——*Susannah* took it off. (*TS*, 1.435/5.9)

Perhaps we, like Susannah, do not care to be reminded of our corruption, but, we remember from the sermon, to deny our flawed nature is to trust our consciences, which are wholly unreliable unless directed by religion, "the fear of God" (*TS*, 1.157/2.17). That is, perhaps we remember. Or perhaps the train of our thoughts moves in a different direction; perhaps, though twisting and untwisting still, we work on a different rope. Perhaps the answer to Tristram's question is "yes" and "no" and *both* at the same time!

Tristram Shandy's nonlinearity is such a critical commonplace, one hesitates to challenge the notion. Certainly the tale is presented neither chronologically nor causally, yet Tristram does follow several chains of thought, and the reader does the same. In fact, Tristram asserts, "some trains of certain ideas . . . leave prints of themselves about our eyes and eye-brows"; we are literally lined with our preoccupations (*TS*, 1.413/5.1). It is therefore difficult for us to hear a word like "whiskers" without setting forth on a train of thought informed by associated ideas. As Tristram puts it, "we see, spell, and put [ideas] together without a dictionary" (*TS*, 1.413/5.1) Many readers of *Tristram Shandy*, Tristram complains, "[run] the scent the wrong way" (*TS*, 1.415/5.1) and find only reasons to take offense, their thoughts centering on the bawdy and licentious. There is plenty of morality and religion in *Tristram Shandy* to counterbalance the lewd. But the moral and the bawdy—like the beautiful and the corrupt—do coexist in *Tristram Shandy*. They form, in Sterne's opinion, "a delicious mixture" and whoever takes offense must have "either a pumkin [*sic*] for his head—or a pippin for his heart" (*TS*, 1.435/5.9). *Tristram Shandy*, instead of being nonlinear, is multi-linear; and all possible lines reflect the delicious mixture of concupiscence and delicacy, bawdiness and morality, wit and judgment, merriness and wisdom, progression and digression. Each line is, in the Shandean sense, an organic machine. To read *Tristram Shandy* is to learn to operate the machine, to become aware of rich resonance within the text itself, within the culture of learning upon which Sterne drew to write the text and within the culture that has grown from *Tristram Shandy*—this last being a resonance that Sterne himself could not anticipate. Attention to such resonance makes it possible for us to hold in our minds contradictory notions without the drive to subordinate one to the other. Such resonance offers a way of reading that opens a text to the fullness of human experience rather than tying it to a single reading, explanation, or hobby-horse. Such resonance, in Tristram's words, "opens the heart and lungs, and . . . makes the wheel of life run long and chearfully [*sic*] round" (*TS*, 1.401/4.32).

  Resonance is not so much a matter of conscious artistry as it is the product of an analogous imagination. This imagination was likely Sterne's by nature, but it was certainly encouraged by his profession as a preacher. The Bible itself reveals what Northrop Frye has called "the expanding of vision through language," through metaphors or images that are not merely rhetorical flourishes.[12] This language—language, for example, of sheep and pastures, harvest and vintage, cities and temples,—resonates richly throughout the Biblical texts. To speak of "shepherd," therefore, is to invoke among other things the wandering nomadic life of the Israelites, the sacrificial death of a lamb in Isaac's place, Jacob's use of lambskin to attain his father's blessing in Esau's stead, David's beautiful psalm, "The Lord is my Shepherd, I shall not want," Jesus' parable of the lost sheep, the sacrificial death of the "lamb of God." Such resonance propels us, in Frye's words, "into the genuinely infinite"; it conquers "the finiteness of the human mind" (Frye, 168). What the Bible achieves is not the unity of "doctrinal consistency or logic . . . but [a] more flexible . . . imaginative unity" (Frye, 218)

Image clusters create in *Tristram Shandy* an imaginative unity similar to the one Frye finds in the Bible. And that is not surprising given that what Frye describes in *The Great Code* is the way "the Bible . . . set up an imaginative framework . . . within which Western literature . . . operated down to the eighteenth century" and beyond (Frye, xi). *Tristram Shandy* draws certain of its key images from the Bible itself and from writers whose imaginations were also heavily indebted to the images of the Bible. Asses, servants who are wiser than their masters, and devils or demons are central images in the Bible, and all are associated with the life of Christ in particular—his humility and his healing power. Some images seem especially central to *Tristram Shandy*. Breeches of various sorts, interruptions, falling or broken things would fit into this category. Whether reverberations draw our imaginations out of the text or direct us to intratextual echoes, it would be difficult to locate the passage in *Tristram Shandy* that is not richer if we read it with an ear to its resonance.

To illustrate the resonances available within the text itself, we can take for example, the scene in which we are told of Tristram's circumcision by the window sash. Figure A is a diagram of various paths our minds might take as we read the description of the event in chapter 17 of volume 5. Of course, any one of these thoughts might call up other resonances: Toby's hobby-horse might give rise to thoughts of hobby-horses in general—Walter's, Tristram's, our own—or of horses—Yorick's, Dr. Slop's, and (later) the horse upon which Gymnast and Tripet acrobatically illustrate polemical debate. Or one's mind might move from hobby-horses to prostitutes because "hobby-horse" was a slang term for prostitute in Sterne's day. If one knew that, one might then allow one's mind to wander from prostitute to fallen women, to Aunt Dinah and the coachman, to the Shandy coat of arms, to the visitation dinner, to the dinner where Toby released the fly.

Extratextual resonances are pertinent too, though they are perhaps less available to today's reader who is not as familiar with Rabelais, Burton, Cervantes, Swift, and Montaigne as Sterne was. But most readers

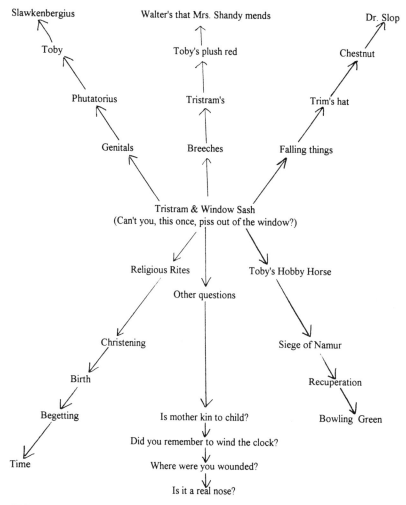

FIGURE A. *Tristram Shandy*'s Multilinear Resonance: Volume 5, Chapter 17.

do respond to Yorick's name as an echo of *Hamlet,* and many recognize Don Quixote's horse, Rosinante, to which Yorick's broken-down horse is compared. The more conversant we are with the texts that form the context of *Tristram Shandy,* the more resonant we find the work itself. The more attentive we are to the text of *Tristram Shandy,* the more resonant we find it as well.

No thesis is being argued by the allusive, echoic structure of *Tristram Shandy;* no system is being proposed. Rather, what resonance seeks to do is to inculcate a habit of mind that stands opposed to the tendency we have of reading straightforward. Yet volumes 5 and 6 do not deny this tendency, which is, after all, the very foundation of narrative. In fact, even the Bible's emphasis on metaphor does not preclude linear narrative structure. The Bible begins, as Frye says, "where time begins"; it ends "where time ends"; and in between "it surveys human history" (Frye, xiii). Thus, if through resonant metaphor the Bible is able to escape the finiteness of the human imagination, it does so within a structure that the human imagination can easily grasp, a linear structure.

Admittedly more narrow in focus than the Bible, *Tristram Shandy* likewise begins with creation—an individual's creation—and will end, Tristram tells us, with that individual's death. In between, we find a rather comprehensive survey of the vast variety of elements that make up the individual life. We find opinions, other people, family histories, fears, stories, conversations, documents, obligations, plans, memories, moments of forgetfulness or incompletion, sexuality, spirituality, pleasures, and pains. We find a wide-ranging, apparently ungoverned imagination, capable at times of surprising mastery of progressive and digressive narrative skill.

The first fourteen chapters of volume 5 of *Tristram Shandy* demonstrate this mastery; they constitute a *tour de force* of the Shandean style. Sterne must have recognized his own achievement, for he pauses to celebrate in chapter 15:

> Had this volume been a farce . . . the last chapter, Sir, had finished the first act of it, and then this chapter must have set off thus.
> Ptr . . . —r . . . —r . . . ing—twing—twang—prut—trut (*TS,* 1.443/5.15)

Indeed, the narrative by which volume 5 commences is so neatly managed, one does not blame the author's documenting his skill, though he does so with "a cursed bad fiddle" (*TS,* 1.443/5.15).

Chapter 1 of volume 5 picks up where volume 4 ended, with Bobby's death. The incident is quite poignant in itself, of course. Sterne had significant personal experience with the deaths of children; his childhood was punctuated with the deaths of siblings, and one of his regular duties as a minister would have been to comfort bereaved parents and to perform burials of children who had fallen victim to the illnesses or accidents that claimed many young lives during the eighteenth century. Sterne would have been all too aware of the pain endured at the death of a child. And we too should be cognizant that although in the eighteenth century childhood mortality was much greater than it is today, the death of a child was nonetheless a cause of human grief and sorrow.

Yet responses to bad news vary, as the Shandy household aptly illustrates. Walter, of course, philosophizes. Like Cicero, he finds comfort—even happiness—in his eloquence and wisdom. When Toby tells him of Bobby's death, many of the innumerable sayings about death offered by philosophers from ancient times until Walter's own day "rushed into . . . [his] head": "He took them as they came," from the Magna Carta to Seneca to Plutarch (*TS*, 1.421/5.3). Toby, the audience of Walter's oration, reacts quite differently. For him, the news of Bobby's death provokes no philosophy, only pity—pity for Bobby's suffering; pity because he fears for the loss of Walter's reason; pity for his sister-in-law, who happens by the room just in time to hear Walter say: "'I have friends—I have relations,—I have three desolate children'" (*TS*, 1.442/5.13). He is quoting Socrates, but Mrs. Shandy does not know it, and she interrupts: "Then . . . you have one more, Mr. *Shandy*, than I know of" (*TS*, 1.442/5.13). Her interruption, as usual, destroys Walter's system; he responds curtly, "By heaven! I have one less" (*TS*, 1.442/5.13). When Walter leaves the room, Toby explains, "They are *Socrates*'s children," and he takes his sister-in-law, "most kindly by the hand, without saying another word, either good or bad, to her, . . . led her out after my father, that he might finish the ecclaircissment himself" (*TS*, 1.443/5.14). Mrs. Shandy's question forces Walter to recognize the sorrow Toby had already admitted and that his wife must soon bear. For all the different tracks and trains upon which their three minds run, the elder Shandys are one in their grief.

We are not told directly of this oneness in grief. Walter enlightens his wife, as it were, off stage, and in fact the only indication we have of Walter's own sorrow (though it is a powerful one) is the abrupt cessation of his catalogue of philosophical truisms. Yet the story of the elder Shandys' response to Bobby's death is itself interrupted in such a way that we can infer their unity in sorrow. For, of course, Tristram does not tell this part of his story straightforward. He leads us to the point in Walter's oration where Mrs. Shandy passes by the door and pauses like "the listening slave, with the Goddess of Silence at his back" (*TS*, 1.427/5.5). Leaving her thus poised, Tristram then digresses to a description of what occurs simultaneously in the servants' hall. Here

Trim, Obadiah, Jonathan, Susannah, and a fat scullion—a kitchen servant—come to terms with the household tragedy.

Obadiah makes the announcement: "My young master in *London* is dead" (*TS*, 1.429/5.7), and Susannah thinks immediately of all her mistress's clothes, gowns that will descend to her when the Shandy family goes into mourning. Like Walter, Susannah finds not only comfort but happiness in the pitiable circumstance. Obadiah himself thinks of the "terrible piece of work . . . stubbing the ox-moor" will be, now that Walter's decision about how to use Aunt Dinah's legacy has been made for him (*TS*, 1.430/5.7). The scullion, sick herself of a dropsy, is likewise solipsistic; she reflects that Bobby is dead and she is not. The thought gives her a sense of superiority. When Trim hears the news, however, his response, like Toby's, is pity for Bobby. Moved to eloquence, his oratory takes a different turn from Walter's speech. Instead of explaining away grief, Trim immediately illustrates its power. "Are we not here now, . . . [said] the corporal, (striking the end of his stick perpendicularly upon the floor, so as to give an idea of health and stability)—and are we not— (dropping his hat upon the ground) gone! in a moment" (*TS*, 1.431/5.7). Suddenly, all the servants recognize in Bobby's death, their own vulnerability. They are sorry, for themselves, to be sure, but for Bobby as well and for his parents and for his uncle too. From the thoughts of green gowns, ox-moors, and dropsy that the news first brought, the servants' minds are suspended in sadness as they "meditate . . . upon *Trim*'s hat" (*TS*, 1.433/5.7).

Trim's hat, like the black page commemorating Yorick's death, like the inevitability of death and God's judgment that underwrites the message of "The abuses of conscience," like the curses that constantly plague us in life—all of these are occasions for reflection on our own mortality. They constitute, as it were, the most fundamental truth for Sterne, for the world of *Tristram Shandy*. It is a moral truth, of course: To live one's life in the belief that after death one must answer for one's conduct should encourage moral behavior and moral awareness. The passages in which *Tristram Shandy* reminds us of our own mortality seem designed for the reflection and meditation occasioned by *memento mori* of any sort.

For the Shandy family servants, reduced to tears by Trim's hat, the effect of the *memento mori* is profound but momentary, for talk soon turns to ways to die, and then to Captain Toby Shandy's sadness at the death of Lieutenant Le Fever. As Tristram concludes the scene, the servants gather around the fire to hear Trim tell the story of the lieutenant's illness and death, a story we will not read until volume 6. Of course, the story of Le Fever is yet another tale of death and sorrow, but it is another tale. And soon the Shandy servants will be following once more their individual lines of thought about green gowns, ox-moors, and dropsy. The elder Shandys too are to experience a momentary oneness, we assume, as Toby takes Mrs. Shandy to her husband, who will tell her the sad news. And we can expect a similarly brief period of contemplation, for from the frayed end of Bobby's fragment of life, threads emerge that twisters of rope begin to weave immediately.

The *Tristrapædia* is Walter's new rope. Having one son left, Walter throws himself into preparing a comprehensive system of education for the child: "The first thing which entered my father's head, after affairs were a little settled in the family . . . —was to sit down coolly . . . and write a TRISTRA-*pædia,* or system of education for me; collecting first for that purpose his own scattered thoughts, counsels, and notions; and binding them together, so as to form an INSTITUTE for the government of my childhood and adolescence" (*TS,* 1.445/5.16). Walter relies on his inventiveness and his resonant learning to write the *Tristrapædia.* Tristram tells us, "[m]y father spun . . . every thread of it, out of his own brain,—or reeled and cross-twisted what all other spinners and spinsters had spun before him, that 'twas pretty near the same torture to him" (*TS,* 1.445/5.16). Walter is determined to follow a straight line in designing his son's education; therefore, he is particularly pleased with John de la Casse's description of writing as "a state of *warfare*" (*TS,* 1.447/5.16). Here, Sterne seems to be tweaking the noses of critics who find his work too bawdy for a clergyman, for it is de la Casse's opinion

that whenever a Christian was writing a book . . . where his intent and purpose was *bonâ fide,* to print and publish it to the world, his first thoughts were always the temptations of the evil one.—This was the state of ordinary writers: but when a personage of venerable character and high station, either in church or state, once turned author,—he maintained, that from the very moment he took pen in hand—all the devils in hell broke out of their holes to cajole him. (*TS,* 1.447/5.16)

The obvious problem with approaching writing as an act of resistance rather than wit is that the restraint under which one labors makes writing a slow, unproductive, and ultimately futile exercise. Because of "the slow progress my father made in his *Tristra-pædia,*" Tristram tells us, "I was . . . totally neglected and abandoned to my mother; and what was almost as bad, by the very delay, the first part of the work, upon which my father had spent the most of his pains, was rendered entirely use-less,——every day a page or two became of no consequence" (*TS*, 1.448/5.16).

Sterne's own narrative preference, of course, is to give in to the devils, to write much, rather than little, to give full play to wit and laughter, which as we noted earlier make up much of the digressive energy of the book. His problem is the opposite of Walter's. Sterne finds the straight line harder and harder to resist. It is significant that volumes 5 and 6 present the important events of Tristram's childhood—his circumcision and his symbolic entry into manhood (albeit at the age of five!)—in the space of a volume and a half as opposed to the four volumes that it took to get Tristram christened.

The figure of the line and its relatives the thread, the ligament, the path, the drawing, the diagram, the polygon, and the parallel are woven throughout volumes 5 and 6 of *Tristram Shandy*. Everything, it seems, from the written word to warfare is amenable to linear represen-tation. "Sir" is instructed to "draw" the Widow Wadman in chapter 38 of volume 6; even memory is a line of sorts, for Walter is "a large uneven thread" in Tristram's brain (*TS*, 2.558/6.23). These figures cul-minate in the linear diagrams at the end of volume 6, where Tristram diagrams the course of his narrative thus far (see Figure B). Tristram hopes to continue to "mend" and to "arrive . . . at the excellency of going on even thus;

---

which is a line drawn as straight," he says, "as I could draw it, by a writ-ing-master's ruler, . . . turning neither to the right hand or to the left" (*TS*, 2.571–72/6.40). We generally read this statement as ironic, as Tris-tram's false capitulation to the demand of critics like Bishop William Warburton, who advised Sterne to write nothing that "priest and vir-gins" would be embarrassed to read (*Letters*, 119). The diagrams illus-trate how boring, how grave, the perfectly pious narrative would be. But they also illustrate the tremendous straightforward drive that occurs even when one allows one's imagination full reign and indulges every digressive impulse along the way. All of the lines are basically straight; deviations resolve themselves into the 180-degree angle, and we read the lines from left to right, that is, from beginning to end. For all of its apparent nonlinearity, *Tristram Shandy* proves that it is as hard to avoid the straight line as it is to achieve it.

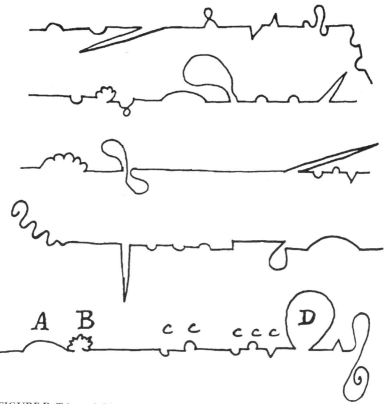

FIGURE B. Tristram's Linear Diagrams of Volumes 1–5: Volume 6, Chapter 23.

The straight line is itself a resonant image in *Tristram Shandy*. The straight line is the line of moral rectitude, the Christian path, the shortest distance between two points, and the line of gravity. It is the line ("plumb") that Trim's hat travels "as if a heavy lump of clay had been kneaded into the crown of it" (*TS*, 1.432/5.7); it is the line ("slap") along which the window sash descends as Tristram follows Susannah's advice to, just this once, "**** *** ** *** ******" (piss out of the window); it is the line Walter tries to pursue in his *Tristrapædia*, proceeding step by step with "caution and circumspection" (*TS*, 1.446/5.16). The straight line is the relentless passage of time that renders the *Tristrapædia* useless. The straight line is a plan, a purpose, a pursuit, contrived and confounded by "human wisdom," for as Tristram observes, "the wisest of us all . . . outwit ourselves, and eternally forego our purposes in the intemperate act of pursuing them" (*TS*, 1.448/5.16).

Despite Tristram's dislike of straightforward narrative, despite Sterne's obvious distaste for anything smacking of gravity, the straight line is not demonized by *Tristram Shandy*. It can be the most moving of figures, as in the case of Trim's hat. It is the most efficient means of fighting in Trim's opinion, and in Yorick's, who agrees that "one home thrust of a bayonet" is preferable to the acrobatic shenanigans of Gymnast and Tripet (1.464/5.29). The straight line is the line of sexual intercourse and the line of cabbage-planting, which according to the editors of the Florida edition, are the same thing (*TS*, 3.442).

The straight line can also be the source of great comfort and resilience, as it becomes in young Billy Le Fever's story. This sad tale concerns an old soldier who dies in an inn close to Toby's country estate, leaving a son (Billy) for whom Toby takes responsibility, as the result of a "line":

> The blood and spirits of *Le Fever,* which were waxing cold and slow within him, and were retreating to their last citadel, the heart,—rallied back,—the film forsook his eyes for a moment,—he looked up wishfully in my uncle *Toby*'s face,—then cast a look upon his boy,——and that *ligament,* fine as it was,—was never broken.——(*TS*, 2.512–13/6.10)

This ligament, the result of the direct line of sight between Toby and Le Fever, spawns other plans, other lines. Toby teaches young Le Fever "to inscribe a regular polygon in a circle" and then sends the boy first to school and next into the army, telling him as he does so that, should fortune fail him, the boy should "come back again to me, . . . and we will shape thee another course" (*TS*, 2.518–19/6.12). When fortune does fail Le Fever, and Toby proposes him as Tristram's tutor, the next course is shaped.

The straight line—the line of gravity, self-importance, and dullness—is also the line of friendship, service, honesty, and humility. Yorick himself uses it to censure his own self-commendation written in praise of his sermon on Le Fever's death:

BRAVO

The straight line is as resonant a figure as any in *Tristram Shandy*, having the ability to expand our imaginations as it invokes the contradictory elements of life without resolving them.

The fundamental source of life's contradictory nature is the fact that it ends in death, that movement ceases, that lines end. But endings are not confined to death; they are part of the rhythm of life as well. What is perhaps the most poignant ending in *Tristram Shandy* is brought about by the Treaty of Utrecht, which puts an end to Toby's hobby-horse:

> STILLNESS, with SILENCE at her back, entered the solitary parlour, and drew their gauzy mantle over my uncle *Toby*'s head;———and LISTLESS-NESS, with her lax fibre and undirected eye, sat quietly down beside him in his arm chair.———No longer *Amberg*, and *Rhinberg*, and *Limbourg*, and *Huy*, and *Bonn*, in one year,—and the prospect of *Landen*, and *Trerebach*, and *Drusen*, and *Dendermond*, the next,—hurried on the blood. (*TS*, 2.561–62/6.35)

This end but signals a new beginning: "the trumpet of war fell out of his hands,—he took up the lute" (*TS*, 2.562/6.35). Toby's war games, we are told, give way to his courtship of the Widow Wadman.

Toby's embarkation on another narrative line requires little effort from him; in fact, the whole household knows that the story has begun over two weeks before Toby himself realizes it: "*Susannah* was informed by an express from Mrs. *Bridget*, of my uncle *Toby*'s falling in love with her mistress, fifteen days before it happened" (*TS*, 2.568/6.39). For Walter, the process of linear movement is more vexed. Finding that Tristram's accident with the window sash has set the rumor mill going ("*poor Master Shandy* * * * * * * * * * * * entirely" [2.521/6.14]), Walter begins to consider putting his son into "breeches." He weighs the pros and cons of such a course of action in what he calls his "beds of justice": "when any difficult and momentous point was to be settled in the family, which required great sobriety, and great spirit too, in its determination,———he fixed and set apart the first *Sunday* night in the month, and the *Saturday* night which immediately preceded it, to argue it over, in bed with my mother" (*TS*, 2.523–24/6.17). But an argument with Mrs. Shandy is an exercise in frustration, leading not to a decisive course of action but to pauses, silences, and unexpected outbursts:

> I am resolved, however, quoth my father, breaking silence the fourth time, he shall have no pockets in them.———
> ———There is no occasion for any, said my mother.———
> I mean in his coat and waistcoat,—cried my father.
> ———I mean so too,—replied my mother.

———Though if he gets a gig or a top———Poor souls! it is a crown and a
scepter to them,—they should have where to secure it.———
Order it as you please, Mr. *Shandy,* replied my mother.———
———But don't you think it right? added my father, pressing the point
home to her.
Perfectly, said my mother, if it pleases you, Mr. *Shandy.*———
———There's for you! cried my father, losing temper———Pleases me!—
—You never will distinguish, Mrs. *Shandy,* nor shall I ever teach you to
do it, betwixt a point of pleasure and a point of convenience.———This
was on the *Sunday* night;———and further this chapter sayeth not. (*TS,*
2.528–29/6.18)

In pursuing the narrative line, Tristram employs a method similar
to Walter's beds of justice. One day, he writes full, without a care in
the world, allowing his pen to take its own digressive path, and the
next he writes empty, with care and discretion. Between the two
methods, Tristram says, "I write a careless kind of a civil, nonsensical,
good humoured *Shandean* book, which will do all your hearts good—
———And all your heads too,———provided you understand it" (*TS,*
2.525/6.17). To do so, again, we have to be able to hold contradictions
in our minds without resolving them. We have to be able to see that
Toby is both morally astute—as he is in his dedication to Le Fever and
his sorrow for Bobby's death—and morally obtuse—as he is in his oration in defense of war, wherein he defines war as "the getting together
of quiet and harmless people, with their swords in their hands" (*TS,*
2.557/6.32). But we have to admit there is a germ of truth to what he
says, for something certainly must be done "to keep the ambitious and
the turbulent within bounds" (*TS,* 2.557/6.32). Similarly, we have to
be able to regard Trim's eloquence as an admirable natural gift, as it
seems when he uses it to deliver the "Abuses of conscience sermon"; as
an intuitive, if glib, response to a situation as it appears in his comments on Bobby's death; and as a mechanical skill, as it seems to be in
his military-style recitation of the catechism. And, in the last case, we
must be prepared to admit that rote memorization, while mechanical,
nonetheless is sometimes accompanied by true understanding. Trim
honors his father and mother by "[a]llowing them . . three halfpence
a day out of [his] pay, when they grew old," leading Yorick to call
him "the best commentator" upon that commandment (*TS,*
1.470–71/5.32).
    Yet, if we must hold contradictions in our minds as we read, Sterne
himself must keep providing resonant material. And if the human imag-

ination is on the one hand drawn to the straight line, it is on the other capable of meaningless, empty flights of fancy. In his own disquisition on invention, Walter asserts that the "North west passage to the intellectual world," lies in the use of *"auxiliary verbs"* (*TS*, 1.484/5.42). He explains that the auxiliary verbs "set the soul a going by herself upon the materials as they are brought her; and by the versability of this great engine, round which they are twisted, to open new tracks of enquiry, and make every idea engender millions" (*TS*, 1.485/5.42). He demonstrates with the example of a white bear and the many questions one can ask oneself about it: "Have I ever seen one? Might I ever have seen one? Am I ever to see one? Ought I ever to have seen one? Or can I ever see one?" (*TS*, 1.487/5.43). It is significant that this nonsensical demonstration of the generative power of the auxiliary verb ends volume 5 and that volume 6 begins with Tristram's declaration that his first five volumes are "better than nothing" (*TS*, 2.491/6.1). We must ask ourselves, are they? Are they sense? Are they nonsense? Are they both and at the same time?

The answer is, of course, that they are both. Although the human imagination is limited, it is also capable of transcending its limitations. It is capable of turning the meaningless into meaning. And it is capable of escaping meaning through fancy. Northrop Frye describes the mind-expanding properties of Biblical language as leading us away from the unity of finiteness to a state of wandering—an imperfect state. But, he explains, "there are two senses in which the word 'imperfect' is used: in one sense it is that which falls short of perfection; in another it is that which is not finished but continuously active, as in the tense system of verbs" (Frye, 168). For Sterne, the resonance of life lies in both senses of imperfection. Although *Tristram Shandy*'s narrative line documents the considerable shortcomings of human existence, it also celebrates that existence as a continuous and joyful state of becoming.

Volumes 7 and 8: Death and Desire

Volumes 1 through 5 of *Tristram Shandy* were published in the span of two years: Volumes 1 and 2 appeared in December 1759, volumes 3 and 4 in January 1761, and volumes 5 and 6 in December 1761. Sterne's life during this period alternated between London and Coxwold where he had become parson in 1760, taking up residence in a cottage he would call Shandy Hall. In fact, by the time Sterne returned from his first trip to London in 1760, he and his wife, as Arthur Cash says, "must have come to an agreement about how they would pattern their lives in the future: they would live as a family in Coxwold during the warm months, when Sterne would superintend the parish and do his writing. In the autumn he would go to London to publish what he had written, while Elizabeth and Lydia would return to York where they could be among friends and enjoy the theatre and other amenities of a 'town life' " (*TLY*, 54). This pattern changed, however, in 1762, and it would be three years (January 1765) before the next installment of Tristram's life and opinions would appear in booksellers' shops. By that time, Sterne's life had been transformed radically and permanently.

The Sterne marriage had never been an easy one, and Sterne's success as a writer, particularly as a writer of the kind of book he was writing, was especially hard on Elizabeth Sterne. In 1759, as Sterne was responding to his loss of church preferment by the raucous Rabelaisian satire that soon yielded to *Tristram Shandy,* his wife suffered a mental breakdown. Cash speculates that she "broke under the strain" of various family crises that included illnesses, deaths, and a relocation from Stillington to York, to say nothing of her husband's newly formed determination to sacrifice future preferment in the church if necessary in order to write an "original" book (*EMY,* 282–85). Sterne had to place his wife under the care of a "Lunatick Doctor" during this period of familial difficulty. The case has a comical side, at least in the version that has come down to us: The nature of Mrs. Sterne's malady was that she thought she was the Queen of Bohemia! This story was told by John Croft, younger brother to Stephen Croft, with whom Sterne travelled to London in 1760 just after the publication of volumes 1 and 2 of *Tristram Shandy.* John Croft, unlike his brother, had limited firsthand knowledge of Sterne; nevertheless, he wrote a memoir and various other anecdotal sketches about his sibling's famous friend. John Croft was notoriously unsympathetic to Sterne. Furthermore, this particular story was not part of Croft's memoir of Sterne but a contribution to a jest-book. Still, as Cash notes, it is "the best known of all anecdotes of Sterne" (*EMY,* 286). The full story Croft told included not only "Mrs. Shandy's" delusion but also her husband's indulgent participation in the fantasy: He " 'treated her . . . with all the supposed respect due to a crowned head' " (quoted in *EMY,* 285).

The image evoked by the story is ludicrous, though some scholars through the years have credited it; others question it, and of course, we will never know the truth beyond the fact that some sort of psychological crisis did occur at this juncture in Elizabeth Sterne's life. She would recover, but the episode marks the beginning of a fracture between husband and wife that never really healed. Between 1762 and 1765, the distance between the Sternes, both psychological and physical, continued to grow. The result was a new sense of self-determination on Elizabeth's part; in some ways, she took the reins of her own life, becoming, metaphorically anyway, empowered. If not the Queen of Bohemia, she at least managed to fashion for herself a comfortable, even pleasurable existence from what must have seemed to her in 1759 and 1760 a precarious set of circumstances. For Sterne, the domestic adjustment was perhaps the source of a new direction as well, an opportunity to look more closely at the relationship between men and women, the nature of sexual longing in particular. It would be the theme of everything he would write from this point on.

What exactly did the Sternes experience between 1762 and 1765? First, Laurence went to France. Alone. He went for his health, having, by his own account, overexerted himself writing and preaching.[13] He planned to send for his wife and daughter, according to a letter he wrote to one correspondent, but in another letter, written to John Hall-Stevenson about a year earlier, he revealed a decided lack of enthusiasm about family, at least married, life. He commiserated with his friend's being "tempted by [his] serving maids and troubled to distraction by [his] wife," for Sterne too was, he confessed, "sick and tired" of Elizabeth.[14] The two letters probably reflect the truth between them—a sense of duty, abiding love (if not passion), and frustration at the difficulties of daily cohabitation.

Sterne spent six months in Paris in 1762, where his health did mend and allow him to enjoy the benefits of being a celebrated author in the cultural center of Europe. In Paris Sterne found freer, more open manners between men and women than he had ever met with in England, even among the bluestocking set. The salons of Paris were sophisticated and worldly; the restraints between men and women, partly imposed by the Anglican orthodoxy that prevailed even in the most intellectual of English circles, were absent among the free-thinking *salonières*. The difference was at first intoxicating to Sterne; then he became bored with what he grew to regard as the superficiality of Parisian social life. He wrote to Hall-Stevenson: the French "are very civil—but civility in itself . . . wearies and bodders one to death" (*Letters,* 186).

Further, the benefits of Paris to Sterne's health were temporary. He became ill during his fifth month there and again suffered a bout of illness six weeks after that. His tubercular lungs were failing gradually, and his physicians advised him to go to Toulouse. Meanwhile in England his fourteen-year-old daughter was weakening from asthma, and Sterne sent for his family so that Lydia too could seek health in the south of France. The Sternes were together from July 1762 until March 1764. It was the last time they were to live together as a family for any extended period of time.

Lydia and Elizabeth fell in love with France; Lydia recovered her health, and Elizabeth enjoyed the change of scene so much that she decided to remain in France with her daughter whatever her husband might decide to do. Laurence's health did not improve, and worse, his work on *Tristram Shandy* was hopelessly bogged down. The diminution of his physical state was nothing compared to waning creativity. After spending two years in search of health, he returned to England still unwell but determined to complete volumes 7 and 8 of *Tristram Shandy*. Sterne was never really healthy after 1762, but by 1765 he had adopted the motto he had heard in Paris: " 'there is nothing so bad as wishing to be better' " (quoted in *TLY,* 206). He would neither wait for death nor flee it; he would simply bid "him come again; and in so gay a tone of careless indifference . . . that [Death would doubt] . . . his commission" (*TS*, 2.576/7.1).

Along with a renewed commitment to life, Sterne also began in 1764 a series of "sentimental" romances. Arthur Cash's explanation of these "love affairs" is persuasively and sensitively observed:

> Sterne . . . neither liked nor respected his own sexual passions, a "lascivi-ous devil" that drove him. He had wanted his marriage to work, and had brought his wife to France determined to patch up their disintegrating relationship. . . . The experiment had failed, and Sterne had lost his faith in marriage. . . .
>   Sterne wanted something more than a battle of the sexes and more than the gratifications of a night. He wanted love. He wanted it to be with gentlewomen, and he wanted it to be sweet, pleasurable and pro-found. And because he wanted it to be free of blame, even for a clergy-man, he wanted it to be public. To supply these moral rather than sexual needs, he invented his own sort of sentimental love. (*TLY,* 182–83)

Sterne would not fully incorporate the idea of sentimental love in all of its ramifications into his works until he wrote *A Sentimental Journey,* but in volumes 7 and 8 of *Tristram Shandy* we see the beginning of the idea. In fact, volume 7 is in a sense an early draft of *A Sentimental Journey,* sharing with the later work both a satire on travel writing and a preoccupation with love and mortality. Volume 8 shifts the focus to the story of Uncle Toby's amours, which itself presents an additional elaboration on the nature of desire and its relationship to love. As such both volumes provide an interesting commentary on what would be one of Sterne's most lasting contributions to western culture—the man of feeling.

Volume 7 begins with a bawdy joke and an interruption. Tristram is telling Eugenius a tale about "a nun who fancied herself a shell-fish, and of a monk damn'd for eating a muscle," when "DEATH himself knocked at my door" (*TS*, 2.576/7.1). The joke is unclear, but the imagery is provocative, and Tristram calls the story "tawdry." What is clear is Tristram's decision to flee: "there is no *living*, Eugenius, . . . at this rate; for . . . this *son of a whore* has found out my lodgings" (*TS*, 2.576/7.1). Tristram finishes his story and goes "off . . . like a cannon, and in half a dozen bounds got into Dover" (*TS*, 2.577/7.1). So, from the very beginning of the volume, the chase is on; Tristram flies, with Death in hot pursuit. "[S]o much of motion," Tristram will tell us in chapter 13, "is so much of life, and so much of joy——and . . . to stand still, or get on but slowly, is death and the devil" (*TS*, 2.593/7.13), and we are tempted to believe him, given earlier associations between death and "the end of the line." The movement that follows Death's interruption is not the movement of life, however, but a frenzied motion, a *danse macabre*—a dance of death. Tristram rushes through France—"CRACK, crack——crack, crack——crack, crack" (*TS*, 2.599/7.17)—seeing little and observing even less: "I know no more of Calais . . . than I do this moment of *Grand Cairo;* for it was dusky in the evening when I landed, and dark as pitch in the morning when I set out" (*TS*, 2.580/7.4).

Of course, in his frantic flight from death, Sterne would have us see, Tristram is the same as most other English travellers in France, where many went to recover in the warm sunshine of the south from the various ailments thought to be caused by the damp English weather. Many of these travellers turned their sabbaticals to account by writing travel books, a hugely popular genre in the eighteenth century. Sterne, however, is skeptical about the worth of the travel-writing enterprise, based as it seems to him to be on the authority of sick people travelling restlessly in pursuit of health. Tristram is one such traveller, and like many he pens his remarks as he goes. He even writes a chapter on Calais, in spite of his admitted ignorance, offering in it the standard travel writer's fare: number and kind of edifices, size of population, history and comments on the quality of the sights to be seen. This kind of information,

Tristram implies, is truly worthless; one can write such a chapter without ever having been to Calais, for it tells the reader nothing about the
true nature of the place. For that one must interact with the people, and
to interact, one must slow down.

It is only when Tristram stops running that he can be said to live
again. When in chapter 42, he changes "the *mode* of [his] travelling" and
rides a mule "as slowly as foot could fall" (*TS*, 2.646/7.42), Tristram's
dance of death becomes a dance of life; his fear is replaced by joy. In
chapter 12 of volume 7 Tristram envisions a death among strangers—
preferable, he says there, to dying amid one's grieving friends; still, it is
a sad picture of a lonely end with "a few guineas" purchasing "the few
cold offices" Tristram would need (*TS*, 2.592/7.12). By the end of volume 7, his vision has changed, and strangers have become partners in
the dance of life. Tristram stops his mule on the road between Nismes
and Lunel: "I'll take a dance," he says and joins a group of "nymphs . . .
and . . . swains" (*TS*, 2.649/7.43). As he dances with a "sun-burnt
daughter of Labour," he is distracted and stimulated by the "slit in [her]
petticoat," and by her apparent lack of inhibition: "I would have given a
crown to have it sew'd up—Nannette would not have given a sous—
Viva la joia! was in her lips—*Viva la joia!* was in her eyes" (*TS*,
2.649–651/7.43). The song to which the peasants dance is the philosophy that Tristram embraces at his journey's end: "VIVA LA JOIA! FIDON
LA TRISTESSA!" Long live joy! Fie on sadness! And for Sterne, Nannette's
unselfconscious expression of sensuality is the essence of joy, the essence
of life itself.

There is, for Tristram, "a great advantage" in travelling, an advantage
that seems to be linked to his interactions with the people of the country
through which he travels. But "people" is too broad a term, for in truth
Tristram's recovery is documented through the women he meets or
hears about or thinks about along his journey. As the dance with Nannette would suggest, health and sexual desire are intrinsically linked for
Tristram, and we measure his convalescence by comparing his shipboard
nausea in the beginning of volume 7 to his free-spirited romp at the volume's close. Of course, even in the throes of illness, Tristram is incorrigi-
bly bawdy as he banters with a fellow passenger, herself violently ill
from the rocking of the ship: "Madam! how is it with you? Undone!
undone! un———O! undone! sir—What the first time?——No, 'tis the
second, third, sixth, tenth time, sir" (*TS*, 2.578/7.2). In this scene, however, the bawdiness seems mechanical; it will become increasingly natural as Tristram moves farther and farther from death.

In the course of describing Tristram's flight, volume 7 offers what we might call an anatomy of desire, exploring many of the nuances of the sexual experience from lust to romance. It does so through a number of female characters whose stories dominate the narrative of Tristram's travels. There are sixteen different women mentioned in volume 7, each of whom offers a slightly different perspective on the subject of sexual longing. The scale ranges from celibacy (represented positively by the Virgin Mary and negatively by the coldhearted "priestess of the cistern," who refuses to water Tristram's horses) to sensuality (represented positively by Nannette and negatively by the gossip who sells Tristram a basket of figs and, he implies, throws herself into the bargain). The other female characters fit along the spectrum as illustrated in Figure C.

The nuns and the saints represent the hypocrisy involved in denying sexual desire. From St. Maxima, who was declared a martyr for walking to Ravenna just to touch the body of St. Germain, to the Abbess of

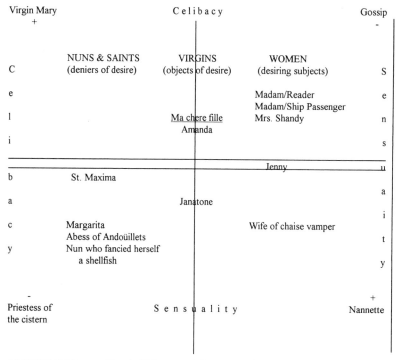

FIGURE C. *Tristram Shandy,* Volume 7: A Spectrum of Desire.

Andoüillets, whose very illnesses seem the result of repression or dis-
placed desire, these religious figures illustrate that institutional celibacy,
as it were, is just a mask for the sensuality that is an inescapable part of
the human condition. Young virgins are poised between the celibate and
the concupiscent states, and they are to varying degrees aware that they
provoke desire in others. "Ma chere fille," whom Tristram addresses as
she returns from church, seems innocent of her latent sensuality and the
sensual thoughts she arouses in Tristram, whereas Janatone is something
of a coquet. Mature women in this volume are treated more as desiring
subjects than desired objects, though of course they can be both just as
young women like Janatone have desires of their own. Some of the
mature women mentioned in volume 7 have desires that are sublimated,
not by policy as is the case with the nuns, but by various exigencies of
daily life. Mrs. Shandy is left at home while her husband travels in
Europe with Tristram and Toby, and she spends her time alone mending
her husband's breeches, an act that suggests the nature of her deprivation. Madam on the ship is, of course, ill. Madam the reader is most like
the nuns—hypocritically pious; she affects a celibate sensibility for
appearance's sake. The maypole loving chaise vamper's wife has a more
natural response to the written word: She puts the papers containing
Tristram's remarks in her hair to curl it.

Of all the women mentioned in volume 7, it is Jenny who, fittingly,
provides Tristram the keenest insight into the nature of desire. She is
open and frank in acknowledging her own needs to her lover Tristram.
She refuses to be deprived because of his incapacity, yet she is kind to
him. She is not promiscuous nor flirtatious nor pious nor proud. Jenny
occupies the median point between ideal celibacy and unrestrained sensuality, neither of which are presented as viable options in the world of
Tristram Shandy. For if a vow of celibacy is an affected denial of the physical nature of the human condition, unrestricted sensual gratification is a
careless rejection of the communal obligations that also attend the
human condition.

Sterne's examination of sexual longing as a principle of life is not
merely an anatomy of desire. It is just as vitally a meditation on the contradictory elements that make up the condition we call "love"—its spiritual dimension and its carnality, which often seem at odds with one
another. On the one hand, we like to believe in romantic stories. Idealized love was described in powerful terms in the eighteenth century by
the very influential Jean-Jacques Rousseau. In *Emile* he gives us the
exemplary story of Emile and his love, Sophie. Sterne had read *Emile*

during his sojourn in France, so it is quite probable that he had the relationship between Emile and Sophie in mind as he wrote volumes 7 and 8 of *Tristram Shandy*. The description of Emile "intoxicated by a nascent passion," was no doubt appealing to Sterne:

> His heart opens itself to the first fires of love. Its sweet illusions make him a new universe of delight and enjoyment. He loves a lovable object who is even more lovable for her character than for her person. He hopes for, he expects a return that he feels is his due. It is from the similarity of their hearts, from the conjunction of decent sentiments that their first inclination was formed. This inclination ought to be durable. He yields confidently, even reasonably, to the most charming delirium without fear, without regret, without remorse, without any other worry than that which is inseparable from the sentiment of happiness . . . . This supreme happiness is a hundred times sweeter to hope for than to obtain. One enjoys it better when one looks forward to it than when one tastes it. O good Emile, love and be loved! Enjoy a long time before possessing. Enjoy love and innocence at the same time. Make your paradise on earth while awaiting the other one.[15]

Emile's education, however, is predicated on Rousseau's belief that, if we resist or avoid human institutions, we can return to the state of nature where "[e]verything is good" (Rousseau, 37) and our "faculties [equal] our desires" (Rousseau, 80). Sterne, of course, holds a different view, for Tristram's experiences occur in the fallen world, a world in which nothing—not nature, not desire—can be restored to its original innocence.

Tristram admits to being inspired by a tale of idealistic, Rousseauesque love. The story of Amanda and Amandus has so touched him that he pauses in Lyons to search for their tomb. Their tale is a sad one, which Tristram read at a very impressionable age, his "brain being tender and fibrillous" (*TS*, 2.627/7.31). The lovers are obviously joined by a "similarity of hearts"—witness their names. They are also prevented from possessing one another by "cruel parents" who separate them (*TS*, 2.627/7.31). Amandus is captured by the Turks and imprisoned by a princess who falls in love with him. But for twenty years he withstands her advances "for the love of his Amanda" (*TS*, 2.627/7.31). For her part, Amanda wanders the world searching for her lover, crying "Amandus! Amandus!" at every town (*TS*, 2.628/7.31). Finally, they meet, coming into Lyons "by different ways," at precisely the same moment. They cry:

Is Amandus
                    } still alive?
Is my Amanda
they fly into each others arms, and both drop down dead for joy.
(*TS,* 2.628/7.31)

They die at the moment of highest happiness, as defined by Jean-Jacques. Tristram later discovers that the tomb of the lovers does not exist anywhere but in the imagination, which suggests the limits of just how far Sterne was finally prepared to go along with Rousseau's idealism. In the years following the publication of volumes 7 and 8 of *Tristram Shandy,* he would travel a bit farther along this road, but he would never go far before he would undercut the vision with ironic bawdiness.

Sexual longing is not merely spiritual. It is physical in its very nature. Tristram's encounter with Janatone, the innkeeper's daughter, prompts a meditation on the physical and, therefore, ephemeral and temporal nature of desire. Janatone is "very handsome" and accomplished (*TS,* 2.588/7.9). She sews, knits, dances, and flirts. Tristram chooses to describe her to us rather than bore us with the description "your worships" want of churches or abbeys or other monuments (*TS,* 2.589/7.9). Those edifices will be around for the next fifty years, "if the belief in Christ continues so long"; anyone can describe them by height, breadth, and façade (*TS,* 2.589/7.9). "[B]ut he who measures thee, Janatone," continues Tristram, "must do it now—thou carriest the principles of change within thy frame" (*TS,* 2.589/7.9). Time may bring a change in shape, in color, or in character. Time may destroy Janatone as an object of desire.

Finally, Tristram does not draw Janatone; he directs us to the original, which of course, we can never see. In a sense she, like Amandus and Amanda, is relegated to the realm of the imagination, but while the two lovers are the imagination's tribute to everlasting love, Janatone is the emblem of transient desire. Even if the reader had put down volume 7 of *Tristram Shandy* upon reading the Janatone passage in 1765 and jumped into a coach bound for Montreuil, and even if that same reader had followed Tristram's instructions and had stopped to see at the chaise door a young woman knitting, sewing, or dancing, he would not have seen the Janatone who provoked Tristram's desire. For even as Tristram instructs his reader to make the journey to see Janatone for himself, the innkeeper's daughter has been transformed by Tristram's own imagination. She is no longer merely the object of desire; she has become a probable sexual conquest: "unless you have as bad a reason for haste as I have—you had better stop:—She has a little of the *devote:* but that, sir, is a terce to a nine in your favour" (*TS*, 2.590/7.9). Sexual longing may indeed be a longing for love, but it is also a longing for sex. Tristram's imagination, which wants to separate the two, finds it difficult to do so.

Such a separation is patently absurd as we see when we examine the story Tristram tells of the Abbess of Andoüillets and her novice travelling companion. This tale is a bawdy, Rabelaisian joke that exploits the phallic reference to sausage ("Andoüillets") in order to suggest the hypocrisy of those who deny their sexuality. The Abbess of Andoüillets, plagued by a stiff knee and having tried all known remedies, including prayers "to every saint who had ever had a stiff leg before her" (*TS*, 2.606/7.21), decides to go to Bourbon for a course of hot baths. Margarita, a seventeen-year-old novice "troubled with a whitloe in her middle finger," which she had aggravated "by sticking it constantly into the abbess's cast poultices, &c." decides to go too (*TS*, 2.607/7.21). The language at the beginning of the tale is titillating, suggesting that cloistered celibacy is but a mask for sexual preoccupation.

This preoccupation is in evidence when the travellers' mules stall halfway up a hill. Margarita immediately imagines "We shall be ravish'd . . . as sure as a gun," and the abbess moans "—why was I govern'd by this wicked stiff joint?" (*TS*, 2.611/7.23). But the novice has a solution: "there are two certain words, which I have been told will force any horse, or ass, or mule, to go up a hill whether he will or no" (*TS*, 2.612/7.24). The words are "bouger" and "fouter"—"bugger" and "fuck." They are words, "sinful in the first degree," Margarita opines, and the abbess agrees (*TS*, 2.612/7.24). Still, she says, it is but a venial sin, and "a venial sin being the slightest and least of all sins,—being halved— . . . in course becomes diluted into no sin at all" (*TS*, 2.613/7.25). So they divide the words up:

Abbess, Bou – – bou – – bou – –
Margarita, ————ger, – – ger, – – ger
Margarita, Fou – – fou – – fou – –
Abbess, ————ter, – – ter, – – ter. (*TS*, 2.614/7.25)

The mules do not budge. "They do not understand us, cried Margarita—But the Devil does, said the abbess of Andoüillets" (*TS*, 2.614/7.25).

Tristram apologizes for the story as he disingenuously speculates that he could have pleased "Madam" better perhaps with "some melancholy lecture of the cross—the peace of meekness, or the contentment of resignation." Or he could have chosen another theme: "the purer abstractions of the soul, and that food of wisdom, and holiness, and contemplation, upon which the spirit of man (when separated from the body) is to subsist for ever" (*TS*, 2.615/7.26). But he knows as Madam herself should know that the soul is not separated from the body while the body lives, and to act as though it is separated is as self-deceiving as the abbess's linguistic chicanery.

Tristram himself praises the Pythagorians' dedication to *"getting out of the body, in order to think well,"* for, he says, he loves this philosophy "more than ever I dare tell my dear Jenny" (*TS*, 2.593/7.13). But Tristram does not succeed in separating himself; no one can do so. In fact, as Tristram admits, even our highest thoughts must be mediated by the body: "the measure of heaven itself is but the measure of our present appetites and concoctions" (*TS*, 2.593/7.13). Moreover, the disasters and disappointments of life that spoil our appetite stand a good chance of embittering us spiritually as well—unless, of course, we can adopt Tristram's "method of book-keeping" and turn disaster to profit (*TS*, 2.624/7.29). To illustrate this point, Tristram admits an "oppressive" failure with Jenny. He pictures himself, obviously impotent, standing "with my garters in my hand, reflecting upon what had *not* pass'd." Tristram's disappointment, however, is not shared by Jenny, who declares herself "satisfied" and whispers in Tristram's ear "**** ** **** *** ******;— **** ** ****." We do not know what she says, but we are certain that she speaks of her own sexual pleasure, for Tristram responds "Every thing is good for something" (*TS*, 2.624/7.29).[16] Tristram feels his own benefit from the episode has to do with a six-week course of goat's whey that he undertook in order to restore his potency, thereby increasing his health and hope for longevity in general. While Jenny's appetite, her sexual needs, may be seen as one motive behind Tristram's search for a cure, his own appetite is his primary concern. He can and does satisfy her without desiring satisfaction of his own, but this kind of selfless love without appetite—without longing—is a meager measure of heaven.

We might conclude from the foregoing discussion that Sterne is offering us a way to understand sexuality as a perfect blend of selfishness and sympathy. But even this notion receives parodic ridicule in volume 7 of *Tristram Shandy*. The most fulfilling relationship Tristram describes in this volume is not between himself and Jenny, Janatone, or Nannette, but between himself and an ass. Tristram has perfect communication, perfect sympathy with the ass, as he tells it:

> 'tis an animal . . . I cannot bear to strike——there is a patient endurance
> of sufferings, wrote so unaffectedly in his looks and carriage, which
> pleads so mightily for him, that it always disarms me; and to that degree,
> that I do not like to speak unkindly to him: on the contrary, meet him
> where I will—whether in town or country—in cart or under panniers—
> whether in liberty or bondage——I have ever something civil to say to
> him on my part; and as one word begets another (if he has as little to do
> as I)——I generally fall into conversation with him; and surely never is
> my imagination so busy as in framing his responses from the etchings of
> his countenance—and where those carry me not deep enough——in fly-
> ing from my own heart into his, and seeing what is natural for an ass to
> think—as well as a man, upon the occasion. (*TS*, 2.630/7.32)

Tristram talks to the ass and gives him a macaroon. He then tries to persuade the ass to move by pulling his halter, which breaks. The ass's countenance seems to plead for mercy, which Tristram promises when the animal suddenly bolts due to a blow from someone else. As the ass runs, an
osier—a stick—protruding from his pannier—his basket—gets caught in
Tristram's pocket and rips his breeches. This accident is Sterne's fitting
commentary on Tristram's sympathy for the beleaguered creature. It is a
self-flattering sympathy, for Tristram reads into the ass's face the conversation he wishes to hold. It is an ideal union of creature with creature, in
Tristram's view, for the ass's identity is completely blended with Tristram's
own. The ass, however, is accorded no autonomy, no "otherness," no
desires of his own. To his credit, Sterne finds such a relationship ludicrous.

Women, while objects of male sexual longing, do have otherness,
autonomy, and desires of their own. In Rousseau's view, they should not,
for women exist solely to complement men. Yet the perfect union he
envisions between Emile and Sophie is possible only because he posits a
perfect original nature for man and an education for Emile that prevents
the corruptions of civilization and allows him to develop into the sort of
man who will care for and be faithful to the woman who loves him. In
the 1790s Mary Wollstonecraft would single out Rousseau's *Emile* for
promulgating oppressive cultural standards for women. Her caustic dis-
missal of Rousseau's ideal union is rooted in life itself:

> to reason on Rousseau's ground, if man did attain a degree of perfection
> of mind when his body arrived at maturity, it might be proper, in order
> to make a man and his wife *one,* that she should rely entirely on his

understanding; and the graceful ivy, clasping the oak that supported it,
would form a whole in which strength and beauty would be equally con-
spicuous. But, alas! husbands, as well as their helpmates, are often only
overgrown children; nay, thanks to early debauchery, scarcely men in
their outward form—and if the blind lead the blind, one need not come
from heaven to tell us the consequence.[17]

Sterne's psychological sympathy with Rousseau's idealistic portrayal of
sexuality in the final analysis yields to a position more akin to Wollstonecraft's realism. For, as divinely inspired as the love between men
and women may be, it is nonetheless between men and women, not
between angelic creatures.

The character in *Tristram Shandy* who comes closest to angelic innocence is Toby Shandy. Wounded in the groin, preoccupied with martial
matters, unable to tell the right end of a woman from the wrong, Toby
would seem an unlikely candidate for carnal love. His amours with the
Widow Wadman, which occupy the remaining volumes of *Tristram
Shandy,* however, reveal much about the nature of love and lust. As Toby
experiences it, love is not so much a dance as it is a state of warfare.
Deprived of his hobby-horse in 1713 by the Treaty of Utrecht, Toby
undertakes a siege of a different sort. He and Trim lay plans for the
courtship of the Widow Wadman as carefully as they had conducted
their military campaigns: "whilst your honour engages Mrs. Wadman in
the parlour, to the right——I'll attack Mrs. Bridget in the kitchen, to
the left; and having seiz'd that pass, I'll answer for it, said the corporal,
snapping his fingers over his head—that the day is our own" (*TS,*
2.715/8.30).

The battle has been raging, however, for much longer than Trim or
Toby suppose, for it was in 1701, twelve years before Toby turned his
attention from war to love, that the Widow Wadman had fallen in love
with him. Captain Shandy and Trim had been her guests "for a night or
two" when they first came to the country from Walter's residence in
London (*TS,* 2.664/8.8). They had come so precipitately, so eager to
begin their campaigns, they had forgotten that "Shandy Hall was at
that time unfurnished"—there was no bed for them to sleep in (*TS,*
2.664/8.8). The Widow Wadman offered one of hers.

This *"perfect woman,"* this "daughter of Eve," had been a widow for two
years when she met Toby (*TS,* 2.664/8.8). Still a young woman when her
husband died, the Widow Wadman had adopted some unusual ways of
coping with the deprivations of widowhood. In particular, there were her
bedroom practices. Each evening her maid, Bridget, would pin her into

bed by pulling the widow's nightgown below her feet, folding it on the sides, pinning the folds together with a corking pin, and tucking "all in tight at the feet" (*TS*, 2.666/8.9). The visit of Toby Shandy put an end to this ritual. The first night he was there, the widow "ruminated till midnight upon both sides of the question"; the second night she read over her marriage settlement; and the third night she kicked the corking pin out of Bridget's hand: "down it fell to the ground, and was shivered into a thousand atoms" (*TS*, 2.667–68/8.9). The widow had fallen in love.

During the twelve years that passed between the widow's falling in love with Uncle Toby and Uncle Toby's falling in love with her, Mrs. Wadman carried on a series of campaigns of her own. Toby lived and conducted his military sieges next door to the widow's home, and she observed his "councils of war" and took her walks near or on the captain's bowling green, even into the sentry box itself (*TS*, 2.673/8.14). Here she began her sieges, coercing the captain into explaining the plans he had hanging on the sentry-box walls. As he pointed to "the little turns and indentings of his works," the widow would follow his finger with her own, maneuvering her hand against, onto, beneath the captain's hand, pressing her leg "against the calf of his" (*TS*, 2.677–78/8.16). Preoccupied though he was, Toby felt some "disorder": "The duce take it," he would exclaim (*TS*, 2.678/8.16).

After the Treaty of Utrecht creates a vacancy in Toby's life, he is more susceptible to love. But it is Trim, not the widow herself, who most effectively turns the captain's thoughts from war to romance. As Toby and Trim work to execute the demolition of Dunkirk, the talk turns to the corporal's story-telling abilities: "Thou hast many excellencies, Trim, said my uncle Toby, and I hold it not the least of them, as thou happenest to be a story-teller" (*TS*, 2.681/8.19). Trim asserts that all the stories he knows are true ones, for they are all about himself, except for one, that is: the story of the King of Bohemia and his Seven Castles. Toby's curiosity is piqued; he asks Trim to tell the Bohemian king's tale.

We do not know what the story is. No editor of *Tristram Shandy* has annotated the King of Bohemia and his Seven Castles, and Sterne himself makes it seem as though the story is a mere fabrication of the ever-inventive Corporal Trim. We know from the little Trim says that the story includes giants, for he tries to set the tale in the year 1712, a detail that raises Toby's objection on the grounds of credibility:

> if there are giants in [the story] . . . thou should'st have carried him [the King of Bohemia] back some seven or eight hundred years out of harm's way, both of cricticks [*sic*] and other people. (*TS*, 2.686/8.19)

Credible or not, the story never gets told, for various digressions lead
Trim into another story—a tale of love.

The mention of Bohemia naturally leads us to wonder if in the title of
this non-story Sterne was glancing back to a moment in his own life
when he played consort to Elizabeth's Queen of Bohemia. Of course, it
seems just as likely that Trim's aborted tale was the hint from which
John Croft fabricated his version of Mrs. Sterne's illness. Whatever the
case the truncated story draws our attention to the interplay between
fact and fiction, between life and the imagination. Toby's insistence on
credibility even in a story that is admittedly not true is a natural
response. Narratives convince us by internal consistency as long as they
do not undermine their own believability by drawing our attention to
their fictive nature. Yet it is also true that if a narrative grips our imagination we often fail to notice even those anomalies that otherwise might
disturb us. Toby, we know, is capable of entering fully into a fantasy
world; otherwise, his bowling green could not have served as long as it
did as the setting for world conflict. It could not have been so many
towns, the home of so many fortifications, the scene of so many sieges.
But Toby resists the story of the King of Bohemia; it fails to capture
him, so to speak. The story of Trim and the young Beguine, on the other
hand, succeeds.

The story Trim tells begins as a war story—the tale of a wound he
suffered on his knee at the battle of Landen. He was attended in his
recovery by a beautiful young Beguine—a secular nun—who nursed
him by "fomenting [Trim's] knee with her hand, night and day" (TS,
2.699–700/8.20). Yet, for many days, Trim tells Toby, he did not "fall in
love." One Sunday, however, the situation changed. As the Beguine
rubbed his knee, Trim reports, "it . . . came into my head, that I should
fall in love":

> The more she rubb'd, and the longer strokes she took——the more the
> fire kindled in my veins——till at length, by two or three strokes longer
> than the rest——my passion rose to the highest pitch——I seiz'd her
> hand——(TS, 2.702–3/8.22)

Toby completes the story for himself: "And then, thou clapped'st it to
thy lips, Trim, . . . and madest a speech." (TS, 2.703/8.22)

The Widow Wadman, listening outside the sentry box, is writing her
own story. When Trim leaves, she enters, ready to "attack." The
"manœuvre of fingers and hands" on which she had previously relied

would no longer serve: "the fair Beguine's" hands had "outdone" her own strategies (*TS,* 2.705/8.23). So the widow tries "a new attack" (*TS,* 2.705/8.23). She asks Toby to look into her eye for a speck of something—she knows not what. Toby peers into the widow's eye, an eye "full of gentle salutations——and soft responses," and he falls in love (*TS,* 2.708/8.25).

The eye is the window to the soul; by a glance Toby forms a lasting bond with Le Fever; by a look he can arouse his brother's sympathy and still his anger. The eye is an organ of human connection. It may even serve, as it does for Toby, to introduce one to romantic love. But that kind of love is not solely an ocular matter. As both Trim and the widow Wadman know, other organs are involved as well. To dismiss the carnality of love is to take Walter Shandy's view—the passions are an ass—or Dr. Slop's Roman Catholic view—" 'Tis Virginity . . . which fills paradise" (*TS,* 2.721/8.33), neither of which seems an adequate rebuttal to the joyful sensuality of Tristram's dance with Nannette at the end of volume 7, a dance in which carnality seems to be a source of spirituality, as Tristram's prayer suggests:

> Just disposer of our joys and sorrows . . . why could not a man sit down
> in the lap of content here—and dance, and sing, and say his prayers, and
> go to heaven with this nut brown maid? (*TS,* 2.651/7.43)

The answer, of course, is that we live in a fallen not an ideal world.

While volume 7 ends with a vision of Edenic innocence, a sensuality that keeps death at bay, the end of volume 8 returns us to the fallen world. As Captain Shandy and Corporal Trim "sally forth" to "attack" the Widow Wadman, Mrs. Shandy says to her husband, "I could like . . . to look through the key-hole out of *curiosity*" (*TS,* 2.729/8.35). "Call it by it's [*sic*] right name, my dear," replies Mr. Shandy, *"And look through the key-hole* as long as you will" (*TS,* 2.729/8.35). By Walter's formulation, Mrs. Shandy's eye is focused voyeuristically on the sensual, the window to her soul peering lasciviously through a key-hole at her brother-in-law and the Widow Wadman. Whether or not Walter has accurately identified his wife's motives, his suspicion is an indication of the distance between men and women, a distance underscored by volume 8's relentless use of the language of war to describe acts of love. For Sterne, to be human is to have a divine but fallen nature. Human nature's best characteristic is that it longs for the innocent pleasures of Edenic bliss; the saddest truth is that we can never fully experience them. In the sublunary state, love is a contest, sex an appetite, and although paradisal harmony may be glimpsed from time to time, it is impossible to keep it steadily in view.

Volume 9: A Cock and a Bull

"All womankind . . . from the highest to the lowest . . . love jokes," Trim tells Toby as they make their way to the Widow Wadman's house for Toby to begin his courtship. "[T]he difficulty," he continues, "is to know how they chuse to have them cut; and there is no knowing that, but by trying as we do with our artillery in the field, by raising or letting down their breeches, till we hit the mark" (*TS,* 2.753/9.8). This observation concludes Trim's story of his brother Tom and the sausage-maker's widow. Tom's tale was partly revealed in volume 2 as "The abuses of conscience sermon" led Trim into a pitiably sad digression on Tom's imprisonment in Portugal:

> [M]y brother *Tom* went over a servant to *Lisbon,*—and then married a *Jew*'s widow, who kept a small shop, and sold sausages, which, some how or other, was the cause of his being taken in the middle of the night out of his bed, where he was lying with his wife and two small children, and carried directly to the Inquisition, where, God help him . . . the poor honest lad lies confined at this hour. (*TS,* 1.144/2.17)

In volume 9, we hear the beginning of the story—how Tom courted the widow in her shop. As "[t]here is nothing so awkward, as courting a woman . . . whilst she is making sausages," Tom chooses to face the matter squarely, talking first "gravely" and then "gayly" about the sausages (*TS,* 2.750/9.7). Seeing "that all he had said upon the subject of sausages was kindly taken," Tom offers to help make them, holding the ring of the sausage open while the widow "stroked the forced meat down with her hand," cutting the strings, and helping her tie the sausages (*TS,* 2.751/9.7). Finally, Tom proposes. The widow had already made up her mind to accept but she feigns surprise and adopts a posture of defense by "snatching up a sausage." Tom, we are told, "instantly laid hold of another," and the widow, "seeing Tom's had more gristle in it. . . signed the capitulation" (*TS,* 2.752/9.7). Tom had hit the mark.

Tom's courtship of the widow turns on a joke, a play on image and word that allows the preoccupations of both Tom and the widow to be addressed playfully but also seriously. Tom's ingenuity at arranging a situation in which puns release the widow to allude to sexual matters must have pleased her greatly. The poor Widow Wadman is not so lucky.

Uncle Toby is no jester. In fact, one might even call him grave, except that he has none of the impulse so often associated with gravity to impose his way of seeing things on others. Yet he is a solemn suitor. Dressed up in his red plush breeches, which Trim has advised against because of their bulkiness, Toby courts the Widow Wadman with as much directness as he can—in a straight line, so to speak: "My uncle Toby saluted Mrs. Wadman . . . then facing about, he march'd up abreast with her to the sopha [*sic*], and in three plain words . . . as he was sitting down, told her, '*he was in love*' " (*TS,* 2.786/9.the eighteenth chapter).[18] The widow, staring at a slit in an apron she was mending, waits for elaboration, but the captain, "having no talents for amplification . . . left the matter to work after its own way" (*TS,* 2.786/9.the eighteenth chapter). Coyly, the widow wonders why Toby would want to marry, but she is disappointed in the answer, for Toby simply refers her to the Book of Common Prayer. The widow presses further, wondering if the sorrows of parenthood might not argue against having children. What compensations, she coquettishly asks Toby, could there be for such pains? His answer again is off the mark: "I declare . . . I know of none; unless it be the pleasure which it has pleased God——" The widow interrupts—"A fiddlestick! quoth she" (*TS,* 2.788/9. the eighteenth chapter).

Toby, feeling out of his depth, proposes quickly, and then he picks up the Bible and reads about the battle of Jericho, "leaving his proposal of marriage, as he had done his declaration of love, to work with her after its own way" (*TS,* 2.789/9.chapter the nineteenth). The widow, however, has a pressing question that she wants answered before she commits herself to wedlock with Toby Shandy. "It was . . . natural," Tristram says, "for Mrs. Wadman, whose first husband was all his time afflicted with a Sciatica, to wish to know how far from the hip to the groin; and how far she was likely to suffer more or less in her feelings, in the one case than in the other" (*TS,* 2.791/9.26). To put it plainly, she wants to know whether or not his wound has rendered him impotent, and she is having a hard time finding out.

Tristram informs us that his Uncle Toby was quite fit for matrimony. Not only was he kind, sweet, gentle, generous, humane, trusting, and tender, but Nature had "considered the other causes for which matrimony was ordained—":

And accordingly * * * * * *
* * * * * * * * * *
* * * * * * * * * *

* * * * * * *.

The DONATION was not defeated by my uncle Toby's wound. (*TS,* 2.777/ 9.22)

Perhaps. But the Shandy men are notoriously sensitive about sexual matters, especially hints of familial weaknesses that might reflect on their own virility. Still, Trim too asserts that the rumor that Toby had been incapacitated was "as false as hell" (*TS,* 2.797/9.28), and Dr. Slop maintains that Toby is quite recovered of his wound (*TS,* 2.791–92/ 9.26).

Still, for whatever reason, Toby's character has no hint of the sexual appetite that so distinguishes his nephew and his servant. Indeed, Toby seems to think very little of bodily matters of any kind, although he does make a very funny bodily joke in volume 6 in response to a discussion of child prodigies:

> what are these, continued my father— (breaking out in a kind of enthusi-asm)—what are these, to those prodigies of childhood in *Grotius, Scioppius, Heinsius, Politian, Pascal, Joseph Scaliger, Ferdinand de Cordouè,* and others—some of which left off their *substantial forms* at nine years old, or sooner, and went on reasoning without them;—others went through their classics at seven;—wrote tragedies at eight; . . .——But you forget the great *Lipsius,* quoth *Yorick,* who composed a work the day he was born;——They should have wiped it up, said my uncle *Toby,* and said no more about it. (*TS,* 2.493–94/6.2)

This exchange is highly unusual, however; it is much more common for Toby to ignore the body. In fact, as we have noted already, his discomfort with speaking about his wound led him to reinterpret questions directed to his physical state as geographical inquiries. By the time he falls in love with the Widow Wadman, his hobby-horsical habit is too entrenched to change. When the widow's interest in his wound reaches such an intensity that she asks "categorically," "whereabouts . . . did you receive this sad blow?" Toby sends for his map. "Unhappy Mrs. Wadman!" Tristram exclaims (*TS,* 2.793–94/9.26).

While Toby remains quite innocent of Mrs. Wadman's true designs, Trim is enlightened by Bridget, whose similar questions have resulted in physical intimacy:

> AND here is the *Maes*—and this is the *Sambre;* said the Corporal, pointing with his right hand extended a little towards the map, and his left upon Mrs. Bridget's shoulder—but not the shoulder next him—and this, said

he, is the town of Namur——. . . and in this cursed trench, Mrs. Bridget, quoth the Corporal, taking her by the hand, did he receive the wound which crush'd him so miserably *here*——In pronouncing which he slightly press'd the back of her hand towards the part he felt for——and let it fall. (*TS*, 2.796/9.28)

Bridget reveals to Trim her mistress's suspicions. Trim defends his master's honor. And it is not long before the entire Shandy family knows "the secret articles which had delay'd the surrender" of the Widow Wadman (*TS*, 2.804/9.32).

Just as he had been the last to find out that he was in love, Toby is the last to discover his mistress's true nature—or actually he and Walter share the honor, just as they had in the first case. Toby's enlightenment comes from an exasperated Trim, who is asked by his master to write down the Widow Wadman's "thousand virtues" as Toby calls them out, taking them "in their ranks" (*TS*, 2.801/9.31). Her best quality is her compassion, Toby avers; "was I her brother . . . she could not make more constant or more tender enquiries after my sufferings" (*TS*, 2.801–2/9.31). Trim writes "H U M A N I T Y" at the top of the page as Toby continues to brag about Mrs. Wadman's attentiveness (*TS*, 2.802/9.31). "[H]ow often does Mrs. Bridget enquire after the wound on the cap of thy knee," he asks Trim. The answer is "never," and Toby gloats (*TS*, 2.802/9.31). If he had been wounded on the knee, Mrs. Wadman would have certainly inquired as to the pain, which is, after all, "equally excruciating," to the pain in a wounded groin. "Compassion has as much to do with the one as the other," Toby tells the corporal. Trim has had enough; he enlightens Toby: "[W]hat has a woman's compassion to do with a wound upon the cap of a man's knee? . . . The knee is such a distance from the main body—whereas the groin, your honour knows, is upon the very *curtin* of the *place*." (*TS*, 2.802–3/9.31). Toby gives a "long whistle," and the two set out for Walter's house.

Toby is, in a sense, a victim of the power of narrative and its ability to persuade us through vicarious identification. He is inspired by the story of Trim and the fair Beguine to look for love, which he finds in the Widow Wadman's eye. But he has no notion of the nature of sexual passion; he thinks love is a matter of fine speeches and Common Prayer Book duties. The story he tries to live is not his story, and he retreats quickly into a more comfortable imaginative realm. By 1718, the year of Tristram's birth, another war has been declared, and Toby is fully immersed once more in his campaigns. While Toby's campaigns are harmless enough in spite of their tacit endorsement of warfare, there is a sense that the Widow Wadman affair is a missed opportunity for Toby, not only in the physical pleasure he misses out on, but also in the unlaughed laughter that Sterne insists is a vital part of sexual intimacy and the best part of life itself.

It is not really surprising that Toby is unable to laugh, to share a joke with the Widow Wadman, for all along Toby has been more responsive to the pathos than to the absurdity of life. The reader feels compassion vicariously for those with whom Toby weeps. In volume 6 the story of Le Fever arouses our sympathy for a dying soldier and his orphaned son; in volume 9 our sensibilities are tapped in the service of a larger human concern.

In 1766, Sterne received a letter from a reader whose reaction to *Tristram Shandy* and *The Sermons of Mr. Yorick* took the form of a personal narrative itself. Ignatius Sancho introduced himself to Sterne as "one of those people whom the illiberal and vulgar call a Nee—gur—" and he went on to tell the writer about his upbringing: "the early part of my Life was rather unlucky; as I was placed in a family who judged that Ignorance was the best Security for obedience: a little Reading and writing, I got by unwearied application—the latter part of my life has been more fortunate; having spent it in the honourable service of one of the best families in the kingdome" (*Letters,* 282). Sancho goes on to relate to Sterne his love of reading, and he praises a passage in Sterne's sermon on Job, which bemoans the tyranny of slavery. Uncle Toby and Corporal Trim receive special mention in Sancho's letter, and he concludes by asking Sterne "to give half an hours attention to slavery" as "that subject handled in your own manner, would ease the Yoke of many, perhaps occasion a reformation throughout our Islands" (*Letters,* 282–83).

Sterne's answer to Sancho indicates that he had written "a tender tale of the sorrows of a friendless poor negro girl," over which he had been crying when he received Sancho's letter (*Letters,* 287). What actually appears in volume 9 of *Tristram Shandy* is not really a tale but an explicit declaration of the common humanity of all races. Trim mentions a "poor negro girl" who was dusting in the sausage-maker's shop when Tom went to court the widow (*TS,* 2.747/9.6). In the course of a conversation that follows, Trim asks Toby, "A Negro has a soul?" and Toby answers, "I suppose, God would not leave him without one, any more than thee or me——" (*TS,* 2.747/9.6). Trim goes on to ask, "[w]hy then, an' please your honour, is a black wench to be used worse than a white one?" (*TS,* 2.748/9.6). Toby can think of no reason, and they agree that she deserves protection not exploitation: " 'tis the fortune of war which has put the whip into our hands *now*——where it may be hereafter, heaven knows!——but be it where it will, the brave, Trim! will not use it unkindly" (*TS*, 2.748/9.6).

Of course, it is ludicrous to imagine the "kind" use of a weapon of pain. Yet our possession of the whip is attributed to fortune, not right, and we are made aware that in the future—heaven knows!—we could change places with the girl, and find ourselves dependent on the kindness of our oppressors. Toby quite rightly (from Sterne's point of view) distinguishes between the equality of our souls—which he asserts—and the equality of our fortunes—which he denies. The story of the "negro girl" is invoked to create a sense of oneness, a vicarious identification that provokes our humanity by allowing us to imagine what it is like to be oppressed. Like the girl herself, who flaps away flies rather than killing them, we learn mercy through the experience of persecution.

The girl's full story is deferred. Trim promises to tell it to Toby at a later date; we never read the tale at all. But we are told another story of pathos—this time by Tristram, who recounts his meeting with poor Maria of Moulins. This young woman was disappointed in love; in fact, her marriage was forbidden by a priest. She has been, Tristram is told, "ever since . . . unsettled in her mind," and her only consolation is to play upon a pipe (*TS*, 2.782/9.24). Tristram, after hearing her tale, sees her—"she was beautiful" (*TS*, 2.783/9.24). His pity and her beauty provoke "an honest heartache," and he takes a seat between her and the goat that keeps her company as she plays her pipe (*TS*, 2.783/9.24). In her madness, Maria stares intently at first Tristram, then the goat, until finally Tristram inquires, "What resemblance do you find?" (*TS*, 2.783/9.24). He assures us that he does so "from the humblest conviction of what a *Beast* man is" (*TS*, 2.784/9.24). He was sincere, he protests, not making a joke at all. Still, he admits he felt guilty and "swore I would set up for Wisdom and utter grave sentences the rest of my days——and never——never attempt again to commit mirth with man, woman, or child, the longest day I had to live" (*TS*, 2.784/9.24). "As for writing nonsense to them," Tristram leaves that to the world. If the world continues to buy, he implies, he will continue to write nonsense.

Tristram, unlike his Uncle Toby, is more inclined to laughter than to tears. He leaves Maria, alone and mad in her melancholy; he feels pity and is touched so much that he can walk back to his chaise only with difficulty, "with broken and irregular steps" (*TS*, 2.784/9.24). Yet his vow to renounce mirth is a rash reaction. For, though pity and compassion do serve as a conduit between individuals, laughter and joy do the same. Finally, in fact, laughter may be preferable to sympathetic tears. When one is laughing, one cannot be grave.

Walter does not see any humor in the Widow Wadman's passion for his brother; when he hears that she is intent on determining for sure that Toby could answer that passion with his own, Walter's Shandy family pride is stung. And his reaction, as usual, is to philosophize. The whole affair, he says in outrage, is "lust" and no wonder: "every evil and disorder in the world of what kind or nature soever, from the first fall of Adam, down to my uncle Toby's (inclusive) was owing one way or other to the same unruly appetite" (*TS*, 2.805/9.32). When Toby arrives, Walter continues his diatribe against a "passion which bends down the faculties, and turns all the wisdom, contemplations, and operations of the soul backwards——a passion . . . which couples and equals wise men with fools, and makes us come out of our caverns and hiding-places more like satyrs and four-footed beasts than men" (*TS*, 2.806/9.33). Lust is worse than just an appetite; it is a shameful thing, even when lawful, Walter asserts. Why else do we blow out the candles "when we go about to make and plant a man" (*TS*, 2.806/9.33)? Why else is there no clean, acceptable way of talking about sex? It is by definition shameful, unlike killing, Walter continues, which is "glorious." We are proud of the weapons of destruction, we bring them out in public and parade around with them: "We carve them——We in-lay them——We enrich them" (*TS*, 2.806–7/9.33). What Walter intends as an indictment against lust suddenly, by the introduction of the subject of war, becomes Sterne's satire against the "gravity" that would glorify the destruction of life and stigmatize its creation.

As usual, Walter's reasoning is based on a logical fallacy—this time the either/or fallacy of reasoning. Our choice as human beings is not love or war, lust or humanity, for the alternative to lust is not killing any more than the alternative to sexual appetite is, as Toby thinks, humanity. The condition of human life is a mixture, full of, as Tristram repeats, "mysteries and riddles" (*TS*, 2.776/9.22). Lust coexists with humanity; war is intertwined with love. Our tendency is to want to reconcile and explain the irreconcilable and inexplicable. But the more appropriate response, Sterne suggests, is laughter.

Tristram Shandy ends with a story and a joke. Just as Yorick is about to "batter . . . to pieces" Walter's "hypothesis" about the dignity of war and the shamefulness of sex, Obadiah enters the Shandy family parlor "with a complaint" (*TS*, 2.807/9.33). His cow had been mated with

Walter's bull on the day that Obadiah married Walter's housemaid: "Therefore when Obadiah's wife was brought to bed—Obadiah thanked God——Now, said Obadiah, I shall have a calf" (*TS*, 2.807/9.33). After six weeks of waiting, "Obadiah's suspicions . . . fell upon the Bull" (*TS*, 2.808/9.33). He has come to complain to Walter about the bull's failings, at the very moment that Walter is rationalizing Toby's similar shortcomings. Obadiah further exacerbates Walter's own sexual insecurity. Walter sets out to defend his bull: "may not a cow be barren?" Dr. Slop says, "[i]t never happens," but he posits another possibility: "the man's wife may have come before her time naturally enough" (*TS*, 2.808/9.33). To determine the matter, Slop asks Obadiah, "has the child hair upon his head" (*TS*, 2.808/9.33). "It is as hairy as I am," Obadiah replies.

Obadiah, we are told, had a three-week's growth of beard as he stood in the Shandy family parlor complaining about the Shandy bull. The sight is too much for Walter. He has to laugh. He responds with a whistle and an elaborate joke:

> Wheu – – u – – – – u – – – – – – – – cried my father; . . . and so, brother Toby, this poor Bull of mine, who is as good a Bull as ever p—ss'd, and might have done for Europa herself in purer times——had he but two legs less, might have been driven into Doctors Commons and lost his character——which to a Town Bull, brother Toby, is the very same thing as his life————(*TS*, 2.808/9.33)

What has tickled Walter's fancy, perhaps, is the idea that the bull has fathered Obadiah's hairy child: The bull is not impotent at all, in spite of Obadiah's charges. And, but for Obadiah's inadvertent admission, the bull could have been taken to court and formally accused of impotence, thereby losing his reputation as a stud, which would have destroyed his life. In Sterne's day "town bull" was slang for "man," so Walter's joke can be read as a comic restatement of his earlier diatribe against lust. Sexual appetite is what we share with the animals; our lust can make us "beasts," a notion underscored by Walter's reference to Europa, who is raped by Zeus in the guise of a bull. But should we therefore deny that aspect of our nature? Of course not. To do so would be the worst sort of gravity.

What began as pique against the Widow Wadman ends in a punch line that stands as an epigraph for the entire of *Tristram Shandy*. Mrs. Shandy interrupts Walter, once more: "L——d! . . . what is all this story about?" Yorick, who we remember opposes gravity in his heart, answers gleefully: "A COCK and a BULL . . . And one of the best of its kind, I ever heard" (*TS*, 2.809/9.33). Tristram has told a long, rambling tale, full of sense and nonsense, laughter and tears, truth and fiction. *Tristram Shandy* is a bawdy joke and a meditation on mortality, a philosophical treatise and a satire on human nature. It is a story that never really gets told, full of stories that do. It is an anti-novel and a novel; a discourse on nothing that covers just about everything. Taken in the spirit in which it was written, *Tristram Shandy* is a powerful assertion of the joy of life, a joy all the more precious because it ends in death. As Tristram himself puts it:

> Time wastes too fast: every letter I trace tells me with what rapidity Life follows my pen; the days and hours of it, more precious, my dear Jenny! than the rubies about thy neck, are flying over our heads like light clouds of a windy day, never to return more——every thing presses on—— whilst thou art twisting that lock,——see! it grows grey; and every time I kiss thy hand to bid adieu, and every absence which follows it, are preludes to that eternal separation which we are shortly to make. (*TS*, 2.754/9.8)

"Heaven have mercy upon us both," Tristram concludes. Tristram's "ejaculation," his spontaneous prayer, asks for comfort in the face of permanent loss. Sterne finds that comfort in laughter at the "infirmities and defects," mental and physical, of human nature (*TS*, 2.761/9.12). In *Tristram Shandy*, we should find such comfort too.

Chapter Four

A Work of Redemption: *A Sentimental Journey* and *The Journal to Eliza*

Laurence Sterne had begun thinking about his *Sentimental Journey Through France and Italy* before he finished volume 9 of *Tristram Shandy*. A month after that volume was printed, his new work was well under way. It was to be, Sterne reported to writer Richard Griffith, a *"Work of Redemption,"* designed, as he told his correspondent Mrs. James, "to teach us to love the world and our fellow creatures better than we do" through an elaboration of the "gentler passions and affections" (*Letters,* 398–99, n.3; 401). To another friend, Sterne wrote, "my Sentimental Journey will, I dare say, convince you that my feelings are from the heart, and that that heart is not of the worst of molds" (*Letters,* 395). It seems that Sterne saw his *Sentimental Journey* as redemptive in at least two senses: as a service to humankind and as a corrective of his own reputation in the world.

Sterne wrote *A Sentimental Journey* as a famous man and as a dying man. His fame was attached, of course, to the nine volumes of *Tristram Shandy* and his *Sermons,* which had introduced readers to the Cervantick Parson Yorick who abhorred gravity, rode a broken-down horse, and died brokenhearted from the world's misunderstanding. Readers would have realized, however, that the Yorick who narrates *A Sentimental Journey* was a flexible mask in Sterne's hands, rather than a consistent character, and while associations with a certain kind of personality—spontaneous, impulsive, sympathetic, and impatient with self-justification—would have certainly informed the first reading of *A Sentimental Journey,* no identification with the biographical details of Yorick's life as readers knew it from Sterne's earlier work would have been expected. In fact, by the seventh volume of *Tristram Shandy,* readers would have been aware that Tristram and Yorick were interchangeable self-portraits of Sterne, for Eugenius, who had appeared in the story of Yorick's illness and death in volume 1, stands in the later volume attendant on Tris-

tram's sickbed. So while *A Sentimental Journey*'s Yorick makes reference
to his friends the Shandys from time to time, we need to realize that the
purpose of his doing so is to underscore the fact that rather than being a
departure from the earlier work, *A Sentimental Journey* is an elaboration
on earlier themes. *Tristram Shandy* was bawdy, to be sure, but it had its
moments of pathos, feeling, and sentiment as well. *A Sentimental Journey*
may be a work of redemption, but it represents no conversion on the
part of its author.

In fact, as an elaboration on the feeling, heart, and sentiment of *Tristram Shandy*, *A Sentimental Journey* strikes us as continuing to partake in
the doubleness of vision we have already witnessed in the earlier work. It
has been a matter of some critical contention just how seriously we can
take Sterne's endorsement of feeling in *A Sentimental Journey*. It is quite
possible, in other words, to read the work as a satire on those who would
argue that sympathy for others is a reliable source of moral behavior.
Sterne's own physical debilitation at the time of the writing of this work
might account for the yearning for renewal through connection with
others—particularly female others—that certainly informs *A Sentimental
Journey,* but it is also quite possible that Sterne could view his own longing as a source of self-delusion. Yorick can be read as a philosopher of
sentiment, but he can also be read as a sensualist who tries to disguise,
even from himself, the truth that his impulses are carnal, not sentimental at all. Part of the purpose of this chapter will be to determine just
how seriously we should take *A Sentimental Journey*'s assertion that there
is an intrinsic relationship between love and morality.

Whether or not Yorick is an object of satire, *A Sentimental Journey* certainly has a satiric thrust in that it ridicules the vogue for travel narratives that existed in the eighteenth century. The public's taste for travel
literature was so decided that anyone who had been anywhere could
make a profit from his or her observations. Sterne himself had indicated
what the standard fare of such narratives was in volume 7 of *Tristram
Shandy,* which is itself a satire on the genre. Descriptions of edifices, sta-
tistics about population and mileage, reports on the standard sights that
visitors should visit, a catalogue of cultural activities or exhibitions,
comments on the natives' habits and customs—such was the expected
content of any work with "travel" in the title.

Of course, such a travel narrative is only as valuable as a source of
information or instruction as the traveller himself, as Sterne suggests in
his ridicule of his fellow travel writers, Tobias Smollett (novelist and
author of *Travels Through France and Italy* [1766]) and Dr. Samuel Sharp

(author of *Letters from Italy* [1766]). "Smelfungus" and "Mundungus," as Sterne calls them, have produced travel narratives colored by their own illnesses, melancholies, miseries, and sour dispositions: "I heartily pity them," Yorick says, "they have brought up no faculties for this work; and was the happiest mansion in heaven to be allotted to Smelfungus and Mundungus, they would be so far from being happy, that the souls of Smelfungus and Mundungus would do penance there to all eternity."[1]

Yet, it is not the limitations of the traveller alone that call the genre into question, for as Yorick's *Desobligeant* preface points out, the idea that travel is somehow innately beneficial is a dubious notion, regardless of the spirit in which the journey is taken:

> Knowledge and improvements are to be got by sailing and posting for that purpose; but whether useful knowledge and real improvements, is all a lottery—and even where the adventurer is successful, the acquired stock must be used with caution and sobriety to turn to any profit—but as the chances run prodigiously the other way both as to the acquisition and application, I am of opinion, That a man would act as wisely, if he could prevail upon himself, to live contented without foreign knowledge or foreign improvements, especially if he lives in a country that has no absolute want of either . . . . (*SJ*, 83–84/12)

As Yorick acknowledges, he lives in such a country, yet he travels anyway.

But Yorick does not aspire to write a standard travel narrative, in any event. The kind of knowledge and improvement he hopes to gain has nothing to do with facts, buildings, and customs. His travels are "sentimental travels," and he seeks feeling, not fact. He admits that "the expatriated adventurer," such as he is, travels under a disadvantage: "we lie under so many impediments in communicating our sensations out of our own sphere, as often amount to a total impossibility" (*SJ*, 78/9). Yet through the course of his travels, Yorick overcomes that "impossibility" in the discovery of a universal means of communication. He records this discovery as he recounts his journey from Calais to "Montriul" to Nampont to Amiens to Paris to Versailles back to Paris to "Moulines," to the "Borbonnois" and to Savoy.[2] Finally, however, the locales Yorick visits are beside the point; for it is not knowledge of place but the regeneration of feeling that he pursues.

Yorick's decision to travel at all is born of impulse, not design. He decides to go to France as the result of a casual conversation with his servant. "They order . . . this matter better in France," Yorick observes as he drinks a toast; and his servant responds, "You have been in France?"

(*SJ*, 65/3). The answer is no, and Yorick departs immediately for Calais to acquire the "right" to comment on French social habits with the authority of firsthand experience. Once in Calais, he drinks the King of France's health after dinner, in accordance with French custom, and he finds himself in harmony with the world. "Just God! said I, . . . what is there in this world's goods which should sharpen our spirits, and make so many kind-hearted brethren of us, fall out so cruelly as we do by the way?" (*SJ*, 68/4). Yorick continues his sentimental observations by noting that such harmony makes one generous; he imagines himself King of France and a benefactor to orphans. Yet the next moment a Franciscan monk asks Yorick for money, and Yorick refuses. He makes excuses: Others—the lame, the imprisoned, the aged, the blind, the sick—have greater claims on his purse. The monk simply wants money for his own subsistence, Yorick charges, and he and his order "have no other plan in life, but to get through it in sloth and ignorance, *for the love of God*" (*SJ*, 74/7). Yorick's irony makes the monk blush. Alone again, Yorick regrets his mean-spirited lecture to the monk, but he reassures himself: "I have only just set out upon my travels; and shall learn better manners as I get along" (*SJ*, 75/8).

Yorick begins his journey therefore as a sentimental traveller, in that he tends from the outset to draw moral lessons from his experience. But he shows himself in this initial episode to be lacking in sensibility, a concept separate from but related to sentimentalism. While the terms were sometimes used interchangeably in the eighteenth century, a subtle distinction often was maintained between the two.[3] In general, sentiment can be defined as "a moral reflection, a rational opinion usually about the rights and wrongs of human conduct" or "a thought, often an elevated one, influenced by emotion." Sensibility, in contrast, denotes "emotional and physical susceptibility," refined and tender emotion, "an innate sensitiveness . . . revealing itself in a variety of spontaneous activities such as crying, swooning and kneeling" (Todd, 7). The difference between the two concepts is really one of emphasis. Sentiment emphasizes the principle of human conduct, whereas sensibility emphasizes the physical and emotional path by which the principle is felt to be true. Sentiment is the product of a rational process that is prompted by an emotional impulse; sensibility is the physical feeling of emotion. Or, as Ann Jessie Van Sant has put it, "*sensibility* is associated with the body, *sentiment* with the mind" (Van Sant, 4). Yorick at the outset of his journey is capable of rationalizing principles of conduct; but only through his encounter with Madame de L*** and through physical (or sensible) contact with her does he begin to allow his conduct to be directed by emotional susceptibility.

The considerable discourse about sentiment and sensibility in the eighteenth century often focused on women. Women were considered to be more sensible in that their nerves were more fragile, their sensory perceptions therefore more acute. Even so, they were not held up as models for imitation on the score of their sensibility as often as they were portrayed as objects of pity that called forth male concern. The emblem of a woman's suffering was portrayed—in literature, anyway— as having an ameliorating effect on the brutish sensibilities of men. The best known eighteenth-century example of such an emblem is Samuel Richardson's Clarissa, whose death reforms the rakish Belford. She is by no means the only example—Henry Fielding's Amelia is another from fiction; Nicholas Rowe's Jane Shore and Thomas Otway's Belvidera are examples from the dramatic canon of the period.

The portrayal of the female victim of abuse or illness or adversity of another sort for the purpose of generating sympathy for her plight per- petuates what some today would call a negative stereotype, emphasizing as such portraits do the fragility, the helplessness, the weakness of the female victim. Even in the eighteenth century, voices were raised in opposition to such a view of the nature of women. Mary Wollstonecraft, in particular, saw the debility and frailty that were assumed natural to women as the result of cultural training, rather than biological necessity. Yet it must be said that in an age when a woman had little power and few opportunities to make her way through the world without the aid of a man—usually a husband whose "right" it was to rule her—a fashion that encouraged sympathy for women probably helped more than it hurt, at least in the short term. Many eighteenth-century male writers contributed to the attempt to transform male sexual urges into such sympathy. Rousseau's Emile, for example, was taught by his tutor Jean- Jacques to desire virtue. Sterne's Yorick, in contrast, makes a virtue of desire.

When Yorick sees the monk whom he had insulted "in close confer- ence with a lady just arrived at the inn" in Calais, he is concerned about the "ill impressions which the poor monk's story, in case he had told it her, must have planted in her breast against me" (*SJ*, 91/16, 98/19). Convinced before he ever sees her face that this lady is "of a better order of beings," imagining a visage and demeanor that charms him, Yorick feels an attachment to the woman that makes him wish to appear gener- ous and good-hearted (*SJ*, 91/16). When he does see the lady's counte-

nance, Yorick imagines an entire history for her, a history that touches
his heart:

> I fancied [her face] wore the characters of a widow'd look, and in that
> state of its declension, which had passed the two first paroxysms of sor-
> row, and was quietly beginning to reconcile itself to its loss—but a thou-
> sand other distresses might have traced the same lines; I wish'd to know
> what they had been—and was ready to enquire, (had the same *bon ton* of
> conversation permitted, as in the days of Esdras)—*"What aileth thee? and
> why art thou disquieted? and why is thy understanding troubled?"* —In a
> word, I felt benevolence for her. . . . (*SJ*, 94–95/17)

Significantly, the language he wishes to speak to the lady is Biblical. It is
a quotation from the Apocryphal book of 2 Esdras, in which the prophet
comforts a grieving woman who is transformed before his eyes into the
restored city of Jerusalem in all the "brightness of her glory, and the
comeliness of her beauty."[4] Yorick's sympathy for his bereaved acquaintance affords him a similar vision of glory.

What the monk could not do for himself, the lady does for him.
Touched by the lady physically and emotionally, Yorick determines to
rectify things with the monk. He offers his snuffbox as a "peace-offering
of a man who once used you unkindly, but not from his heart" (*SJ*,
99/20). The monk blushes, makes his own apologies, and offers his
snuffbox in return. Yorick tells us "I guard this box, as I would the
instrumental parts of my religion, to help my mind on to something
better" (*SJ*, 101/20), and when he recounts his later visit to Father
Lorenzo's grave, where he sat holding the snuffbox, crying, "as weak as a
woman," we hear echoes of "Alas, poor Yorick!" and we remember the
black page of *Tristram Shandy*'s *memento mori* (*SJ*, 103/21).

In addition to reminding us of mortality, the monk's snuffbox
includes a lesson in living, one that was not lost on the eighteenth-century readers who found in the tale an argument for religious harmony.
Part of Sterne's redemptive purpose here seems to have been to reject
the anti-Catholicism of *Tristram Shandy* and to offer a vision of harmony
between Protestants and Catholics. Certainly the episode was so read in
the late eighteenth century, particularly on the continent, where it
became fashionable to exchange snuffboxes in emulation of Yorick and
the monk.[5]

Yet we must not overlook the fact that it was Madame de L*** who
precipitated such a unification. And this episode as a whole seems to
offer support of Yorick's stated credo:

having been in love with one princess or another almost all my life, and I
hope I shall go on so, till I die, being firmly persuaded, that if ever I do a
mean action, it must be in some interval betwixt one passion and
another: whilst this interregnum lasts, I always perceive my heart locked
up—I can scarce find in it, to give Misery a sixpence; and therefore I
always get out of it as fast as I can, and the moment I am rekindled, I am
all generosity and good will again; and would do any thing in the world
either for, or with any one, if they will but satisfy me there is no sin in it.
(*SJ*, 128–29/34)

Yorick maintains that erotic attraction—love—makes one generous,
openhearted and sympathetic. Certainly, after his remise (coachhouse)
flirtation with Madame de L*** in Calais, Yorick demonstrates a much
more obliging character than he had before. At his next stop in Montriul, finding he needs a servant, Yorick hires the amorous La Fleur, who
has no qualifications for servitude except a willingness to serve; Yorick
lets his intuitive identification with La Fleur guide his behavior, his heart
rule his head, so to speak, and, he tells us, he never regretted doing so
because "by the festivity of his temper . . . I had a constant resource . . .
in all difficulties and distresses of my own" (*SJ*, 126/33). Leaving Montriul, Yorick's heart continues to prompt his actions as he opens his
purse to all who ask for charity—quite a contrast to his initial retentive-
ness with Father Lorenzo.

   The fragment that is included in volume 1 of the journey again
makes the case for the linking of eroticism and morality. This fragment
presents a town (Abdera) initiated into a new golden age by the pathetic
speech of Perseus in Euripides's *Andromeda* "*O Cupid, prince of God and
men*" (*SJ*, 131/34). The entire town is transformed; "the whole city, like
the heart of one man, open'd itself to Love" (*SJ*, 131/35). War ceased; a
new age of pastoral simplicity ensued. According to the fragment:
"'Twas only in the power . . . of the God whose empire extendeth from
heaven to earth, and even to the depths of the sea, to have done this" (*SJ*,
131/35). The fragment presents a city of glory, similar to the one in the
vision of Esdras, and Sterne suggests that the transforming power is not
merely sympathy but a sensibility born of erotic love that is a spiritual as
well as a carnal gift.

   As we discussed in the previous chapter, in volume 7 of *Tristram
Shandy*, Tristram maintains that our bodily desires provide us a foretaste
of heaven: "the measure of heaven itself is but the measure of our present appetites and concoctions" (*TS*, 2.593/7.13). We have no other way
of conceiving eternal happiness but by drawing on our imperfect earthly

joys. As erotic passion is one of the chief of those joys, it is surely one of the chief ways by which we can glimpse heaven.

Of course, erotic passion is but one appetite to which human beings are subject. There are others, all of which can be described as self-centered, as all appetite emanates from the desires of the self. Basically, the redemption of sexual desire that occurs in Yorick's encounter with Madame de L*** consists of the transforming of erotic passion into concern for another; the same alchemical change can occur with any desire. In the episode entitled "The Dead Ass," Sterne presents the universal principle by which such change occurs. Yorick and La Fleur are stalled in their egress from Montriul by a dead ass in the road, which La Fleur's post horse refuses to go around. Farther along the road, in Nampont, they meet the ass's owner, who sits on a stone bench sighing and weeping. His sad tale lugubriously emphasizes the friendship between man and beast:

> [T]his poor creature . . . had been a patient partner of his journey. . . .
> [I]t had eat the same bread with him all the way, and was unto him as a
> friend. . . . The ass, he said, he was assured loved him—and upon this
> told them a long story of a mischance upon their passage over the Pyre-
> nean mountains which had separated them from each other three days;
> during which time the ass had sought him as much as he had sought the
> ass, and that they had neither scarce eat or drank till they met. (SJ,
> 139–140/40–41)

The mourner's lament prompts Yorick to say to himself, "Did we love each other, as this poor soul but loved his ass—'twould be something" (SJ, 141/41). Yorick's insight is as old as the gospels; it is, in fact, a comic restatement of the second "great commandment" (Matthew 22:36–39): Each of us should love the world as he loves his own ass. More decorously put, in the words of Christ, we should love our neighbor as we love ourselves. This sentiment is not a cold moral principle but one that is underwritten by the emotions. And it is best understood in spontaneous bursts of feeling for another, as Yorick's later adventures demonstrate.

Spontaneity characterizes both the vision of Esdras and Yorick's own spiritual improvement through his encounter with Madame de L***. "When the heart flies out before the understanding," Yorick says, "it saves the judgment a world of pains" (SJ, 91/16), and such impulsiveness seems crucial to the spiritual benefit to be derived from such encounters.

Once sympathy becomes a premise of duty or custom, it loses its ability to prompt the kind of unselfconscious openheartedness that Sterne/Yorick seems to value. Yorick's second encounter with Madame de L*** suggests as much. He meets her again in Amiens and considers accompanying her to Brussels at her invitation. It now occurs to him that he has a prior obligation: He is in love with someone else, Eliza, to whom he has "sworn . . . eternal fidelity" (*SJ*, 147/43). He vows not to go: "Eternal fountain of happiness! . . . be thou my witness—and every pure spirit which tastes it, be my witness also, That I would not travel to Brussels, unless Eliza went along with me, did the road lead me towards heaven" (*SJ*, 148/44). Realizing the implication of his vow, Yorick admits, "[i]n transports of this kind, the heart, in spite of the under-standing, will always say too much" (*SJ*, 148/44). The heartfelt insight Yorick has gleaned from his encounter with Madame de L*** is in conflict with his duty to Eliza. His vision of heaven remains a glimpse only, not a sight he can hold steadily in view. Yet duty is not the only impediment to a sustained experience of heavenly bliss. Sterne, like his contemporaries, would have been quite aware that sexuality did not produce universal beneficence, that in fact, sexuality was responsible for much evil in the world. Sterne himself underwent a cure for venereal disease while he was writing *A Sentimental Journey* and certainly he was aware that his lust and licentiousness were at least partly responsible for the domestic discord that characterized his marriage. In addition, as a priest, Sterne would have presided over cases of adultery or fornication in the spiritual courts; he would have witnessed the human cost of such behavior, the degradation and the shame. He also would have seen another dimension of erotic passion—children who became parish wards as the result of illegitimate birth. Sex was certainly a spiritual gift, but like all such gifts, it was subject to human abuse.

After his remise flirtation with Madame de L***, Yorick finds himself susceptible to other "princesses" he encounters in his travels. All women are to him avenues to fine feelings, from shop-girls to members of the French aristocracy. Yet each of these encounters serves more to undermine the notion that there is some moral benefit to "love at first sight" rather than to support it (*SJ*, 161/51). One of the most famous episodes in *A Sentimental Journey* is the flirtation between Yorick and a Paris *grisset*, a shop-girl. Yorick pauses to ask the young woman for directions to the Opera *comique,* and the two begin an elaborate flirtation that prompts Yorick to take the *grisset*'s pulse on the pretext of establishing that her courtesy and kindness are the result of "one of the best pulses of any woman in the world" (*SJ*, 164/53). Yorick's comment to Eugenius bespeaks a self-consciousness on Yorick's part that argues little for the chastity of his imagination or the spontaneity of his behavior:

> —Would to heaven! my dear Eugenius, thou hadst passed by, and beheld me sitting in my black coat, and in my lack-a-day-sical manner, counting the throbs of it, one by one, with as much true devotion as if I had been watching the critical ebb or flow of her fever—How wouldst thou have laugh'd and moralized upon my new profession?—and thou shouldst have laugh'd and moralized on—Trust me, my dear Eugenius, I shouldst have said, "there are worse occupations in this world *than feeling a woman's pulse.*"—But a Grisset's! thou wouldst have said—and in an open shop! Yorick—
> —So much the better: for when my views are direct, Eugenius, I care not if all the world saw me feel it. (*SJ*, 164–165/53)

Yorick's openness, he maintains, is a sign of his guiltlessness, the directness of his motives and his intentions. But the triumphant tone in which he celebrates his "new profession," to say nothing of his surprise that the *grisset*'s husband merely tips his hat to Yorick as he passes through the shop, gives us pause. It is just possible that Yorick's sensibility serves not only as a mask for his sensuality but as a means of hiding that sensuality from himself as well.

A later episode underscores the notion of a certain duplicity on the part of the narrator. At the Opera *comique*, Yorick is moved to pity by the sight of a dwarf straining for a view behind a large and impervious German. Yorick spies a French soldier with whom he feels an instant kinship because of another soldier whom he had loved,—none other than "Tobias Shandy, the dearest of my flock and friends, whose philanthropy I never think of at this long distance from his death—but my eyes gush out with tears" (*SJ*, 170/56). In accord with Yorick's expectations, the French officer relieves the dwarf's discomfort by arranging for the dwarf to be placed in front of the German so that he could see. "This is noble!" exclaims Yorick (*SJ*, 179/61).

Yorick and the French officer strike up a conversation in which the officer remarks on the benefits of travel: "[I]t taught us mutual toleration; and mutual toleration. . . taught us mutual love" (*SJ*, 181/62–63). This sentiment is a rearticulation of the lesson of Father Lorenzo's snuffbox, which, significantly, Yorick is using when the officer notices his distress over the dwarf's dilemma. This restatement of the importance of mutual understanding at the end of Part One has the effect of bringing the narrative full circle as it draws to a temporary close. But Part One also ends with a cry of *"Haussez les mains, Monsieur l'Abbe"*; the crowd at the opera insists that a priest, standing behind "a couple of grissets," must hold his hands up during the performance so that he will not be tempted to put them where they should not be (*SJ*, 180/62). Yorick expresses shock "that an ecclesiastick would pick the Grisset's pockets," but the French officer tells him that the *abbé* is being accused of other designs (*SJ*, 180/62) and dismisses the crowd as advancing "an illiberal sarcasm at the church," though he admits that there is "good and bad every where" (*SJ*, 180–81/62)—and in everybody, Sterne might add, including priests. To maintain otherwise is as ludicrous as the final image of volume 1 of *A Sentimental Journey,* which depicts Yorick reverently attending Madame de Rambouliet as she pisses by the side of the road: "had I been the priest of the chaste CASTALIA, I could not have served at her fountain with a more respectful decorum" (*SJ*, 183/63).

It is certainly characteristic of Sterne to undercut sentiment with bawdiness, and Yorick's quixotic idealism in the presence of the nasty necessities of biological life is laughable. However, such idealism is preferable to disgust, and if sensibility can serve to guard against bitterness it should be encouraged. In volume 2 of *A Sentimental Journey,* Sterne does just that.

At the beginning of volume 2, Yorick recounts that the French officer's observations about the benefits of travel have prompted him to seek a copy of *Hamlet* in a Paris book shop so that he can reread Polonius's speech to Laertes on the same subject. Polonius's famous advice, of course, speaks eloquently of, among other things, the benefit of self-knowledge: "This above all, to thine own self be true/And it must follow as the night the day/Thou canst not then be false to any man."[6] Yorick finds a set of Shakespeare's works, but he cannot purchase them. The bookseller tells him that a French Count de B****, who loves English books and Englishmen, owns the volumes and the books are there to be bound and then sent to the count in Versailles.

Just as Yorick has difficulty locating a copy of Polonius's advice, he has trouble following it as well, because he, like most human beings, has a great capacity for self-delusion. He is brought face to face with that fact when he discovers that he has left England so precipitately that he has forgotten to bring along his passport—a serious oversight as England and France are at war. The police, La Fleur informs him, are looking for him; the prospect of the Bastille looms large, but instead of being terrified, Yorick falls back on sentiment:

—And as for the Bastile! the terror is in the word—Make the most of it
you can, said I to myself, the Bastile is but another word for a tower—
and a tower is but another word for a house you can't get out of—(*SJ*,
196/70)

While he is thus philosophizing, he hears a voice crying "'I can't get
out—I can't get out,'" and his "affections [are] . . . tenderly awakened";
his "dissipated spirits, to which [his] reason had been a bubble, were. . .
suddenly call'd home" (*SJ*, 197)–8/71–72).

The voice belongs to a starling in a cage, an English bird, it turns out,
brought to Paris by an English boy who caught it on the Cliffs of Dover
as he waited with his master to board the ship to France. The lad had
taught the bird to bemoan his captivity in English and had left him
behind in France where no one could understand what he was saying, no
one until Yorick happened to overhear him, that is. Upon hearing the
starling, Yorick's "systematic reasonings upon the Bastile" give way to
empathy for the enslaved and abhorrence for the state of slavery: "Disguise thyself as thou wilt, still slavery! . . . —still thou art a bitter
draught; and though thousands in all ages have been made to drink of
thee, thou art no less bitter on that account" (*SJ*, 198–99/72).

Yorick continues to ponder the issue of freedom and captivity, but he
finds that he cannot think about it properly when he thinks about it in
the abstract. He, therefore, engages in an imaginative exercise in which
he thinks of "a single captive," in all his misery, his "sickness of . . .
heart," his fever, his separation from family and friends. Meditating on
this scene of hopelessness and pain, Yorick "burst into tears": "I could
not sustain the picture of confinement which my fancy had drawn" (*SJ*,
201–3/73). Yorick determines to try to save himself from such misery;
he sets forth to seek a passport in Versailles.

Failing to get an interview with the powerful Duc de C*****, Yorick
goes to visit the count who loved English books instead. Once there,
Yorick remains puzzled by himself:

> There is not a more perplexing affair in life to me, than to set about
> telling any one who I am—for there is scarce any body I cannot give a
> better account of than of myself; and I have often wish'd I could do it in
> a single word—and have an end of it. (*SJ*, 221/85)

In this instance, he gets his wish: "[i]t was the only time and occasion in
my life, I could accomplish this to any purpose" (*SJ*, 221/85). Shakespeare's works lie on the table; help is at hand. Yorick picks up a vol-

ume, turns to the fifth act of Hamlet and puts his "finger upon YORICK": "*Me, Voici!* said I" (*SJ,* 221/85).

The count is thrilled to have—as he takes it—one of Shakespeare's characters in the room with him, and he embraces Yorick and then leaves to prepare a passport for the jester to the King of Denmark. While the count is gone, Yorick amuses himself by reading *Much Ado About Nothing,* a play whose title seems an ironic comment on the whole passport episode. But the play charms him, he asserts, as literature often does—a matter upon which Yorick meditates. He marvels at the "[s]weet pliability of man's spirit," which can lose itself in the "illusions" of literature in spite of the sadness and anxiety that characterize life (*SJ,* 224/87). His life would have been shorter, he is sure, were it not for the "enchanted ground" of "fancy" that provided a "velvet path" for him to tread when his way was "too rough" or "too steep" (*SJ,* 225/87). "When evils press sore upon me," Yorick asserts, "and there is no retreat from them in this world, then I take a new course" (*SJ,* 225/87). He visits, like Aeneas, the "elysian fields" where he meets the "pensive shade" of Dido and sees "the injured spirit wave her head, and turn off silent from the author of her miseries and dishonours." "I lose the feelings for myself in hers—and in those affections which were wont to make me mourn for her when I was at school" (*SJ,* 225/87).

In this passage, Yorick invokes an episode from Virgil's *Aeneid,* which would have had a deep resonance for the eighteenth-century reader who would have been as familiar with the Roman epic as he or she was with the Bible. In one of the most moving narratives ever written, Virgil tells of the Queen of Carthage's love for the Trojan hero Aeneas, who for a time returns her love, and then abandons her to fulfill his fate as the founder of Rome. Left alone and desperate, Dido kills herself, to the sorrow of her people and—when Aeneas finally hears of it—to his sorrow as well. When Aeneas meets Dido in the underworld, she refuses to acknowledge him in either reproach or forgiveness. Her silence after such passion in life is even more affecting than her suicide. Most readers, in Sterne's time and in ours, find Dido's death and her later meeting with her lover poignant and stirring.

Certainly Yorick had found it so, and he clearly approves of the "pliability of spirit" that opens the heart to such powers of the imagination. His approval is a challenge to another reader of the Dido episode—St. Augustine himself. As a schoolboy, Augustine, like Yorick, was so touched by Dido's passion for Aeneas and her tragic death that he wept, but in his *Confessions* he castigates himself for what he finds to be worse than youthful folly. He describes his response to Virgil's powerful tale as sinful, as a deliberate choice of this world over the next:

> For what [is] more miserable than a miserable being who commiserates not himself; weeping the death of Dido for love to Æneas, but weeping not his own death for want of love to Thee, O God. Thou light of my heart, Thou bread of my inmost soul, Thou Power who givest vigour to my mind, who quickenest my thoughts, I loved Thee not. I committed fornication against Thee, . . . *for the friendship of this world is fornication against Thee.* . . . And all this I wept not, I who wept for Dido slain, and "seeking by the sword a stroke and wound extreme," myself seeking the while a worse extreme, the extremest and lowest of Thy creatures, having forsaken Thee, earth passing into the earth. And if forbid to read all this, I was grieved that I might not read what grieved me.[7]

For Augustine, the attractions of literature are distractions from Christian duty. He abhors the sensuality and feeling that he once felt for Dido; he rejects the very quality of the imaginative experience that Sterne finds not only a source of pleasure but a source of moral improvement as well. "I was never able to conquer any one single bad sensation in my heart so decisively," Yorick maintains, "as by beating up as fast as I could for some kindly and gentle sensation, to fight it upon its own ground" (*SJ*, 226/87).

In Sterne's own time, the Dido episode had received attention from Bishop William Warburton, the same Warburton who advised Sterne to approach his *Tristram Shandy* with decorum and gravity. Warburton reads the Dido episode, like Augustine, as a contest between religion and emotion, though from a slightly different perspective. Dido was portrayed and described by Virgil, according to Warburton, "to set off [Aeneas's] Piety."[8] Dido was a "Woman immersed in voluptuous pleasures" who had contempt for the gods. Aeneas succumbed to her charms, but he "recovered" himself by overcoming his "impotent and unruly passion" and going on to fulfill his pious—his religious—duty, the founding of Rome. "[T]he episode of Dido and AEneas," Warburton elaborates, "was not given to ornament his [Virgil's] poem with an amusing tale of a love adventure, but to expose the public mischiefs which arise from Rulers' indulging themselves in the voluptuous weakness" (Warburton, 1.241).

Sterne disagrees with both St. Augustine and Bishop Warburton. Instead of finding an emotional, sensual response to literature or to another person wrong and undutiful, Sterne finds it admirable—even spiritual—and in fact he shows that it is through the sympathetic imagination, whether it be exercised on literary characters or actual individuals, that one redeems one's baser impulses. Sterne suggests that the only sure way we can follow the directive of Christ to love each other as we love ourselves is to imagine what it is like to be another—to feel, as the young Augustine did for Dido and as Yorick does for his imagined captive, what it is like to experience another's pain.

Of course, Sterne recognizes that art is closely allied to artifice and that it might provoke not honest feeling and true sympathy but merely the form of emotion, the fashion of sentiment, the outward show of sensibility. And, in fact, Yorick eventually decides that his sympathy with others has become artificial. Back in Paris, he tells us, "I was of every man's opinion I met," but he soon grew tired of "the children of Art" and he "languish'd for those of Nature" (*SJ,* 266/112). He decides to leave France for Italy. Interestingly, however, as he begins his journey toward Italy, Yorick seeks out the acquaintance of a literary character—Maria of Moulines, whom Tristram Shandy had described in volume 7 of his life and opinions. The story of "that disorder'd maid," Yorick says, had "affect'd me not a little in the reading," so he goes "half a league out of the road . . . to enquire after her" (*SJ,* 269/113). Unlike St. Augustine, Yorick finds such "melancholy adventures" spiritually reassuring: "I am never so perfectly conscious of the existence of a soul within me, as when I am entangled in them" (*SJ,* 270/113).

Maria has changed slightly since Tristram described her. Her goat has been replaced by a dog, her sorrow for her lover has yielded to sorrow for her father who has recently died. Yorick sits beside her wiping her tears and crying himself. Eventually, he admits that he finds Maria appealing physically, not merely affecting emotionally. She was "of the first order of fine forms," Yorick says (*SJ,* 275/116). And if he could forget Eliza he could be content to stay with Maria forever, holding her in his arms "as a daughter" (*SJ,* 275/116). The description is admittedly erotic, but it should not negate our sense that Yorick has been emotionally affected by Maria's hardships. She is quite vulnerable, but he does not turn that vulnerability to his sexual advantage. Instead, his carnal impulses become the basis for sympathetic, imaginative identification with another.

The same may be said of Yorick's earlier encounter with the *fille de chambre* he meets in the Paris book shop. Yorick puts a coin in the young girl's nearly empty purse, telling her that if she will be as good as she is pretty, heaven will fill her purse—an act and a sentiment that even a

naive young girl could find ambiguous. She and Yorick walk together
along the Quai de Conti, Yorick moralizing as he goes about her virtue
and the importance of her maintaining it. When they part, he is
tempted to kiss her, but instead he "bid God bless her" (*SJ*, 191/67).

Later the *fille de chambre* comes to Yorick's hotel to show him a purse
she made to hold the coin he gave her. He admits her to his room, and
they discuss the purse, she mends his stock, he buckles her shoe, and
suddenly the "fair *fille de chambre*" is thrown "off her center" into the
middle of the bed (*SJ*, 236/93). In a section entitled "The Conquest,"
Yorick concludes the episode in language that is thoroughly ambiguous:
"As I finish'd my address," he says, "I raised the fair *fille de chambre* up by
the hand, and led her out of the room . . . *and then*—the victory being
quite decisive—and not till then, I press'd my lips to her cheek, and,
taking her by the hand again, led her safe to the gate of the hotel" (*SJ*,
238/94). While we assume that Yorick's victory has been a victory over
himself and his carnal desires, the ambiguity of the language celebrates
rather than condemns the desires themselves. For, as Yorick explains,
"[i]f nature has so wove her web of kindness, that some threads of love
and desire are entangled with the piece—must the whole web be rent in
drawing them out?" (*SJ*, 237/94). He is not to blame for having such
desires, but for the way he acts in response to them: "Wherever thy
providence shall place me for the trials of my virtue—whatever is my
danger—whatever is my situation—let me feel the movements which
rise out of it, and which belong to me as a man—and if I govern them as
a good one—I will trust the issues to thy justice, for thou hast made
us—and not we ourselves" (*SJ*, 237–38/94).

Finally, his search for the natural expression of sympathy and fellow
feeling leads Yorick to a meal and a dance with a peasant family in the
Bourbonnois. In the dance, Yorick thinks he sees the expression of religion, though he almost dismisses this notion as "one of the illusions of
an imagination which is eternally misleading me" (*SJ*, 284/120). But the
father of the family confirms Yorick's insight, saying that it was a custom in the family to "dance and rejoice" after each supper in the belief
that "a chearful [*sic*] and contented mind was the best sort of thanks to
heaven that an illiterate peasant could pay" (*SJ*, 284/120). "Or a learned
prelate either," Yorick replies (*SJ*, 284/120). Such a clear echo of Tristram's dance with Nannette at the end of volume 7 of *Tristram Shandy*
suggests that the peasant family's dance is a redeemed version of Tristram's joyful but desirous dance with the "daughter of labour." For
desire, while it partakes in joy, does not necessarily produce the "chearful

and contented mind" that the peasant finds a proper expression of gratitude to heaven. In fact, unfulfilled desire does just the opposite.

It is difficult finally to read *A Sentimental Journey* as a repudiation of desire. Almost every passage is infused with double entendre—even Yorick's "prayer" speaks of "movements" which "rise" and provoke "issues." And Yorick's dance, while communal rather than partnered, is nonetheless a sensual dance. Our conviction that *A Sentimental Journey* is on some level always about sexual longing is partly attributable to the fact that while he was writing this work, Sterne was himself involved in a "sentimental" relationship characterized by intense desire. And, fortunately, we have a record of that desire in a journal that Sterne wrote contemporaneously with *A Sentimental Journey. A Journal to Eliza* illuminates the relationship between desire and religion in a way that enriches our reading of *A Sentimental Journey.* Before examining the conclusion of Yorick's journey of sentiment, therefore, we will look closely at Sterne's day-by-day record of his own feeling during the first months of his writing *A Sentimental Journey.*

A Journal to Eliza bears witness to Sterne's determination to love as long as he lived. The journal was addressed to the Eliza he mentions from time to time in *A Sentimental Journey,* Eliza Draper, a young married woman whom Sterne knew but three months before she left England to join her husband in India. She is the most famous of his sentimental attachments, largely because of the journal and because of his immortalizing of her picture and her name in *A Sentimental Journey.* Sterne designed the lasting fame, he tells Eliza, and elaborates the nature of their relationship in an entry in the journal dated June 17:

> I have brought your name *Eliza!* and Picture into my work—where they will remain—when You and I are at rest for ever—Some Annotator or explainer of my works in this place will take occasion, to speak of the Friendship which Subsisted so long and faithfully betwixt Yorick and the Lady he speaks of—Her Name he will tell the world was Draper—a Native of India—married there to a gentleman in the India Service of that Name—, who brought her over to England for the recovery of her health in the Year 65—where She continued to April the Year 1767. It was about three months before her Return to India, That our Author's acquaintance and hers began. Mrs Draper had a great thirst for Knowledge—was handsome—genteel—engaging—and of such gentle dispositions and so enlightend [*sic*] an understanding,—That Yorick, (whether he made much Opposition is not known) from an acquaintance—soon became her Admirer—they caught fire at each other at the same time—

and they would often say, without reserve to the world, and without any Idea of saying wrong in it, That their Affections for each other were *unbounded.*[9]

The two carried on a sentimental "affair" for three months in London, writing each other letters, sharing meals, interesting friends in their emotional attachment and their sadness at parting when Eliza Draper was called back to India by her husband. The relationship was quite pleasant for both—Eliza Draper enjoyed the prestige of being publicly worshiped by a famous author, and Laurence Sterne at fifty-four was flattered by the attentions of this young, attractive woman of twenty-three who looked up to him as her "Bramin" or teacher. That Sterne, in turn, called Eliza his "Bramine" suggests a playful refusal to inhabit the role of superior; and indeed the journal makes it clear that, despite the difference in their ages, Sterne configured the relationship as equal in a very special sense.

Sterne wrote the *Journal to Eliza* as a private record "of the miserable feelings of a person separated from a Lady for whose Society he languish'd" (*JE,* 135). He states at various points in the course of the journal that he intends for Eliza to have the journal and that he expects to read a similar account of her miseries when they are reunited. The portion of the journal that survives, however, does not seem to have been turned over to Mrs. Draper, and indeed, it remains unclear whether or not Sterne planned the journal for a private correspondence only or for publication in some form. The journal may have served as an exercise in sentimental expression that fueled Sterne's writing of *A Sentimental Journey,* or it may represent the heartfelt private passion of a sick and lonely man. Or, as is usual with matters relating to Sterne, all alternatives may in some sense be true—and at the same time.

For our purposes, the journal is interesting in that it reflects a view of love as redemptive in the same sense that informs *A Sentimental Journey.* Sterne calls Eliza his "Help-mate" (*JE,* 136), and he tells her, "I find myself more your Husband than contracts can make us" (*JE,* 169). Their souls are so sympathetic as to be one soul: "I resemble no Being in the world so nearly as I do You" (*JE,* 161). Sterne believes that although he and Eliza are separated by thousands of miles as she makes her way across the ocean to India, they nevertheless enjoy a perfect communion. "Surely no evil can have befallen You—" Sterne writes, "for if it had—I had felt some monitory sympathetic Shock within me, which would have spoke like Revelation" (*JE,* 154).

Although Sterne's love for Eliza Draper leads him into some fantastical reveries that we cannot see as innocent—such as his vision of the convenient deaths of Daniel Draper and Elizabeth Sterne—he nevertheless insists that the relationship is not only blameless, but virtuous. In fact, he and Eliza ensure each other's virtue, as he explains to her: "Remember You are mine—and stand answerable for all you say and do to me—I govern myself by the same Rule—and such a History of myself can I lay before you, as shall create no blushes, but those of pleasure" (*JE,* 182). Their love is ordained by Providence and directed by God, Sterne asserts, and somehow the two of them will escape their current, unfulfilling marriages to enjoy "the Elysium we have so often and rapturously talk'd of" (*JE,* 137). Their life together will be "a Paradice" (*JE,* 179); Sterne will install Eliza as the "Goddesse of this Temple," if they just "leave all to that Being—who is infinitely removed above all Straitness of heart . . . and is a friend to the friendly, as well as to the friendless" (*JE,* 159–60). "Some Haven of rest will open to us," Sterne promises Eliza and himself, "assuredly—God made us not for Misery and Ruin—he has orderd [*sic*] all our Steps—and influenced our Attachments for what is worthy of them—It must end well—Eliza!—" (*JE,* 160).

That Sterne is sincere in his portrayal of a paradisal love is reinforced by the language he employs to describe the reintroduction of his wife into his existence in the summer of 1767. In June, he received a letter from his daughter Lydia announcing that she and her mother were coming to Coxwold to discuss with Sterne their making France their permanent home. Sterne was agreeable to the plan but suspicious that the visit was motivated by "pure Interest—to pillage What they can from me" (*JE,* 156). He hated the thought of "waging War" with Elizabeth (*JE,* 181), and he took great offense at several letters Elizabeth sent in advance of her visit. The terms in which he expressed his complaint reinvoke the notion of marriage as, above all, a spiritual union; he speaks of the "vexation of heart" he suffers "at a couple of ungrateful unfeeling Letters from that Quarter, from whence, had it pleas'd God, I should have lookd for all my Comforts" (*JE,* 179). "[B]ut he has will'd they should come from the east," Sterne concludes, "—and he knows how I am satisfyed with all his Dispensations" (*JE,* 179). Eliza Draper is, for Sterne, the kindest dispensation of all.

The joy of the dreams of elysian bliss that punctuates the journal is balanced by the tears of misery at separation. Sterne often reports weeping during conversations about Eliza, crying over dinners that she is not sharing, sobbing at the thought of her ill health and the hazards of her journey. One conversation with their mutual friend, Mrs. James, leaves Sterne so weak that, he says, "I had like to have fainted, and to that Degree was my heart and Soul affected, it was with difficulty I could reach the Street door" (*JE*, 147). His increasing sensibility is not a burden to him; in fact, he feels "pleasure" in the misery of a "heart unsupported by aught but its own tenderness"(*JE*, 137).

Like Yorick who finds confirmation of his soul in his pity for another, Sterne discovers in his heightened sensibilities a spiritual regeneration. It comes as a shock then, in the midst of reveling in the finer sensations of the soul, to find the sentimental lover diagnosed with venereal disease! Sterne himself is amused: "I have as whimsical a Story to tell you, and as comically disastrous as ever befell one of our family—Shandy's Nose— his *name*—his Sash-Window are fools to it" (*JE*, 141).

Protesting that he had had "no commerce whatever with the Sex— not even with my wife . . . these 15 Years," Sterne finds himself being "treated as a *Sinner*, in a point where I had acted like a *Saint*" (*JE*, 141). He undergoes a painful mercury cure for his ailment, which was in all likelihood an effect of his tuberculosis, not a venereal complaint at all (*TLY*, 290). Still, we should not take too seriously his claim of chastity, for it is almost certainly untrue. What is most interesting about this passage, in any event, is Sterne's invocation of the mishaps that befall poor Tristram in spite of Walter's designs for his perfection. Whatever the nature of Sterne's physical debilitation, he certainly saw it at this juncture as an ironic and telling counter-movement to the lofty sentimentality of his journal. He complains to Eliza that "with all his sensibilities, [he is] suffering the Chastisement of the grossest Sensualist" (*JE*, 142), but he is less impressed with the injustice than with the ridiculousness of the situation.

Although the whimsical, ridiculous Sterne is less in evidence in the *Journal to Eliza* than he is in *Tristram Shandy* and *A Sentimental Journey,* the artist is still there. In fact, as Cash has pointed out, Sterne manipulated dates in the journal so that it seems a consecutive chronological record of a lover's misery, when in fact there are gaps in time—most notably a three-week gap at the end of July, after Sterne receives a packet of letters from Eliza. Sterne records his reaction to this packet in an entry dated July 27, but he must have written the passage much later because he makes reference to the "nonsensical Festivity" of the York Races, which were always held—and still are—during the third week of August (*JE*, 185). Possibly, Eliza's packet was a source of disappointment to him in that it may have contained the letters of a friend not a lover. For whatever reason, Sterne cut off his journal early, telling Eliza that his wife had arrived a full month before she actually joined him in Coxwold.

In other words, the journal contains a great deal of artifice, a fact underscored by numerous references to Sterne's looking at Eliza's picture: "I pore so much on thy Picture—I have it *off by heart*—dear Girl—oh tis sweet! tis kind! tis reflecting! tis affectionate! tis—thine my Bramine—I say my matins and Vespers to it—I quiet my Murmurs, by the Spirit which speaks in it" (*JE,* 146). Although the journal tries to sustain the spontaneity (the "catching fire") of new love, as all lovers' diaries do, it eventually and inevitably cannot do so, for it is impossible to remain at the point of bliss that Rousseau described as a "nascent passion," that we have all experienced as infatuation. By the end of the journal, the longing that fueled Sterne's dreams of elysian happiness with Eliza is gone.

Sterne did not suffer and pine for Eliza until his death in March 1768. He continued to flirt, to emote, to long for other "princesses," just as Yorick does in *A Sentimental Journey.* Yet Sterne was sincere in his dream of absolute fulfillment and earthly happiness with "my second self" (*JE,* 154), with a help-mate, with one other whose sensibilities were tuned to precisely the same pitch as his were. He had suffered loneliness, and, as he told Eliza, by his sufferings, by his love, he had earned or purchased the right to happiness he would eventually enjoy with her (*JE,* 155). His sufferings are a debt owed him by God; Eliza redeems (or cancels) that debt.

Eliza Draper represents, then, what Madame de L***, Maria de Molines, the *fille de chambre* and the *grisset* represent, a figurative compensation for the travails of life. If this formulation seems sexist, remember that Sterne is a man who finds love with women. There is nothing essential about the doctrine that prevents anyone from identifying the objects of his or her longing as compensatory. Indeed, Sterne's point is not even restricted to romantic love. The old man's pity for his ass and Yorick's feeling for the dwarf he sees at the opera also provide compensation for life's hardships in the pleasing sensation of feeling itself. As Yorick exclaims, it is in empathy, in feeling our connectedness to one another, that we "know we have a soul." That such feeling is basically egocentric does not render it less worthy, as Yorick discovers in "The Act of Charity" that he witnesses in Paris. In this encounter, Yorick observes two ladies approached by a poor man who asks a twelve-sous piece of each of them. "Poo! said they—we have no money" (*SJ*, 258/108). The poor man continues to press until they agree to give him one sous. He needs twelve, he insists, and continues:

> What is it but your goodness and humanity which makes your bright eyes so sweet, that they outshine the morning even in this dark passage? and what was it which made the Marquis de Santerre and his brother say so much of you both as they just pass'd by. (*SJ*, 259/109)

They each give him twelve sous, and Yorick discovers that flattery is the secret of the beggar's success. Yorick does not dismiss the charity as meaningless; instead, he praises flattery: "Delicious essence! how refreshing art thou to nature! how strongly are all its powers and all its weaknesses on thy side! how sweetly dost thou mix with the blood, and help it through the most difficult and tortuous passages to the heart!" (*SJ*, 260/109). Flattery, like all other human skills, can be used for base ends, but it is also the surest path to the heart and a sure means by which the heart can be opened to the needs of another.

The language of sensibility is essentially flattery, and as such it is a universal language, bridging the gap, in Yorick's case, between French and English. It takes no translator, no interpreter to explain what it means to hold another's hand, to look into another's eye, to respond to tears or smiles. Sensibility is a language everyone can understand. In France it is as though Yorick hears his own language spoken by the women he meets, by the weak and incapacitated, by the oppressed, and the victimized. It makes sense then that Sterne would liken the sentiments he draws from the observation of people to the Biblical text "Capadosia, Pontus and Asia, Phrygia and Pamphilia," for this text is taken from the description in Acts 2 of the day of Pentecost (*SJ*, 257/107). The apostles, preaching in Jerusalem to a group of Jews, "devout men, out of every nation under heaven," are understood by all who gather to hear them.[10] The crowd is amazed: "how hear we every man in our own tongue, wherein we were born?"[11] Peter explains to them that the apostles are prophesying, through the Holy Spirit, to let the Jews know that Christ "whom ye have crucified" has risen.[12] Peter tells the crowd that they should "[r]epent, and be baptized . . . for the remission of sins," and they do: "the same day there were added *unto them* about three thousand souls."[13] The message of Pentecost is a message of a community of belief that includes Gentiles and Jews alike: "whosoever shall call on the name of the Lord shall be saved"[14] It is a message, Yorick says, "as good as any one in the Bible" (*SJ*, 257/107).

For Sterne, true redemption is the gift of God, whereby all we have to do is call upon the name of the Lord to be redeemed from our lives of sin and pain. Yet while such redemption refers ultimately to the forgiveness of Christ that makes eternal life possible in spite of sinfulness, there are moments in life when we feel its benefits as well. And it is precisely human love and the imagination that govern those moments, as we see in Yorick's final adventure.

Sterne concludes *A Sentimental Journey* with the tale he entitles "The Case of Delicacy." Due to some unforeseen road trouble (a stone that blocks the way), Yorick stops in an inn in Savoy, between St. Michael and Madane, on a "wet and tempestuous" night, five miles short of his intended resting place (*SJ,* 286/121). He takes possession of the bedroom, orders supper, and is "thanking heaven it was no worse" when a lady and her maid arrive at the inn (*SJ,* 286/121). The inn has only one bedchamber; the hostess, pointing out that the chamber has two beds and a closet with another bed, shows the women into Yorick's room. They are attractive women; and they, as well as Yorick, are self-conscious about the arrangement. "There were difficulties every way," so they make a pact (*SJ,* 287–88/122). The lady will sleep in the bed nearest the fire, by Yorick's stipulation. That bed's curtains, which are flimsy and transparent, will be fastened by the *fille de chambre* with corking pins or thread. Yorick, not having a robe, will sleep in his breeches all night. After the candle is put out, Yorick will not speak a word—except to utter his prayers. The reader is told to imagine the way the lady and Yorick undressed—but delicately: "if it is not the most delicate in nature, 'tis the fault of his own imagination—against which this is not my first complaint" (*SJ,* 290/124).

After the candle is out, Yorick finds he has difficulty sleeping. He tosses and turns, "till a full hour after midnight," at which time he exclaims in frustration "O my God!" The lady objects—"You have broke the treaty, Monsieur"—but Yorick protests—"it was no more than an ejaculation," and "provided for in the clause of the third article" of their pact (*SJ,* 290/124). The lady continues to argue, and "in the warmth of the dispute, . . . two or three corking pins fall out of the curtain to the ground" (*SJ,* 290/124). Yorick reaches out from his bed to reassure her that he is completely committed to decorum, to delicacy, but before he can get the words out, his hand encounters the *fille de chambre* who had come from her closet "into the narrow passage which separated" Yorick from the lady (*SJ,* 291/125).

The case of delicacy ends with an indelicate insinuation. Yorick tells us "when I stretch'd out my hand, I caught hold of the Fille de Chambre's"—and that is all. The *fille de chambre*'s what? Her hand? Perhaps. Or perhaps not. The sentence is left incomplete. But the scene itself is interestingly resonant. The echoes of Toby's courtship of the Widow Wadman; the admonition that we the readers have smutty minds that we should reform; the highly charged sexual situation; the use of the word "ejaculation," which can mean, in this context, either prayer or sexual orgasm; the prayer itself, which echoes Peter's injunction to call upon the Lord—all of these elements remind us that the world of *A Sentimental Journey*, like the world of *Tristram Shandy*, is a world of lust and delicacy, riddles and mysteries, desire and sentiment, bodies and souls, laughter and tears. Although on the surface *A Sentimental Journey* seems to exchange Tristram's bawdiness for Yorick's acute sensitivity to the feelings of others, the final scene suggests that such sensitivity—the longing for communion with another—is not the attribute of the celibate saint but of the desiring sinner. And that had been Sterne's point all along.

Chapter Five

Laurence Sterne's Other Visitors

This book is entitled *Laurence Sterne Revisited* because of the existence of an earlier book in the Twayne English Authors series, written by William Bowman Piper, published in 1965 under the title of *Laurence Sterne*.[1] Piper's volume presents close readings of *Tristram Shandy* and *A Sentimental Journey*, with particular attention to the way these works address the relationship between the individual and society. Piper's argument explores the difference between the narrative positions staked out by Tristram and Yorick, a strategy that yields a provocative reading of each of Sterne's works. Like others at the time who practiced what we still call the "new criticism," Piper proceeds on two assumptions: 1. The text is a self-contained, discrete unit that can be understood without reference to the life and beliefs of the author; and 2. the text is an example of a specific genre such as novel, sonnet, or epic and shares the formal properties of its generic category.

Without rejecting either of these assumptions, Melvyn New, in 1969, initiated a new era in Sterne studies by a simple generic dispute. While it had become commonplace to read and talk about *Tristram Shandy* as a novel—indeed, in Viktor Shklovsky's much (too much?) quoted phrase "the most typical novel" ever written—in *Laurence Sterne as Satirist: A Reading of Tristram Shandy*, New argues that it is not a novel at all, but a satire, and once that definition is accepted, one must look outside the text for meaning.[2] Satire is a genre of indirection, an ironic discourse aimed at correction toward positive norms that are usually assumed or implied. If *Tristram Shandy* is a satire, what is Sterne ridiculing and what is he affirming? New answers the question. *Tristram Shandy*, he says, is best understood within "the mainstream of the conservative, moralistic Augustan tradition," the norms of which are defined by the Anglican church (*Sterne as Satirist*, 1).

New's was not a voice in the wilderness, by any means, nor was it the first to articulate this position. D.W. Jefferson's 1951 article *"Tristram Shandy* and the Tradition of Learned Wit" is probably the earliest sounding of the theme, for Jefferson linked Sterne to earlier satirists such as Rabelais, Burton, and Swift.[3] Arthur Cash's 1966 study of *A Sentimental*

Journey and John Stedmond's 1967 *The Comic Art of Laurence Sterne* are
two additional critical analyses that de-emphasize the novelistic elements
of Sterne's works.[4] But it was New who most clearly set up the battle
lines: Are *Tristram Shandy* and *A Sentimental Journey* novels or satires?
New admits that such a question sets up a false dichotomy, but he also
maintains that the generic tradition in which one places an author determines much of what one sees and says about that author's works.[5]

To read *Tristram Shandy* as a satire is to recognize Sterne's orthodox
belief in the limitations of human nature, a belief shared by the Augustan satirists, particularly Swift and Pope. It is also to see, New argues,
that Tristram himself is an object of Sterne's satire, as are Walter and
Toby Shandy. Walter's rationality, Toby's sentiment, Tristram's futile
effort to tell his story, all aspects of human endeavor are shown to fall
short; only the admission of human limitation can ensure an escape from
that limitation—in transcendence, salvation, eternal life in Christian
terms. *Tristram Shandy* and *A Sentimental Journey,* as satires, exist to
remind us of human limitations, Sterne's own limitations included. As
Arthur Cash puts it:

> . . . Sterne took a moral stand in his fiction which differed hardly at all
> from that of his sermons. The only change was a subtle shift from clerical
> optimism to humorous pessimism. To his parishioners, he had held out a
> cheerful hope for salvation; when he turned to writing the histories of
> Tristram and Yorick, he offered the reader an amusing picture of man
> forlornly inadequate to his own ideals. (*Sterne's Comedy,* 126)

New's and Cash's insistence that we read *Tristram Shandy* and *A Sentimental Journey* as a continuation of, rather than a departure from,
Sterne's lifelong commitment to Christianity was offered as a corrective
of what was already in 1966 a well-established tendency to see Sterne as
"one of us." Sterne's vision of the fragmentary, self-centered, relativistic,
uncertain world is underwritten by his firm belief in heavenly permanence. The temporal world is, in New's and in Cash's view, the object of
his satire. We see the same fragmentary, self-centered, relativistic, uncertain world today, but as a rule, we as modern secular readers share neither Sterne's belief in permanence nor his Christian perspective. Yet
Sterne's own sense was that Christianity was being challenged in his
own time by secularism with its concomitant confidence in human reason and human perfectibility. As New and Cash argue, *Tristram Shandy*
and *A Sentimental Journey* are responses to these challenges.

John Traugott's study of *Tristram Shandy, Tristram Shandy's World: Sterne's Philosophical Rhetoric,* represents the view opposite to New's.[5] Traugott's argument de-emphasizes the certainty of Sterne's Christian belief and finds in *Tristram Shandy* a work that confronts the modern world, particularly the isolation of the individual in it. Regarding *Tristram Shandy* as a critique of Lockean rationalism, Traugott argues that *Tristram Shandy* shows that the limits of human reason can be transcended through sympathy and nonrational communication. Tristram, in this reading, is not an object of satire, but a master rhetorician instead, skilled in defining our perceptions through the cumulative building of contexts rather than through direct, determinant communication. Traugott sees Sterne as a philosopher, concerned primarily with epistemology—how we know what we know: "The point is that Sterne is concerned much less with Christianity, if we are to judge from the space allotted it, than with describing pretenders to wisdom, and less with describing pretenders to wisdom than in making a rhetorical and satiric demonstration of human passions" (Traugott, 26). We know what we know, Traugott's Sterne conveys, through our attempt to express what we know, the ordering rhetoric of our imaginations.

Traugott's book was published in the 1950s, but his argument continued to appeal in the following decades to those readers and critics who find in the treatment of the characters and in the narratorial presence of Tristram a fundamental and endearing humanity. Further, Traugott's approach is attractive in that it paints Sterne as a "serious" moralist without involving too much discussion of Christianity, a topic that causes considerable discomfort in modern "intellectual" circles. It is not surprising, then, that following Traugott's lead, a "philosophical" secular Sterne began to emerge in the criticism of the 1970s and 1980s alongside the more orthodox Christian Sterne presented by New and Cash.

Helene Moglen's 1975 study, *The Philosophical Irony of Laurence Sterne,* agrees with Traugott that *Tristram Shandy* is essentially a critique of Lockean rationalism.[6] She goes further, however, to insist that Sterne's skepticism about the universality of our knowledge forms the basis of a new ethical system, one based on "uncorrupted . . . benevolence and good will" such as, Moglen maintains, we see in Trim and Toby (Moglen, 24). Sterne, Moglen argues, embraces relativism and the absurd, even as he abandons the hope that reason can provide any access to the truth. He departs from Locke at precisely that point, for while "Locke, despite all, continues to place his hope in reason, in the power of the mind to master the abstract, to order experience, to give scientific validity to the concept of God if to nothing else," Sterne places his faith in "instinctual reaching out in mute sympathy toward his fellows" (Moglen, 10–11). This Sterne, Moglen says, is a prophet, prefiguring as he does the insights of Freud, Bergson, and James, and figuring those insights, as the twentieth century would figure them, in the psychological novel.

James Swearingen's Sterne is also prophetic in that he anticipates the phenomenological philosophy of Edmund Husserl. Swearingen's *Reflexivity in Tristram Shandy: An Essay in Phenomenological Criticism* asserts that Sterne's work reflects an understanding of consciousness as "intentional" in the Husserlian sense; that is, consciousness is directed, partial, and incomplete.[7] Perceptual reality is built through the course of time; thus consciousness can be seen as ever-accumulating, never complete. *Tristram Shandy*'s insight into this "truth," Swearingen argues, would not be fully articulated until the twentieth century.

The sense that Sterne anticipates the modern (and the postmodern) world continues to inform criticism of *Tristram Shandy* and *A Sentimental Journey.* Jonathan Lamb's 1989 study, *Sterne's Fiction and the Double Principle,* most notably, extends the discussion of associationism and individual psychology that is at the heart of earlier studies such as Traugott's, Moglen's, and Swearingen's.[8] Lamb, like the earlier critics, reads Sterne's exploitation of Locke's association of ideas as Humean in the sense that it rejects the notion of thought that is separate from sense. Sterne, Lamb argues, recognizes that all thought is located in sense. The rhythm of nonarticulated sensual perception enables one to avoid the act of naming, of limiting perception to a specific referent, and this avoidance is, according to Lamb's Sterne, freedom. To name something, to yearn for certainty, is to adopt narrow, restrictive, "grave" views, to walk the straight line which is anathema to Tristram and to Sterne.

Lamb moves from a celebration of Sterne's celebration of indeterminacy to a discussion of the difficulty of maintaining indeterminacy in the face of narcissism. All readers tend to read themselves into any narrative (witness Trim's reading of his family history in the sermon's reference to the Inquisition); therefore, any story is potentially defining, not indeterminate, potentially limiting rather than liberating. Sterne's own solution to this problem is, in Lamb's view, "sublime" in that it partakes of what Harold Bloom and Thomas Weiskel have termed as the essence of the sublime—the Oedipal (Lamb, 107). Lamb says that in Sterne, the sublime is less a projection of the father as God than a displacement of

Sterne's own conflicts with his mother and Uncle Jaques. *Tristram Shandy*'s references to *Hamlet* invite a comparison: Sterne feels betrayed by his mother (Gertrude) through her alliance with his uncle (Claudius). Only through the symbolic slaying of his mother in the portrayal of Mrs. Shandy turned to a statue (*TS,* 1.426–27/5.5) and the symbolic killing of his cleric uncle in the report of the cleric Yorick's death (*TS,* 1.33–36/1.12) is Sterne (Tristram) freed to write and to publish his self-vindication. For Lamb, then, *Tristram Shandy*'s insights into the operations of the individual consciousness are very personal—not universal— insights, a logical corrective to Traugott's reading, which celebrated Sterne's rejection of the Lockean universal by asserting the universality of individual isolation.

The link between Sterne and the twentieth century continues to interest critics, particularly with regard to important twentieth-century figures who acknowledged their indebtedness to *Tristram Shandy* and *A Sentimental Journey*. Melvyn New's 1994 study *Tristram Shandy: A Book for Free Spirits* is centered on Friedrich Nietzsche's reading of Sterne.[9] It was Nietzsche who called Sterne "the most liberated spirit of all time" and who celebrated him as a "great master of *ambiguity*."[10] Nietzsche shares with Sterne a distrust of rationalism, an appreciation for "the energies and joys" to be found in ambiguity (*Free Spirits,* 10). New ultimately places Sterne's own acceptance of uncertainty within the context of the tradition of Christian skepticism. Nietzsche's admiration of Sterne is not, however, an admiration of the tradition of Christian skepticism per se. That Sterne, whose frame of reference lies squarely within that tradition, could seem so "relevant" to those whose frame of reference is so far outside it speaks to the pivotal cultural position Sterne seems to occupy.

In an essay entitled "Sterne, Our Contemporary," Denis Donoghue addresses the issue of Sterne's contemporaneity and finds him a man of his own age, not one of ours:[11]

> We say that Sterne is modern and that Swift, Pope, and Johnson are not.
> . . . Sterne is fascinated by . . . obstacles, he prefers them to the truth they impede. As a comedian he loves to rebuke the axioms of common sense. We think of this as a modern stance, critical, comic, and subversive. But . . . [t]here is no reason to speak of Sterne as if he were Kafka, Musil, or Beckett. He is a man of his time, though he complicates our sense of that time. . . . He does not undermine the common assumptions of his age, though it is the nature of his comedy to ensure that those assumptions are not too glibly held. (Donoghue, 57–58)

While some critics have explored Sterne's philosophical kinship with twentieth-century thinkers, others have followed Donoghue's lead in examining the way Sterne "complicates our sense" of the eighteenth century. Elizabeth Harries, for example, has discussed the fragmented nature of Sterne's fictions, not as a precursor to our own sense of life's chaos and incompleteness, but as an affirmation of the eighteenth century's belief in an ultimate order.[12] Although Sterne's fragments point to the subjectivity of experience and of aesthetic expression, they do so, Harries argues, in a "deeply analogical context" (*Unfinished*, 53). The notion of fragment is deeply resonant, especially in a Biblical context, Harries argues, in which the implication is not that human life is meaningless but that ultimate meaning is to be fulfilled in a heavenly rather than a human order: "By giving us fragments and thwarting ordinary coherence, Sterne forces us to contemplate a different kind of order—an order not governed by 'any *man's* rules' . . . but by rules more inscrutable and divine" (*Unfinished*, 52).[13]

Since 1954 the critical trend with regard to Sterne has been to take him seriously whether as an orthodox Christian moralist or as a philosopher of the self. Richard Lanham's 1973 *Tristram Shandy: The Games of Pleasure* attempted to stem this tide.[14] Lanham asserts that the only seriousness to be found in *Tristram Shandy* is "the seriousness of the gamesman and the game" (Lanham, 37). While the Victorians dismissed Sterne's playfulness as "trivial," Lanham laments that we have ignored it altogether in our determination to find him "philosophical." We need to recognize that *Tristram Shandy* is not a book about "all of human experience"; it is a book about the pleasures of private life: "It is the *nature* of the private life to seek pleasure. This is Sterne's point and the novel's," Lanham maintains; finally, *Tristram Shandy* "does not tell us how to endure time and chance but how to play games with them, capitalize on them, make them our own" (Lanham, 166–67).

While, as the above survey would suggest, Lanham's effort did not set the tone of critical debate for the following decades, it did reintroduce the idea that reading Sterne is fun and that our primary experience as readers of *Tristram Shandy* is one of pleasure. Whether or not Lanham should be credited for the emergence of a lighter tone in articles and books about Sterne, the fact is that the abstract, highly philosophical prose of Traugott and Swearingen has yielded (in general) in the 1990s to a critical style that attempts to convey as well as discuss the rewards of reading Sterne. While Melvyn New's *Tristram Shandy: A Book for Free Spirits,* for example, adumbrates, as discussed above, the philosophical side of Sterne, it does so in a playful way. The organization of the study, drawn from Stuart Gilbert's study of *Ulysses,* is a schematized, obviously artificial format that is highly appropriate for literary criticism, though such criticism usually tries to hide its artificiality. Yet criticism is a game—a serious game, but a game nonetheless. New's approach highlights both the joy of the critical game and Sterne's celebration of the joy of life.

The notion that *Tristram Shandy* and *A Sentimental Journey* continue to confer pleasure is featured as well in John Allen Stevenson's essay on Sterne in *The Columbia History of the British Novel.*[15] Stevenson begins his consideration of Sterne with the question: "Why read Sterne?" (Stevenson, 154). His answer, ultimately, is that Sterne continues to make us laugh: "the gift of laughter is the soul of Sterne, and for those who see it, that gift is still enough" (Stevenson, 179). Unfortunately, Stevenson notes, there are many who do not "see it," who do not get the jokes and who therefore find no "foothold in the book" (Stevenson, 178). Stevenson here refers to women readers of Sterne, particularly the "recent feminist opposition to his work" (Stevenson, 177). Here Stevenson invokes a debate—for, as he notes, Sterne has his feminist defenders—that has been fueling the last decade of Sterne studies. Feminist readings of *Tristram Shandy* and *A Sentimental Journey* constitute perhaps the liveliest segment of Sterne criticism today, and while most do not center on the issue of what is funny to women versus what is funny to men, the debate pits the sensibility of Sterne against his female readers, against Madam and her daughters, so to speak.

Ruth Perry's 1988 article "Words for Sex: The Verbal-Sexual Continuum in *Tristram Shandy*" sets out the feminist case against Sterne.[16] *Tristram Shandy,* she argues in agreement with Clara Reeve's 1789 observation, is a man's book. Women appear in the narrative only as foils for male action; and, in fact, a subliminal distrust of women pervades the entire work. Even impotence is more often in *Tristram Shandy* a thwarting of women than a frustrating of male desire. Most significantly, the emphasis on language marks the text as phallocentric, for men control language. Even the erotic core of the book is homosocial: "The marriage between Toby and Trim is the emotional center of the book" (Perry, 37). They are domestic partners and even share a child, Le Fever's son. With its focus on male friendship, *Tristram Shandy* exhibits little interest in women's desire or experience.

The homoerotic dimension of Sterne's work has been noted elsewhere. Eve Kosofsky Sedgwick, for example, discusses the homosocial bond between *A Sentimental Journey*'s Yorick and La Fleur in her 1984 study "Sexualism and the Citizen of the World: Wycherley, Sterne, and Male Homosocial Desire."[17] Sedgwick sees homoeroticism as a product of early capitalism and the weakening importance of the family. Yorick in a sense translates all relationships and occurrences into sexual terms, thus rewriting impersonal connections with men and with women into a familial-like intimacy.

Other critics insist that although there is homoeroticism in *Tristram Shandy* and *A Sentimental Journey,* the works comment significantly upon heterosexual relationships. These arguments tend to suggest that, far from being misogynistic and phallocentric, Sterne's works in fact affirm the centrality of women. Leigh A. Ehlers's article "Mrs. Shandy's 'Lint and Basilicon': The Importance of Women in *Tristram Shandy*" asserts that *Tristram Shandy* is a "'woman's book,' in which women are invested with considerable, though untapped, restorative powers."[18] It is the Shandy males, not Sterne, who relegate women to the periphery. Walter, Toby, and Tristram are blind to the restorative and generative powers of women—powers that Sterne recognizes clearly. The Shandy family is endangered by its misogyny; isolation and extinction will result "if they continue in their patriarchal, rationalistic pursuit of power at the expense of love and respect for women" (Ehlers, 70). Yet Tristram, unlike his father and his uncle, evidences some "progress toward respect for . . . women [which] becomes a journey toward self-knowledge" (Ehlers, 70). In this education, Sterne holds out hope for the "salvation and restoration of the Shandy family" (Ehlers, 70).

Other critics have found much to say about the enigmatic Mrs. Shandy and about *Tristram Shandy*'s representation of the female "other" in general. J. Paul Hunter's "Clocks, Calendars, and Names: The Troubles of Tristram and the Aesthetics of Uncertainty" explores the nature of Mrs. Shandy's power. Hunter sees Tristram's mother as a "subversive creative imagination" that undermines the male line in a celebration of "uncertainty and disorder."[19] Melvyn New finds that Mrs. Shandy represents additional qualities that Sterne regards highly: wit, perception, and intelligence.[20] Helen Ostovich argues that Mrs. Shandy, like Madam the reader, only *seems* passive: "[B]oth are active manipulators of the verbal play around them, not merely silent receptors."[21] Mrs. Shandy makes Walter articulate both sides of his argument about putting Tristram into breeches by simply agreeing with everything he says. Madam the reader makes Tristram progress and digress in an effort to keep her interested in his tale. In both cases, the relationship is the collaborative marriage of "stimulating wit and sympathetic judgment"—as dependent on female presence as on male language (Ostovich, 171). Elizabeth Harries, in contrast, admits that upon first reading most will find *Tristram Shandy*'s jokes misogynistic; yet many will also find, as she herself does, great pleasure in the text in spite of "its serious limitations."[22] *Tristram Shandy* is a puzzle, Harries remarks, in that "while undermining conventional expectations about narrative and language, at the same time [it] shores up many prejudices and cultural myths about gender" ("Sorrows," 117). In saying so, Harries reflects the overall sense of Sterne as both one of us and a man of his own time.

There is one aspect of Sterne's work, however, for which the twentieth century has not claimed kinship—his sentimentalism. Patricia Meyer Spacks and Wolfgang Iser are two critics who have commented on the twentieth century's lack of interest in the sentimental, and certainly the validity of their observation is attested by the overwhelming critical preference for *Tristram Shandy*—where the sentimental makes but an occasional appearance—over *A Sentimental Journey*—where the sentimental is the defining tone and subject.[23] Yet it was this very trait in Sterne's writing that appealed to the generation immediately following his own. In her essay, "On the Origin and Progress of Novel-Writing," with which she prefaced her fifty-volume edition of *The British Novelists,* Anna Barbauld praised the sentiment of *Tristram Shandy* and *A Sentimental Journey,* which she admired despite the "indelicacies" of the works:

> It is the peculiar characteristic of . . . [Sterne], that he affects the heart, not by long drawn tales of distress, but by light electric touches which thrill the nerves of the reader who possesses a correspondent sensibility of frame. . . . [T]he feelings are awakened as really by the story of *Le Fevre,* as by the narrative of *Clarissa.* . . . It is one of the merits of Sterne that he has awakened the attention of his readers to the wrongs of the poor negroes, and certainly a great spirit of tenderness and humanity breathes throughout [*Tristram Shandy*].[24]

Barbauld's admiration of Sterne's sentiment has not been shared, in general, by twentieth-century readers and critics. In fact, sentimentalism itself has been regarded with great suspicion in the post–World War II world, for obvious reasons. The sentimental view depends on the definition of "man" as fundamentally good, and the twentieth century has simply provided too much evidence to the contrary.

While there are no signs that our skepticism about the goodness of the human race is abating, there has been a recent surge of intellectual interest in the subjects of sentimentalism and sensibility. With this interest has come renewed attention to *A Sentimental Journey*. John Mullan's *Sentiment and Sociability: The Language of Feeling in the Eighteenth Century* (1988) begins with a discussion of David Hume's "attention to the nature of social instinct" and his positing of "the universality of social understanding," which the novel of sentiment, Mullan argues, would question and ultimately reject.[25] His chapter on Sterne, "Laurence Sterne and the 'Sociality' of the Novel," examines the creation of the sentimental Sterne in the public imagination of the eighteenth century. Extracts from *Tristram Shandy*—Le Fever's story, Yorick's tale—could sustain such an image, but the work in its entirety, Mullan asserts, could not be read innocently. *A Sentimental Journey* can. In *A Sentimental Journey*, Mullan argues, Sterne deliberately conflates the sentimental and the suggestive in Yorick, whose "sentimental inclination" may lead him "to the brink of immorality" but who can be read as innocent in motive and in action (Mullan, 199). Mullan observes that "the sanctioning of erotic encounter as sentimental innocence was generally acceptable to readers of the text in the eighteenth century," though the twentieth-century reader is usually more skeptical (Mullan, 199). Yet, whether or not we credit Yorick's innocence, we must regard it as eccentric, determined by his individual bodily responses to situations and people, not a model for social behavior or "proof of a universal propensity" to sympathy for others (Mullan, 193). Finally, Mullan says, "Sterne . . . does not hold out a life of sentiment as a practical way of being in society. The gestures by which feeling is communicated are, in his fiction, the prerogative of those who cannot be imitated because innocence is inimitable" (Mullan, 200).

While Mullan does not see *A Sentimental Journey* as a satire on sentimentalism as Arthur Cash does in his 1966 study of the work, he does regard it as a critique of sentimentalism. Ann Jessie Van Sant's *Eighteenth-Century Sensibility and the Novel* likewise presents *A Sentimental Journey* as an examination of the nature of sensibility rather than an uncritical endorsement of the concept.[26] Sensibility, she argues, combines the physiological man with an idealized, feminized delicacy of nerve. Such delicacy miniaturizes experience, but it also sexualizes it. The juxtaposition of refined feeling and carnality in the ordinary body of sensibility is complicated in Yorick's case, Van Sant suggests, by his impotence, which causes him to intellectualize his experience of sensation. Thus sensibility in *A Sentimental Journey* is a thoroughly parodic field combining the idealized, the carnal, the intellectual, and the physical. Van Sant sees Sterne's purpose, ultimately, as teaching, through the presentation of the parodic nature of sensibility, the philosophical examination of the nature of the self: "In Sterne's fiction, episodes that begin with observation take the attention to organic sensitivity, which, giving rise to parody, leads back to observation" (Van Sant, 110). Thus Sterne evokes from us "the interior scrutiny that philosophers require their readers to adopt as a rhetorical stance for proper reading" (Van Sant, 110).

Barbara Benedict's *Framing Feeling: Sentiment and Style in English Prose Fiction, 1745–1800* also focuses on the readers of *Tristram Shandy* and *A Sentimental Journey*.[27] *Tristram Shandy*, she argues, "establishes rhetorical methods that will characterize sentimental literature until the end of the century" (Benedict, 88). These strategies create the "illusion of intimacy" in public presentation of characters with whom the reader does not merge his or her identity (Benedict, 88). *A Sentimental Journey*, she maintains, also employs the rhetorical strategies of sentimentalism for the purpose of satirizing the assumptions of sentimentalism. Sentimental exchange in the work is nothing but commercial exchange, she argues; "[m]oney is the form of 'sentimental commerce' plied to the lower-class women Yorick meets as a 'sentimental' substitute for sex"; flattery is the currency of the upper class (Benedict, 91). Thus, "Sterne modifies his celebration of delicate sensation by casting it in language that emphasizes its materiality" (Benedict, 92).

Robert Markley also discusses sentimentalism in terms of its ideological impact. He reads *A Sentimental Journey* as an apology for and example of middle-class duplicity.[28] The work, he argues, employs "a series of strategies designed to mystify the contradictory impulses of sentimentality, to celebrate and mock Yorick's faith in human nature, and to attempt to reconcile ideas of innate virtue with demonstrations of moral worth" (Markley, 223). *A Sentimental Journey*'s representation of charity is, according to Markley, "the rationalization of a middle-class culture that cannot reconcile its virtuous self-image with its dependence on economic inequality" (Markley, 224). He castigates Sterne for his failure to understand the political oppressiveness of the ideology he reinforced from the pulpit and in his literary works.

Patricia Meyer Spacks is more generous. She regards *A Sentimental Journey* and sentimental fiction in general as including admission of "the essential impossibility of resolving life's experiential inequities" in its acknowledgment of "the infinite duplication of distress in the world" (Spacks, 130). If this admission is ineffectual, it is only because those who could help the situation—men of power—refuse to respond to the distress and the inequities they perceive. The language and values of benevolence, Spacks argues, were in the eighteenth century associated with women. Sterne is one of several writers of the time who "argue[s] for taking feelings seriously," and in doing so, argues also for making virtue the cause of men as well as women (Spacks, 130). Spacks admits, however, that sentimental protagonists—Yorick included—more often than not "dramatize altruism's futility, its incapacity to produce sustained, complex action," though she values sentimentalism's challenge to power more than she blames its failure to fully articulate an alternative (Spacks, 132).

The reader who has followed this critical summary closely has encountered the satirical Sterne, the sentimental Sterne, the misogynistic Sterne, the feminist Sterne, the philosophical Sterne, the Christian Sterne, the Sterne of class oppression and the Sterne of potential revolution; she may now be throwing up her hands in frustration: Where is the real Sterne? What do the books really mean? To think of literary criticism, however, as a visit with a text is to recognize that one must answer that question oneself. It is with books, as it is with people: Critics can give only their views based on their readings of the text, just as people can give only their opinions of other people based on their observations and conversations. The third party, the reader of criticism or the listener to gossip, has a duty to compare the opinion of the writer or the speaker with her own observations, her own conversations, her own reading of the text.

This author finds Spacks more persuasive than Markley on the question of Sterne and sentimentalism, though she admits that Markley is more provocative and therefore worth reading too. She finds New more persuasive than Traugott with regard to the subject and strategy of *Tristram Shandy,* but less persuasive than Harries on the matter of Sterne's treatment of women. The Sterne of *Laurence Sterne Revisited* is more profound than Lanham's, but less serious than Swearingen's—all of which is probably apparent to the readers of the first four chapters of this book, despite every attempt to keep bias out of the foregoing summary.

So what are we to conclude? We shall conclude as Sterne began, with a recognition of the fundamental subjectivity and fragmentation of human experience and a refusal to give up the pursuit of truth. In his book-length study of *Tristram Shandy,* Wolfgang Iser makes the following observation: "Sterne has imbued his novel with consciousness that narration is the conceivability of the otherwise elusive, and at the same

time he shows clearly that this insight leads not to resignation, but to a
process of stimulating the reader's imagination" (Iser, 10). Language,
Sterne has shown us, is at best an unreliable tool for communication
because it is always informed by the speaker's subjectivity when uttered
and the reader's subjectivity when heard (Iser, 41). Iser argues that in
Sterne this limitation is often transcended by a nonverbal, physical
understanding. But it is also addressed by the idea of eccentricity, the
notion of the hobby-horse, which is not, Iser points out, identical to a
person's true nature, but which serves several functions with regard to
the definition of the self:

> As a phantasm it fills the hollow space from which subjectivity emerges;
> consequently it congeals into an oddity which delineates the singularity
> of the self. Indeed, as frozen fantasy this phantasm conveys an experience
> of singularity whose bizarre manifestation proves to be resistant to inter-
> pretation. (Iser, 53–54)

While the hobby-horse signals the ungraspability of the self, it also provides a means of access to the self. The crucial point is that the hobby-
horse should be recognized as a stimulation for the reader's imagination
with regard to, say, Uncle Toby's character and not taken for Uncle
Toby's character itself.

In a sense, all literary criticism is hobby-horsical. It is limited, partial, thesis-driven. Critics tend to see what they look for, their attention
directed to the questions that interest them. For all of the polemical
strategies of interpretation, each corrective view tends to reveal not
"the whole truth" previously unnoted by other commentators, but
another view, a different slant on things, yet another hobby-horse.
Does this then mean that criticism is of no value? Iser has suggested
the answer to that question. A critical reading, like any other hobby-
horse, reveals the subjectivity of the critic, fixes that subjectivity into an
identity, and (ideally) stimulates the imagination of the reader to look
beyond, into the "space from which subjectivity emerges." That space,
in the context of this discussion, is *Tristram Shandy* or *A Sentimental Journey*. If criticism inspires us to revisit these texts with renewed interest
and stimulated imaginations, it has done its job. After all, no critic can
"compel you or me to get up behind him" (*TS*, 1.12/1.7), so that if we
do not find inspiration or elucidation, we are free to let the critic ride
on without us. As Tristram puts it, in that case, "pray, Sir, what have

either you or I to do with it?" (*TS*, 1.12/1.7). We can just saddle up our own pads, "ride out and take the air" in our turn (*TS*, 1.13/1.8). As for Laurence Sterne, who wrote to be famous and whose fame has endured, one suspects his feeling would be the more visitors, however mounted, the better.

Notes and References

Preface

    1. *The Four Loves* (New York: Harcourt, Brace, 1960), 140; hereafter cited in text.

Chapter One

    1. *Letters of Laurence Sterne,* ed. Lewis Perry Curtis (1935; reprint, Oxford: Clarendon, 1965), 101; hereafter cited in text.

    2. "A Poetical Epistle To Doctor Sterne Parson Yorick And Tristram Shandy," in *Boswell's Book of Bad Verse,* ed. Jack Werner (London: White Lion, 1974), 136.

    3. "Memoirs of the Life and Family of the Late Rev. Mr. Laurence Sterne" was first published by Sterne's daughter Lydia de Medalle in 1775. Until 1985 it was assumed that Sterne wrote the entire "Memoirs" in 1767, as Lydia maintained he had done. Kenneth Monkman, however, has shown that the first 1400 words of the "Memoirs" were written by Sterne in 1758. See his *Sterne's Memoirs: A Hitherto Unrecorded Holograph Now Brought to Light in Facsimile* (Coxwold, North Yorkshire: The Laurence Sterne Trust, 1985). Curtis includes the "Memoirs" on pages 1–5 of the *Letters,* and for ease of reference (as Monkman's monograph is not widely available) textual citations will refer to the Curtis edition and will be noted parenthetically as "Memoirs."

    4. *A Sentimental Journey Through France and Italy by Mr. Yorick,* ed. Gardner D. Stout, Jr. (Berkeley: University of California Press, 1967), 221.

    5. Although I use Sterne's cryptic "Memoirs" to organize my discussion, I am heavily indebted to Cash's *Laurence Sterne: The Early and Middle Years* (London: Methuen, 1975) and *Laurence Sterne: The Later Years* (London: Methuen, 1986), as is everyone who writes about Sterne. These two volumes are hereafter cited in text as *EMY* and *TLY.*

    6. Kenneth Monkman speculates that Sterne may have been the author of an April 1738 essay printed in the *Gentleman's Magazine* that refutes natural religion. This essay, Monkman argues, was Sterne's effort to portray himself as serious and worthy of a clerical career. His appointment to Sutton-in-the-Forest was made in August 1738. See "Did Sterne Contrive to Publish a 'Sermon' in 1738?" *The Shandean* 4 (1992), 111–33.

    7. In *The Politicks of Laurence Sterne,* Lewis P. Curtis indentifies only two periods of pre-*Shandy* writing by Sterne (Oxford: Oxford University Press, 1929). Kenneth Monkman has asserted more recently that Sterne wrote rather extensively during a third period—the 1745 Jacobite Rebellion, an assertion I

take seriously though conclusive proof is lacking. "Sterne and the '45 (1743–48)," *The Shandean* 2 (1990), 45–136; hereafter cited in text.

8. "The Unknown World," *Gentleman's Magazine* 13 (1743), 376.

9. *Seasonable Advice to the Inhabitants of Yorkshire* (York: John Hildyard, 1745), 6. Monkman reprints *Seasonable Advice* in a facsimile insert between pages 52 and 53 of "Sterne and the '45." Page numbers are to the facsimile.

10. *A Political Romance* in *"A Sentimental Journey Through France and Italy by Mr. Yorick"* with *"The Journal to Eliza"* and *"A Political Romance,"* ed. Ian Jack, The World's Classics (Oxford: Oxford University Press, 1968), 197; hereafter cited in text as *PR*.

11. *Rape of the Lock,* Canto 1.2.

12. The "fragment" was first published in a bowdlerized version by Sterne's daughter Lydia, who included it in the collection of her father's letters she prepared seven years after Sterne's death. A more reliable edition based on a holograph was edited and published by Melvyn New in "Sterne's Rabelaisian Fragment: A Text from the Holograph Manuscript," *PMLA* 87 (1972), 1088–91; hereafter cited in text as "Fragment." For ease of reading, I silently omit the slant marks (/) by which New indicates page breaks in the manuscript.

Chapter Two

1. William Kenrick, Review of *Tristram Shandy, Monthly Review* 21 (1759), 568. Reprinted in *Tristram Shandy: An Authoritative Text,* The Norton Critical Edition, ed. Howard Anderson (New York: Norton, 1980), 472. In referring to the sermons by title, I follow the practice of Melvyn New of capitalizing only the first word and proper names in each title (Melvyn New, ed., *The Sermons of Laurence Sterne.* Vol. 4 of *The Florida Edition of the Works of Laurence Sterne* [Gainesville: The University of Florida Press, 1996]). I would like to acknowledge here my appreciation to Melvyn New for allowing me to read in manuscript his introduction to the sermons from which I gleaned much insight into Sterne's theology, reflected (I hope) in the following discussion.

2. Letter to Sir David Dalrymple, 4 April 1760 in *Horace Walpole's Correspondence,* Vol. 15, ed. W.S. Lewis, Charles H. Bennett, and Andrew G. Hoover (New Haven, Conn.: Yale University Press, 1951), 66. Also reprinted in *Tristram Shandy: An Authoritative Text,* The Norton Critical Edition, 473.

3. Review of *The Sermons of Mr. Yorick, Monthly Review* 22 (1760), 422.

4. "A Poetical Epistle to Doctor Sterne, Parson Yorick, and *Tristram Shandy,"* in *Boswell's Book of Bad Verse,* ed. Jack Werner (London: White Lion Publishers, 1974), 137–38.

5. *Book of Common Prayer* (Oxford, 1700). Subsequent quotations from the Thirty-Nine Articles are from this edition of the *Book of Common Prayer* and are cited parenthetically by number.

6. Melvyn New, "Introduction," in *The Sermons of Laurence Sterne: The Notes.* Vol. 5 of *The Florida Edition of the Works of Laurence Sterne* (Gainesville: The University of Florida Press, 1996), 2–3.

7. *The Sermons of Mr. Yorick,* 2 vols. in Vol. 5 of *The Complete Works and Life of Laurence Sterne,* ed. Wilbur L. Cross (New York and London: The Clonmel Society, 1904), xlviii–xlix, an inadequate edition, now superseded by the Florida edition of Sterne's sermons in press at the time of this writing. Further references to the sermons are (alas) to the 1904 edition and are indicated in parentheses by title, volume number, and page number. I note here, too, that often Sterne repeats passages verbatim in more than one sermon. I have made no attempt to identify the duplications of passages I cite. I give one reference only, and I simply mention Sterne's habit (a perfectly natural one for a lecturer of any sort) to alert readers that no quotation should be considered as "belonging to" one sermon only.

8. An early attempt to identify some of Sterne's sources was Lansing Van der Heyden Hammond's *Laurence Sterne's Sermons of Mr. Yorick,* Yale Studies in English, vol. 108 (New Haven, Conn.: Yale University Press, 1948). Again, the notes to the University of Florida edition of *The Sermons of Laurence Sterne* offer more complete identification of sources.

9. The nature of eighteenth-century Anglicanism is the subject of ongoing controversy among scholars who disagree as to the extent to which "Latitudinarism" turned religion into a mere rational moral system, empirical and expedient rather than metaphysical in nature. Sterne clearly does not equate rationality with morality, and as will be apparent in the forthcoming discussion, he finds reason a completely inadequate basis for morality. For those interested in the scholarly debate, begin with Donald Greene, "Augustinianism and Empiricism: A Note on Eighteenth-Century English Intellectual History," *Eighteenth-Century Studies* 1 (1967), 33–68. See also Greene's "Latitudinarianism and Sensibility: The Genealogy of the 'Man of Feeling' Reconsidered," *Modern Philology* 75 (1977), 159–83; his "How 'Degraded' was Eighteenth-Century Anglicanism," *Eighteenth-Century Studies,* 24 (1990), 93–108; John A. Vance, "Eighteenth-Century Anglicanism: A Layman's View," *Eighteenth-Century Studies* 25 (1992), 361–66; Richard Nash, "Benevolent Readers: Burnet's *Exposition* and Eighteenth-Century Interpretation of the Thirty-Nine Articles," *Eighteenth-Century Studies* 25 (1992), 353–60; Gregory F. Scholtz, "Anglicanism in the Age of Johnson: The Doctrine of Conditional Salvation," *Eighteenth-Century Studies,* 22 (1988–89), 182–207; and Chester Chapin, "The Inseparability of Faith and Works in Anglican Thought: Reflections on a Recent Debate," *The Age of Johnson: A Scholarly Annual,* ed. Paul J. Korshin, 6 (1994), 283–319.

10. Cross actually reads "We are decided. . . ." I am indebted to Melvyn New for the corrected reading of this passage.

11. See also "Philanthropy recommended": "*Humanity* . . . [is] so great and noble a part of our nature, that a man must do great violence to himself, and suffer many a painful conflict, before he has brought himself to a different disposition" (1:48–49).

12. Imlac says this in chapter 11 of *Rasselas. Rasselas and Other Tales,* ed. Gwin J. Kolb, Vol. 16, *The Yale Edition of the Works of Samuel Johnson* (New Haven, Conn., and London: Yale University Press, 1990), 50.

13. For a discussion of Sterne's relationship with Catherine Fourmantel, see Cash, *EMY,* 291–96, and *TLY,* 47–52; for Eliza Draper, see *TLY,* 250–304.

14. Cash's translation, *TLY,* 105–6.

Chapter Three

1. Quotations from *Tristram Shandy* are from *The Life and Opinions of Tristram Shandy, Gentleman,* ed. Melvyn New and Joan New, Vols. 1–3 of *The Florida Edition of the Works of Laurence Sterne,* (Gainesville: University of Florida Press, 1978–1984). Future citations are made parenthetically by volume and page number of the Florida edition, followed by volume and chapter number of *Tristram Shandy,* so that students and instructors using classroom paperbacks will find citations easy to collate with the discussion. The passages to which I have just referred are found in 1.1–2/1.1, that is, in volume 1, pages 1–2, of the Florida edition and volume 1, chapter 1, of *Tristram Shandy.*

2. Theodore Baird, "The Time-Scheme of *Tristram Shandy* and a Source," *PMLA* 51 (1936), 803–20.

3. Baird lists the "few errors, gaps, and loose ends" on pages 818–19.

4. Walpole was not being complimentary here, finding the strategy, finally, dull: "It makes one smile two or three times at the beginning, but in recompense makes one yawn for two hours." Letter to Sir David Dalrymple, 4 April 1760 in *Horace Walpole's Correspondence,* Vol. 15, ed. W.S. Lewis, Charles H. Bennett, and Andrew G. Hoover (New Haven: Yale University Press, 1951), 66. Also reprinted in *Tristram Shandy: An Authoritative Text,* The Norton Critical Edition, 473.

5. Here, this chronology continues to reflect Baird's analysis of the events of *Tristram Shandy,* but we should note that the exact dates for the events surrounding Toby's confinement in London and removal to the country are inconsistently indicated in *Tristram Shandy* and, therefore, are a matter of some critical dispute as the editors of the Florida edition note. See *Tristram Shandy,* 3.103, 1–2.

6. Among his many projects, Swift's hack writer in *A Tale of a Tub* plans to write a treatise on "the *Art of being Deep-learned, and Shallow read.*" In *A Tale of a Tub with Other Early Works, 1696–1707,* ed. Herbert Davis (Oxford: Basil Blackwell, 1957), 80.

7. John Locke, *An Essay Concerning Human Understanding,* ed. Peter H. Nidditch (Oxford: Clarendon, 1975), 156; hereafter cited in text.

8. Alexander Pope, *Essay on Criticism,* lines 82–83 in *Pastoral Poetry and An Essay on Criticism,* ed. E. Audra and Aubrey Williams, Vol. 1 of the Twickenham Edition of *The Poems of Alexander Pope* (London: Methuen, 1961), 248.

9. The notes to the Florida edition comprise the whole of volume 3 and are an invaluable tool to the fullest reading of *Tristram Shandy.* For example, they make available to the twentieth-century reader levels of meaning that would have been clear to the eighteenth-century reader familiar with slang and

colloquial expressions but that are lost to us. In my discussion of *Tristram Shandy,* I have often silently drawn upon the notes to the Florida edition, but here I document the reference to Phutatorius's "flap or fall," 3.325.

10. Genesis 3:16.

11. Book of Common Prayer, article 9.

12. Northrop Frye, *The Great Code: The Bible and Literature* (New York: Harcourt Brace Jovanovich, 1982), 167; hereafter cited in text.

13. See *Letters of Laurence Sterne,* 150.

14. The letter, written in Latin, is translated by Cash, *The Later Years,* 105–6.

15. Jean-Jacques Rousseau, *Emile, or On Education,* ed. Allan Bloom (New York: Basic Books, 1979), 419; hereafter cited in text.

16. See Melvyn New's discussion of this episode in his *Tristram Shandy: A Book for Free Spirits,* Twayne's Masterwork Studies, Robert Lecker, gen. ed. (New York: Twayne, 1994), 108–9.

17. *A Vindication of the Rights of Woman,* in Vol. 5 of *The Works of Mary Wollstonecraft,* ed. Janet Todd and Marilyn Butler (New York: New York University Press, 1989), 91.

18. Chapters 18 and 19 are left blank in their "natural" order in volume 9; Tristram includes them (complete with black letter headings) between chapters 25 and 26. To reflect their unusual status, I document them by writing out "the eighteenth chapter" and "chapter the nineteenth."

Chapter Four

1. *A Sentimental Journey Through France and Italy by Mr. Yorick,* ed. Gardner D. Stout, Jr. (Berkeley: University of California, 1967), 120. *"A Sentimental Journey Through France and Italy by Mr. Yorick" with "The Journal to Eliza" and "A Political Romance,"* ed. Ian Jack, The World's Classics (Oxford: Oxford University Press, 1968), 29. Subsequent references to *A Sentimental Journey* will be made parenthetically to the standard edition—Stout's—first, followed by the paperback classroom text.

2. As in *Tristram Shandy,* Sterne's spellings of the French cities and regions was inexact, but I do not correct him in the text of my discussion. Those readers interested in tracing Yorick's journey, however, should note that "Montriul," "Moulines," and "Borbonnois" are not the conventional spellings for Montrieul, Moulins, and Borbonnais.

3. See Janet Todd, *Sensibility: An Introduction* (London: Methuen, 1986), 6–9; and Ann Jessie Van Sant, *Eighteenth-Century Sensibility and the Novel: The Senses in Social Context* (New York: Cambridge University Press, 1993), 4–8; both works are hereafter cited in text.

4. 2 Esdras 10:31; 2 Esdras 10:50.

5. See "The Lorenzo cult" in *Sterne: The Critical Heritage,* ed. Alan B. Howes (London: Routledge and Kegan Paul, 1974), 429–31.

6. *Hamlet* 1.3.78–80.

7. *The Confessions of Saint Augustine,* trans. E.B. Pusey, Everyman Library edition (London: Dent, 1907), 13.

8. William Warburton, *The Divine Legation of Moses Demonstrated,* 10th ed., 3 vols. (London: Thomas Tegg, 1846), 1:240; hereafter cited in text.

9. *Journal to Eliza,* 166. Citations of this work refer to the Oxford World's Classics edition cited above and are noted parenthetically in the text.

10. Acts 2: 5.

11. Acts 2: 8.

12. Acts 2: 36.

13. Acts 2: 38; Acts 2: 41.

14. Acts 2: 21.

Chapter Five

1. William Bowman Piper, *Laurence Sterne,* Twayne English Authors Series, Sylvia E. Bowman, gen. ed. (New York: Twayne, 1965).

2. Melvyn New, *Laurence Sterne as Satirist: A Reading of "Tristram Shandy"* (Gainesville: University of Florida Press, 1969); hereafter cited in text. Viktor Shklovsky, "A Parodying Novel: Sterne's *Tristram Shandy*" in *Laurence Sterne: A Collection of Critical Essays,* Twentieth-Century Views, ed. John Traugott (Englewood Cliffs, N.J.: Prentice-Hall, 1968), 89.

3. D.W. Jefferson, *"Tristram Shandy* and the Tradition of Learned Wit," *Essays in Criticism* 1 (1951), 225–48.

4. Arthur H. Cash, *Sterne's Comedy of Moral Sentiments: The Ethical Dimension of the "Journey,"* A Modern Humanities Research Association Monograph, Duquesne Studies Philological Series 6 (Pittsburgh, Penn.: Duquesne, 1966); hereafter cited in text; and John M. Stedmond, *The Comic Art of Laurence Sterne: Convention and Innovation in "Tristram Shandy" and "A Sentimental Journey"* (Toronto: University of Toronto, 1967).

5. John Traugott, *Tristram Shandy's World: Sterne's Philosophical Rhetoric* (Berkeley: University of California Press, 1954); hereafter cited in text.

6. Helene Moglen, *The Philosophical Irony of Laurence Sterne* (Gainesville: University of Florida Press, 1975); hereafter cited in text.

7. James E. Swearingen, *Reflexivity in Tristram Shandy: An Essay in Phenomenological Criticism* (New Haven, Conn.: Yale University Press, 1977).

8. Jonathan Lamb, *Sterne's Fiction and the Double Principle,* Cambridge Studies in Eighteenth-Century English Literature and Thought 3, Howard Erskine-Hill and John Richetti gen. eds. (Cambridge: Cambridge University Press, 1989); hereafter cited in text.

9. Melvyn New, *Tristram Shandy: A Book for Free Spirits,* Twayne's Masterworks Studies, Robert Lecker, gen. ed. (New York: Twayne, 1994); hereafter cited in text as *Free Spirits.*

10. Quoted by New from Friedrich Nietzsche's *Human, All Too Human: A Book for Free Spirits* in *Free Spirits,* 16.

11.   Denis Donoghue, "Sterne, Our Contemporary," in *The Winged Skull: Papers from the Laurence Sterne Bicentenary Conference,* ed. Arthur H. Cash and John M. Stedmond (Kent State, Ohio: Kent State University Press, 1971), 42–58; hereafter cited in text.

12.   Elizabeth Wanning Harries, "Gathering Up the Fragments: Hamann, Herder, Sterne," chapter 2 of her *The Unfinished Manner: Essays on the Fragment in the Later Eighteenth Century* (Charlottesville: University Press of Virginia, 1994), 34–55; hereafter cited in text as *Unfinished.*

13.   Other critics continue to explore Sterne's pivotal position in Western culture, his mediation of the forces of his own cultural moment, and his prescience with regard to the preoccupations of our own time. One notable work in progress is that of Manuel Schonhorn, who argues that the concept of the creative artist that emerges in *Tristram Shandy* is Sterne's refiguring of the cultural authorities of the past—the soldier, the parson, and the scholar—into a new comic, life-affirming agency. He presented this argument in an essay entitled "Tristram Shandy, Paradigm Change, and the Heroization of the Artist," at the 1995 International Congress on the Enlightenment in Münster, Germany.

14.   Richard A. Lanham, *"Tristram Shandy": The Games of Pleasure* (Berkeley: University of California Press, 1973); hereafter cited in text.

15.   John Allen Stevenson, "Sterne: Comedian and Experimental Novelist," in *The Columbia History of the British Novel,* ed. John Richetti (New York: Columbia University Press, 1994), 154–80; hereafter cited in text.

16.   Ruth Perry, "Words for Sex: The Verbal-Sexual Continuum in *Tristram Shandy,*" *Studies in the Novel* 20 (1988), 27–42; hereafter cited in text.

17.   Eve Kosofsky Sedgwick, "Sexualism and the Citizen of the World: Wycherley, Sterne, and Male Homosocial Desire," *Critical Inquiry* 11 (1984), 226–45.

18.   Leigh A. Ehlers, "Mrs. Shandy's 'Lint and Basilicon': The Importance of Women in *Tristram Shandy,*" *South Atlantic Review* 46.1 (1981), 61–75. Quotations are from p. 61; hereafter cited in text.

19.   J. Paul Hunter, "Clocks, Calendars, and Names: The Troubles of Tristram and the Aesthetics of Uncertainty," in *Rhetorics of Order/Ordering Rhetorics in English Neoclassical Literature,* ed. J. Douglas Canfield and J. Paul Hunter (Newark: University of Delaware Press, 1989), 173–98. Quotations are from p. 196.

20.   Melvyn New, "Job's Wife and Sterne's Other Women," in *Out of Bounds: Male Writers and Gender(ed) Criticism,* ed. Laura Claridge and Elizabeth Langland (Amherst: University of Massachusetts Press, 1990), 55–74.

21.   Helen Ostovich, "Reader as Hobby-horse in *Tristram Shandy,*" in *New Casebooks: "The Life and Opinions of Tristram Shandy, Gentleman,"* ed. Melvyn New (New York: St. Martin's Press, 1992), 155–73. The quotation is from p. 164; hereafter cited in text.

22.   Elizabeth W. Harries, "The Sorrows and Confessions of a Cross-Eyed 'Female Reader' of Sterne," in *Approaches to Teaching Sterne's "Tristram*

Shandy," ed. Melvyn New (New York: The Modern Language Association of America, 1989), 111–17. The quotation is from p. 114; hereafter cited in text as "Sorrows."

23. Patricia Meyer Spacks, "The Sentimental Novel and the Challenge to Power," chapter 5 of her *Desire and Truth: Functions of Plot in Eighteenth-Century English Novels* (Chicago: University of Chicago Press, 1990), 114–16; and Wolfgang Iser, *Laurence Sterne: "Tristram Shandy,"* trans. David Henry Wilson, Landmarks of World Literature (Cambridge: Cambridge University Press, 1988), 129; both works are hereafter cited in text.

24. Anna Letitia Barbauld, "On the Origin and Progress of Novel-Writing," in *The British Novelists: with An Essay; and Prefaces, Biographical and Critical* (London: F.C. and J. Rivington, et al., 1810), 1:1–62. The passage cited is on pp. 40–41.

25. John Mullan, *Sentiment and Sociability: The Language of Feeling in the Eighteenth Century* (Oxford: Clarendon, 1988), 56; hereafter cited in text.

26. Ann Jessie Van Sant, *Eighteenth-Century Sensibility and the Novel: The Senses in Social Context* (Cambridge: Cambridge University Press, 1993); hereafter cited in text.

27. Barbara M. Benedict, *Framing Feeling: Sentiment and Style in English Prose Fiction, 1745–1800* (New York: AMS Press, 1994); hereafter cited in text.

28. Robert Markley, "Sentimentality as Performance: Shaftesbury, Sterne, and the Theatrics of Virtue," in *The New Eighteenth Century: Theory, Politics, English Literature,* ed. Felicity Nussbaum and Laura Brown (New York: Methuen, 1987), 210–30; hereafter cited in text.

Selected Bibliography

PRIMARY SOURCES

The Life and Opinions of Tristram Shandy, Gentleman, ed. Melvyn New and Joan New. Vols. 1–3 of *The Florida Edition of the Works of Laurence Sterne.* Gainesville: University of Florida Press, 1978–84. Soon to be released in paperback by Penguin. The Penguin edition will include the Florida text and a reduced version of the notes. Other paperback editions include the Norton Critical Edition, ed. Howard Anderson (New York: Norton, 1980), which includes the text of *Tristram Shandy,* a chronology of Sterne's life, contemporary comments by Sterne and others about the work and a selection of twentieth-century criticism. Also available are the Riverside edition, ed. Ian Watt (Boston: Houghton, 1965) and the Oxford edition, ed. Ian Campbell Ross (Oxford: University Press, 1983).

A Sentimental Journey Through France and Italy by Mr. Yorick, ed. Gardner D. Stout, Jr. Berkeley: University of California Press, 1967. Paperback editions include Oxford's World's Classic edition (Oxford: Oxford University Press, 1968), ed. Ian Jack, which also includes *The Journal to Eliza* and *A Political Romance,* and the Penguin paperback (New York: Penguin, 1968), ed. Graham Petrie.

A Political Romance. Facsimile Reprint. Menston, UK: Scolar, 1971.

"Fragment in the Manner of Rabelais." In "Sterne's Rabelaisian Fragment: A Text from the Holograph Manuscript," ed. Melvyn New. *PMLA* 87 (1972), 1083–92.

Sermons of Mr. Yorick, 2 vols. in Vol. 5 of *The Complete Works and Life of Laurence Sterne,* ed. Wilbur L. Cross. New York and London: The Clonmel Society, 1904. Superseded by *The Sermons of Laurence Sterne,* ed. Melvyn New. Vols. 4 and 5 of The Florida Edition of the Works of Laurence Sterne. Gainesville: University of Florida Press, 1996, in press at the time of this writing.

Letters of Laurence Sterne, ed. Lewis Perry Curtis. 1935; reprint, Oxford: Clarendon, 1965.

SECONDARY SOURCES

Bibliographies

Hartley, Lodwick. *Laurence Sterne in the Twentieth Century: An Essay and a Bibliography of Sternean Studies 1900–1965.* Chapel Hill: University of North Carolina Press, 1966.

151

————. *Laurence Sterne: An Annotated Bibliography, 1965–1977.* Boston: G.K. Hall, 1978.

New, Melvyn. "Surviving the Seventies: Sterne, Collins and Their Recent Critics." *Eighteenth-Century Theory and Interpretation* 25 (1984), 3–24.

Biographies

Cash, Arthur H. *Laurence Sterne: The Early and Middle Years.* London: Methuen, 1975.

————. *Laurence Sterne: The Later Years.* London: Methuen, 1986. Cash's two-volume study is the standard biography of Sterne.

New, Melvyn. "Laurence Sterne," in *British Novelists: 1660–1800. Dictionary of Literary Biography,* ed. Martin C. Battestin. Vol. 39, part 2. Detroit: Gale Research, 1985, 471–99.

Journals

The Shandean. This is the one journal devoted exclusively to the works and life of Laurence Sterne. It has been published annually since 1989, and it contains much of interest to the devoted reader of Sterne. It is particularly recommended for its production standards. Many materials are reprinted in facsimile, and there are usually several color reproductions of items such as versions of the marbled page in *Tristram Shandy* and watercolor illustrations of scenes from *Tristram Shandy.* Occasionally critical articles and reviews are included, but the journal is devoted primarily to bibliographical, biographical, and textual matters.

Books

Bloom, Harold, ed. *Laurence Sterne's Tristram Shandy: Modern Critical Interpretations.* New York: Chelsea House Publishers, 1987. A selection of critical essays on *Tristram Shandy,* all published previously elsewhere from 1953–84. The book contains an introduction by Bloom and seven essays from the four decades represented. Included are essays by Dorothy Van Ghent, Ian Watt, Ronald Paulson, and Martin Price.

Byrd, Max. *Tristram Shandy.* Unwin Critical Library. Claude Rawson, gen. ed. London: George Allen and Unwin, 1985. An introductory analysis of *Tristram Shandy* aimed at students, teachers, and non-academic readers. Byrd emphasizes Sterne's self-portraiture in *Tristram Shandy* and his concern with identity in general. Particularly useful is the chapter on "Literary Backgrounds," in which Byrd discusses Sterne's affinity with Rabelais, Cervantes, and Swift.

Cash, Arthur Hill. *Sterne's Comedy of Moral Sentiments: The Ethical Dimension of the Journey.* A Modern Humanities Research Association Monograph. Duquesne Studies Philological Series 6. Pittsburgh: Duquesne University

Press, 1966. A study of *A Sentimental Journey* that treats it as a satire on sentiment rather than as a celebration of feeling. Cash's argument makes ample use of *The Sermons of Mr. Yorick* and includes an appendix in which he discusses *The Journal to Eliza*. This book should be the starting point for any study of Sterne and sentiment.

Cash, Arthur and John M. Stedmond, eds. *The Winged Skull: Papers from the Laurence Sterne Bicentenary Conference.* London: Methuen, 1971. A selection of essays delivered at the Sterne Bicentenary Conference held at the University of York in September 1968. All essays were published here for the first time, including Denis Donoghue's essay, "Sterne, Our Contemporary."

Howes, Alan B. *Sterne: The Critical Heritage.* London: Routledge and Kegan Paul, 1974. Supplies early reactions to Sterne's works from contemporaries and from nineteenth-century commentators as well. A useful resource for tracking Sterne's reputation in the generations immediately following his own.

Iser, Wolfgang. *Laurence Sterne: Tristram Shandy,* trans. David Henry Wilson. Landmarks of World Literature. Cambridge: University Press, 1988. A study of *Tristram Shandy* centered around the notion of subjectivity, which yields a particularly interesting discussion of the hobby-horse.

Lamb, Jonathan. *Sterne's Fiction and the Double Principle.* Cambridge Studies in Eighteenth-Century Literature and Thought. Cambridge: University Press, 1989. "The most complex and powerful sentiments," Lamb explains, "arise from a coalition of an impression and an idea which cannot conceal the imperfection of their union, but can exploit it." That imperfect union is the "double principle" that Lamb finds essential to an understanding of Sterne's work, for this principle emphasizes the complexity of any given experience, the essential contradictory nature of life, the presence of the past in the present, and the need for renewal and flexibility in the face of tragedy and compunction. The book is a challenging read, for Lamb blends rhetorical analysis, narrative theory, and Freudian psychoanalytic criticism. Most examples are drawn from Sterne's own time, but the slant is decidedly postmodern.

Lanham, Richard A. *Tristram Shandy: The Games of Pleasure.* Berkeley: University of California Press, 1973. Examines the "rhetorical play" of *Tristram Shandy* in elaboration of the thesis that what Sterne is serious about in this work is pleasure.

Loveridge, Mark. *Laurence Sterne and the Argument About Design.* Totowa, N.J.: Barnes and Noble, 1982. Loveridge combines the concerns of structural critics and literary historians to examine the concept of design as it was configured in the eighteenth-century in general and in *Tristram Shandy* and *A Sentimental Journey* in particular. These works—and indeed the novel in general—address questions of form and design, not merely as matters of aesthetic interest but as concerns with ethical and moral ramifications as well.

Moglen, Helene. *The Philosophical Irony of Laurence Sterne.* Gainesville: University of Florida Press, 1975. Using Locke's *Essay Concerning Human Understanding* as a point of departure, Sterne develops the notion of subjectivity in ways that anticipate the insights of Bergson, James, and Freud.

Myer, Valerie Grosvenor. *Laurence Sterne: Riddles and Mysteries.* Critical Studies Series. London: Vision Press, 1984. A collection of eleven essays arranged in four parts: "Sex, Laughter and Death," "The Intellectual Background," "Interpretation," and "Afterword." Includes a valuable annotated bibliography by W.G. Day, focusing on the years 1977–83.

New, Melvyn. *Laurence Sterne as Satirist: A Reading of Tristram Shandy.* Gainesville: University of Florida Press, 1969. New argues that *Tristram Shandy* is related to Augustan satire, which takes its norms from the conservative, orthodox Anglican church. Like Swift before him, Sterne views "man" as limited, reason as flawed, sentiment as untrustworthy. Sterne's belief in the ultimate authority of the Christian religion as configured by the eighteenth-century Church of England lies behind the satire of *Tristram Shandy.*

New, Melvyn, ed. *New Casebooks: The Life and Opinions of Tristram Shandy, Gentleman.* New York: St. Martin's Press, 1992. A collection of essays, all previously published elsewhere, that represent, according to New, a critical tradition different from the one established by John Traugott in *Tristram Shandy's World: Sterne's Philosophical Rhetoric.* The essays include selections by Wayne Booth, Donald Wehrs, Elizabeth Harries, D.W. Jefferson, and Sigurd Burckhardt, and in general they examine *Tristram Shandy* in contexts other than that of the eighteenth-century novel.

New, Melvyn. *Tristram Shandy: A Book for Free Spirits.* Twayne Masterwork Studies. Robert Lecker, gen. ed. New York: Twayne, 1994. Focusing on Friedrich Nietzche's comments on Laurence Sterne, New presents an engaging discussion of *Tristram Shandy.* Organized by topics such as "satire," "sentimentalism," "narrative," and "gender," the book offers an accessible guide to the text for readers at all levels. It offers particularly thought-provoking treatments of Sterne's representation of women and his place within the tradition of Christian skepticism.

Piper, William Bowman. *Laurence Sterne.* Twayne English Authors Series. New York: Twayne, 1965. A reading of *Tristram Shandy* and *A Sentimental Journey* as confrontations between individual and society. Tristram is a defensive narrator in conflict with society as he tells a private story that is fundamentally unsuitable for public utterance because of its oddity, sadness, and obscenity. Yet his accommodative narrative strategies in effect universalize the eccentric, make comic the tragic, and morally redeem the obscene elements of his life. *A Sentimental Journey* presents a "publicly oriented narrator" (Yorick) whose message is that universal benevolence enables us to transcend the limitations of individual experience.

Stedmond, John M. *The Comic Art of Laurence Sterne: Convention and Innovation in "Tristram Shandy" and "A Sentimental Journey."* Toronto: University of Toronto Press, 1967. Like New (1969) and Cash (1966), Stedmond examines Sterne's works as comic satires rather than novels, emphasizing the Christian norms from which Sterne's vision emanates and Sterne's laughter at human imperfections, particularly at the human tendency to take oneself too seriously.

Swearingen, James E. *Reflexivity in Tristram Shandy: An Essay in Phenomenological Criticism.* New Haven, Conn.: Yale University Press, 1977. Swearingen argues that *Tristram Shandy* is phenomenological in the sense that it is concerned with the structures of Tristram's consciousness. Sterne's treatment of this consciousness is discussed as prescient, involving insights that would not be fully articulated until the twentieth century. Swearingen treats *Tristram Shandy* as a philosophical novel, though he does include a discussion of comedy and play as these relate to the serious examination of the self offered by Sterne.

Traugott, John, ed. *Laurence Sterne: A Collection of Critical Essays.* Englewood Cliffs, N.J.: Prentice-Hall, 1968. A selection of essays, previously published elsewhere, including the famous essay by Viktor Shklovsky in which he asserts that *Tristram Shandy* is the most typical novel ever written. Also included are D.W. Jefferson's "*Tristram Shandy* and the Tradition of Learned Wit" and a selection from W.B.C. Watkins's 1939 study, *Perilous Balance: The Tragic Genius of Swift, Johnson, and Sterne,* a dated, but still interesting psychological analysis.

Traugott, John. *Tristram Shandy's World: Sterne's Philosophical Rhetoric.* Berkeley: University of California Press, 1954. Considers Sterne as a rhetorician rather than a novelist. Traugott is particularly interested in the way that Sterne undermines Locke's rationalism with his own preference for wit.

Parts of Books

Alter, Robert. "Sterne and the Nostalgia for Reality." In *Partial Magic: The Novel as a Self-Conscious Genre.* Berkeley: University of California Press, 1975. Seemingly "nonrealistic" in its playful intent and form, *Tristram Shandy* does in fact provide a reflection of the operations of the mind attempting to cope with the multifarious nature of the external world.

Benedict, Barbara. "The Sensitive Reader: *The Life and Opinions of Tristram Shandy* and *A Sentimental Journey Through France and Italy*" in her *Framing Feeling: Sentiment and Style in English Prose Fiction 1745–1800.* New York: AMS Press, 1994. Benedict sees in the fragmentation and ambiguity of Sterne's sentimental fictions an undermining of sentimentalism and a challenge to the feminization of culture.

Carnochan, W.B. " 'Which Way I Fly . . .' " In *Confinement and Flight: An Essay on English Literature of the Eighteenth Century*. Los Angeles: University of California Press, 1977. Discusses *Tristram Shandy, Caleb Williams,* and *Vathek* as presenting examples of flights—earthbound, sublunary flights (as is Tristram's flight from death) that suggest no real transcendence or escape from the gravitational pull of the earth. An interesting and unusual contextualization of *Tristram Shandy*.

Harries, Elizabeth. "Gathering Up the Fragments: Hamann, Herder, Sterne" in her *The Unfinished Manner: Essays on the Fragment in the Later Eighteenth Century*. Charlottesville: University Press of Virginia, 1994. Sterne's fragmentary vision, like that of his contemporaries, Johann Georg Hamann and Johann Gottfried von Herder, is an expression of his belief in a stable, ordered universe grounded in Christian theology.

Kraft, Elizabeth. "*Tristram Shandy* and the Parody of Consciousness" in her *Character and Consciousness in Eighteenth-Century Comic Fiction*. Athens: University of Georgia Press, 1992. *Tristram Shandy* satirizes the definition of the self assumed by the novel as a genre by exposing the novel's tendency to ennoble the individual through an immersion in the processes of one character's consciousness. Tristram's search for identity rejects the narrative structuring of consciousness, finding the revelatory moment of awareness more central to the acquisition of true self-knowledge.

McNeil, David. "Sterne: Military Veterans and 'Humours' " in his *The Grotesque Depiction of War and the Military in Eighteenth-Century English Fiction*. Newark: University of Delaware, 1990. Following Wolfgang Kayser and Mikhail Bakhtin, McNeil sees Sterne as a writer of the grotesque, positioned somewhere between satire and sentiment, particularly with regard to war. A reading that attempts to account for Sterne's (and Tristram's) sincere affection for the military man and the horror of war that Sterne recognizes as well.

Mullan, John. "Laurence Sterne and the Sociality of the Novel" in *Sentiment and Sociability: The Language of Feeling in the Eighteenth Century*. Oxford: Clarendon, 1988. Discusses *A Sentimental Journey* as a critique of sentimentalism. The work is not, in Mullan's view, a satire on sentimentalism, yet neither is it an argument for sentiment as the foundation of social relations. It is instead the story of one man's (Yorick's) conflation of the erotic and the sentimental.

Nuttall, A.D. "*Tristram Shandy*." In *A Common Sky: Philosophy and the Literary Imagination*. London: Chatto and Windus, 1974. *Tristram Shandy* exploits the comic potentialities of Locke's *Essay Concerning Human Understanding* and other aspects of the scientific world view.

Preston, John. "*Tristram Shandy*: (i) The Reader as Author" and "*Tristram Shandy*: (ii) The Author as Reader." In *The Created Self: The Reader's Role in Eighteenth-Century Fiction*. New York: Barnes and Noble, 1970. An examination of Tristram as creator and Sterne as character. Through

Tristram's writing of Yorick, Sterne explores the ramifications of the creative and the created self.

Price, Martin. "Sterne: Art and Nature." In *To the Palace of Wisdom: Studies in Order and Energy from Dryden to Blake.* New York: Doubleday, 1964. Through an exquisite and elaborate attention to gesture and sound, Sterne exposes the artifice of language, which can approximate but never reproduce the natural, and more communicative, expression of the body or the voice.

Spacks, Patricia Meyer. "The Beautiful Oblique: *Tristram Shandy.*" In *Imagining a Self: Autobiography and Novel in Eighteenth-Century England.* Cambridge, Mass.: Harvard University Press, 1976. Tristram's sense of self (as well as Sterne's) is organized around his failures and limitations. *Tristram Shandy* argues that ultimately self-knowledge is a matter of balancing reason and passion, internal realities with external realities, and conscience with desire—a balancing that results in the recognition of one's limitations and the ability to transcend them.

Van Sant, Ann Jessie. "Locating Experience in the Body: The Man of Feeling." In *Eighteenth-Century Sensibility and the Novel: The Senses in Social Context.* Cambridge: Cambridge University Press, 1993. In a discussion of several fictional "men of feeling," Van Sant argues that *A Sentimental Journey* provides an examination of the essentially parodic nature of Yorick's sensibility in which the delicacy of nerves generally associated with the female governs the responses of the male body.

Essays

Baird, Theodore. "The Time-Scheme of *Tristram Shandy* and a Source," *PMLA* 51 (1936), 803–20. A still useful explanation of the chronological care with which Sterne composed his chaotic tale.

Booth, Wayne. "Did Sterne Complete *Tristram Shandy?*" *Modern Philology* 47 (1951), 172–83. Reprinted in the Norton Critical Edition of *Tristram Shandy,* 532–48. Booth's answer is yes.

Booth, Wayne. "The Self-Conscious Narrator in Comic Fiction Before *Tristram Shandy,*" *PMLA* 67 (1952), 163–85. Reprinted in *New Casebooks,* ed. Melvyn New, 36–59. Traces the self-conscious narrator from Cervantes's *Don Quixote* through Fielding's *Tom Jones* to the little known *Adventures of Captain Greenland.*

Briggs, Peter M. "Locke's *Essay* and the Tentativeness of *Tristram Shandy.*" *Studies in Philology* 82 (1985), 493–520. Argues that Sterne was in basic agreement with Locke about the processes of cognition, but that he reversed Locke's valuation of reason over imagination.

Brown, Homer Obed. "Tristram to the Hebrews: Some Notes on the Institution of a Canonic Text," *Modern Language Notes* 99 (1984), 727–47. An examination of the textual authority of Yorick's sermon as it sheds light on the question of the authority of any text, including Tristram's own.

Burckhardt, Sigurd. "*Tristram Shandy*'s Law of Gravity." *ELH* 28 (1961), 70–88. Reprinted in the Norton Critical Edition, 595–610, and in *New Casebooks,* ed. Melvyn New, 60–76. Argues that gravity is the law of *Tristram Shandy* because it is the law of mortal life itself.

Ehlers, Leigh A. "Mrs. Shandy's 'Lint and Basilicon': The Importance of Women in *Tristram Shandy*," *South Atlantic Review* 46.1 (1981), 61–75. Argues that women in *Tristram Shandy* are powerful, despite the dismissive attitude of the Shandy males who do not represent Sterne's own view.

Hunter, J. Paul. "Clocks, Calendars, and Names: The Troubles of Tristram and the Aesthetics of Uncertainty." In *Rhetorics of Order/Ordering Rhetorics in English Neoclassical Literature,* ed. J. Douglas Canfield and J. Paul Hunter. Newark: University of Delaware Press, 1989, 173–98. Considers the oddness of *Tristram Shandy* as a cultural issue emanating from eighteenth-century anxieties about patriarchal identity.

———. "From Typology to Type: Agents of Change in Eighteenth-Century English Texts" in *Cultural Artifacts and the Production of Meaning: The Page, the Image, and the Body.* Margaret J.M. Ezell and Katherine O'Brien O'Keeffe, eds. Ann Arbor: University of Michigan Press, 1994, 41–69. Pairing Sterne with Alexander Pope, this essay demonstrates that print technology links the avowed innovator (Sterne) with the professed opponent of innovation (Pope).

Jefferson, D.W. "*Tristram Shandy* and the Tradition of Learned Wit." *Essays in Criticism* 1 (1951), 225–48. Reprinted in *New Casebooks,* ed. Melvyn New, 17–35, and in *Laurence Sterne,* ed. John Traugott, 148–67. Explores Sterne's affinities with Rabelais and Burton in an effort to understand the wit of *Tristram Shandy.*

MacLean, Kenneth. "Imagination and Sympathy: Sterne and Adam Smith." *Journal of the History of Ideas* 10 (1949), 399–410. Discusses *A Sentimental Journey* in relationship to Adam Smith's *Theory of Moral Sentiments.* Both works adumbrate the notion that sympathy is more often than not a version of self-indulgence.

Madoof, Mark S. " 'They caught fire at each other': Laurence Sterne's Journal of the Pulse of Sensibility." In *Sensibility in Transformation,* ed. Syndy McMillen Conger. Rutherford: Fairleigh Dickinson University Press, 1990, 43–62. A reading of *Journal to Eliza* as a self-reflexive drama.

Markley, Robert. "Sentimentality as Performance: Shaftesbury, Sterne, and the Theatrics of Virtue." In *The New Eighteenth Century: Theory, Politics, English Literature,* ed. Felicity Nussbaum and Laura Brown. (New York: Methuen, 1987), 210–30. Examines *A Sentimental Journey* and the sentimental philosophy of Shaftesbury as equivocations of middle-class morality in that they justify the economic inequality upon which the middle class depends for its self-definition.

New, Melvyn. "Sterne, Warburton, and the Burden of Exuberant Wit." *Eighteenth-Century Studies* 15 (1982), 245–74. Examines Warburton's reactions to Sterne's wit and Sterne's responses to those reactions.

Ostovich, Helen. "Reader as Hobby-Horse in *Tristram Shandy*," *Philological Quarterly* 68 (1989), 325–42. Reprinted in *New Casebooks*, ed. Melvyn New, 155–73. A reader-response essay that explores the relationship between Tristram and "Madam," his female reader.

Thomas, Calvin. "*Tristram Shandy*'s Consent to Incompleteness: Discourse, Disavowal, Disruption." *Literature and Psychology* 36.3 (1990), 44–62. A Lacanian reading of *Tristram Shandy*.

Wehrs, Donald R. "Sterne, Cervantes, Montaigne: Fideistic Skepticism and the Rhetoric of Desire." *Comparative Literature Studies* 25 (1988), 127–51. Places Sterne within the tradition of classical skepticism.

Zimmerman, Everett. "*Tristram Shandy* and Narrative Representation." *The Eighteenth-Century: Theory and Interpretation* 28 (1987), 127–47. Reprinted in *New Casebooks*, ed. Melvyn New, 111–32. Examines *Tristram Shandy* in the context of the controversy between deist Anthony Collins and Anglican Richard Bentley over the authority of scripture, arguing that Sterne's awareness of textual criticism informs his own attitude toward the authority of narrative representation.

Index

The Author

Elizabeth Kraft is an associate professor of English at the University of Georgia. She is the author of several studies of eighteenth-century British fiction, including *Character and Consciousness in Eighteenth-Century Comic Fiction* (University of Georgia, 1992) and "The Two Amelias: Henry Fielding and Elizabeth Justice," *ELH,* 62 (1995), 313–28. She is also the coeditor (with William McCarthy) of *The Poems of Anna Letitia Barbauld* (University of Georgia, 1994).

The Editor

Herbert Sussman, Professor of English at Northeastern University, is the author of *Victorian Masculinities: Method and Masculine Poetics in Early Victorian Literature and Art; Fact into Figure: Typology in Carlyle, Ruskin, and the Pre-Raphaelite Brotherhood;* and *Victorians and the Machine: The Literary Response to Technology.*